HAKESPEARE'S
USE OF MUSIC:
A STUDY OF THE MUSIC
AND ITS PERFORMANCE
IN THE ORIGINAL PRO-
DUCTION OF SEVEN COMEDIES

Da Capo Press Music Reprint Series

MUSIC EDITOR
BEA FRIEDLAND
Ph.D., City University of New York

HAKESPEARE'S USE OF MUSIC:
A STUDY OF THE MUSIC AND ITS PERFORMANCE IN THE ORIGINAL PRODUCTION OF SEVEN COMEDIES

by

JOHN H. LONG

DA CAPO PRESS · NEW YORK · 1977

Library of Congress Cataloging in Publication Data

Long, John H
    Shakespeare's use of music.

    (Da Capo Press music reprint series)
    Reprint of the ed. published by University of
Florida Press, Gainesville.
    Bibliography: p.
    1. Shakespeare, William, 1564-1616—Knowledge—
Music. 2. Shakespeare, William, 1564-1616—Stage
history—To 1625. I. Title.
[ML80.S5L72]   782.8'3   77-5643
ISBN 0-306-77423-2

This Da Capo Press edition of *Shakespeare's Use of Music: A Study of the Music
and Its Performance in the Original Production of Seven Comedies* is an unabridged
republication, with a few minor corrections by the author, of the first edition published
in Gainesville, Florida in 1955. It is reprinted by arrangement with The University of Florida Press.

Published by Da Capo Press, Inc.
A Subsidiary of Plenum Publishing Corporation
227 West 17th Street, New York, N.Y. 10011

Manufactured in the United States of America

Shakespeare's Use of Music

HAKESPEARE'S
USE OF MUSIC:
A STUDY OF THE MUSIC
AND ITS PERFORMANCE
IN THE ORIGINAL PRO-
DUCTION OF SEVEN COMEDIES

by

JOHN H. LONG

UNIVERSITY OF FLORIDA PRESS
GAINESVILLE~1955

In Memory of J. A. L.

Acknowledgments

HE WRITER HERE WISHES TO ACKNOWLEDGE THE
generosity of the following organizations in
permitting him to quote and to transcribe
from works in their custody: The American
Book Company, New York City; Christ
Church Library, Oxford, England, whose man-
uscript settings of Ford's "Sigh no more, ladies" and Morley's "O
mistris mine" were transcribed by permission of the Governing
Body of Christ Church; The Clarendon Press, Oxford, England;
E. P. Dutton & Company, Inc., New York City; The Folger Shakespeare Library, Washington, D. C.; Galaxy Music Corporation,
New York City, by permission of Galaxy Music Corporation, Sole
Agents for Stainer & Bell, Ltd., London, England, the owners of
the copyright to E. H. Fellowes' *The English School of Lutenist
Song Writers*; G. Schirmer, Inc., publishers of *The Musical Quar-
terly,* copyright, 1938, by G. Schirmer, Inc., New York City; The
Huntington Library, San Marino, California, for permission to
reproduce "The Fairie Round" found in A. Holborne's *Pavans,
galliards, almains . . . 1599*; J. Curwen & Sons, Ltd., London,
England; Kamin Dance Bookshop and Gallery, New York City;
Lawrence & Wishart, Ltd., London, England; The New York
Public Library, New York City; Oxford University Press, New
York City; *Studies in Philology,* The University of North Carolina,
Chapel Hill; Theodore Presser Company, Bryn Mawr, Pa., for
transcriptions from Vincent's *Fifty Shakspere Songs,* used by per-
mission of the copyright owner, Oliver Ditson Company, Bryn
Mawr, Pa.

Contents

Plates

Introduction

T IS THE PURPOSE OF THIS STUDY TO PRESENT THE results of an examination of the use of music, both instrumental and vocal, as a dramatic device in seven comedies by Shakespeare: *The Two Gentlemen of Verona, Love's Labour's Lost, A Midsummer Night's Dream, The Merchant of Venice, Much Ado About Nothing, As You Like It,* and *Twelfth Night. (The Taming of the Shrew* is omitted because its position in sequence is uncertain.) By the term "dramatic device" is meant the use of music as an aid not only to the intensification of the impact of the language, but also to the forwarding of the action, the portrayal of character, the delineation of settings, and the creation of an appropriate atmosphere, such as a mood of mystery or awe. Also included in the term "dramatic device" is the use of music in solving problems of stage production in instances where music covers the sound of stage machinery, denotes a lapse of time, or indicates off-stage action.

This study includes only those performances of the plays given before the publication of the First Folio. I have used as texts the Folio of 1623 and contemporary quartos, on the assumption that a greater degree of eclecticism is justifiable in this study than in the establishment of a severe and completely defensible verbal text. Hence, I have taken my evidence wherever I could find it clear. However, I have tried to assess the authority for each shred of evidence and to avoid combining data, except with the justification of a sound textual theory. For instance, I have never used as the basis for any piece of evidence a text arrived at by a modern editor.

In view of the admitted importance of music in the plays of Shakespeare and his contemporaries, it is surprising that the subject has received slight attention from scholars. Several books have been written on the background of Elizabethan music against which Shakespeare's plays appear, but their focus of interest is not upon the way he used the music. A number of scholarly articles such as those by Richmond Noble and Edmund H. Fellowes have treated the subject, but these are concerned with isolated problems and do not constitute a survey of the phenomena. Only one book, so far as I know, contains a serious and sustained study of Shakespeare's use of music, and it omits a consideration of the purely instrumental music in the plays. This book is Richmond Noble's *Shakespeare's Use of Song*. It is possible that research has been handicapped by complete lack of musical scores which can be assigned to the plays of Shakespeare. This lack is indeed a serious one, but much can still be learned from a careful assessment of the available evidence.

The procedure followed is necessarily complex. I first made an intensive study of the text and stage directions of the Shakespeare plays in the versions described above, and an evaluation and interpretation of the interior evidence found. This part of the study, in itself, was inadequate for a clear presentation of the use and performance of the music. I therefore turned to plays contemporaneous with Shakespeare in order to determine from their stage directions and dialogue what could at this point be learned about the habits and conventions governing the use of music in the Elizabethan theaters. The next step involved an examination of contemporary accounts of the drama and music of the times as found in early records, in reliable reprints of relevant documents and texts, and in quotations from writers of the period found in secondary studies of both subjects. Finally, I assessed the conclusions reached by authors of secondary studies and in editorial comments concerning the use of music by Shakespeare and contemporary dramatists.

Of the materials thus considered, the contemporary accounts and the interior evidence from the plays are the most important. An explanation of the treatment of this material is therefore pertinent.

If we wish to discover how music was performed in Elizabethan

plays, the best source of information is perforce the plays themselves. And if we are interested in the performance of music in
plays during Shakespeare's productive period, we need consider
only those plays written or produced in or bordering that period.
In selecting these plays, I made it a general rule to take the earliest
date of publication of the dramas in determining their place in
time. This procedure, of course, is not entirely accurate, but I
could hardly set out to determine the exact chronology of hun-
dreds of plays.

Having thus limited the number of plays to be examined in the
study, I reduced the number to be given close scrutiny by eliminat-
ing those plays which contained no significant use of music. The
remaining core of plays given serious study were those which, in
each case, met two requirements: (a) they were probably produced
within or bordering the chronological period assigned; and (b)
they contained a significant use or amount of music.

Turning to the internal evidence provided by the plays, I found
that the performance of music therein was described in three ways:
by stage directions per se supplied by the author, the prompter,
or a reporter of the play; by stage directions and cues which, em-
bedded in the actors' speeches, are most nearly sure to be within
the intention of the author; and by comments on the music made
by actors in character, again largely attributable to the author.

The stage directions per se may be trusted, generally, to describe the actual performance of the music in a particular play,
but they do not necessarily reflect the intentions of the playwright.
On the other hand, the spoken stage directions most likely express
the author's wishes, but do not necessarily mean that the players
followed his intentions. Therefore, for the purpose of this study,
all three sources of information were considered and carefully
weighed.

The stage directions supplied by an author, editor, or prompter
are usually brief and cryptic notes such as "Song," "Musicke,"
"They sing," or "Musicke playes"—just enough reminder to assure
the correct introduction of the music. Occasionally, however, particularly in the late Elizabethan drama when staging becomes

more elaborate, stage directions appear such as the following from Marston's *Sophonisba* (1606), V, iv: *"Organ and recorders play to a single voice. Enter in the meantime the mournful solemnity of Massinissa's presenting Sophonisba's body."*

Stage directions supplied by a reporter are apt to be more informative than prompter's cues, since they are usually parts of a reading version rather than parts of the actors' "book." For example, a reporter's version of *Tancred and Gismund* (1592) contains this stage direction: *"Introductio in Actum tertium. Before this Acte the Hobaies sounded a lofty Almain, and Cupid Ushereth after him, Guizard and Gismund hand in hand. . . . The measures trod, Gismunda gives a cane into Guiszards hand. . . ."*

Stage directions supplied by the actors' lines are even more informative. One such in the anonymous *Wily Beguiled* (1606) provides an outline description of the number of musicians involved, their costume, the instruments they played, and the type of music performed. Thus: *"Enter Sylvanus. Sylvanus. . . .* Whilst old Sylvanus send a lovely traine/ Of Satyrs, Driades, and watrie Nymphes,/ Out of their bowers to tune their silver strings,/ And with sweete sounding musicke sing,/ Some pleasing Madrigalles and Roundelayes,/ To comfort Sophos in his deepe distresse. *Exit Sylvanus. Enter the Nymphes and Satyres singing."*

A more precise picture of the performance of stage music is given in this short excerpt from Middleton's *A Mad World, My Masters* (1608): *"Sir B. . . .* My music! give my lord a taste of his welcome. *A straine played by the consorts: Sir Bounteous . . . seems to foot the tune. . . . Sir B.* My organists! *The organs play, and servants with covered dishes pass over the stage."*

It can hence be seen that interior evidence on the dramatic use of music on the Elizabethan stage is plentiful. Even the brief notations "Musicke" and "Song" are informative; the first is used only to signify music played by an instrumental consort; the second is applied to the performance of vocal music with or without instrumental accompaniment.

The body of contemporary evidence outside the plays is not large. Scattered references to stage music appear in the letters of visiting foreigners, in the pamphlets printed by the Puritans and their opponents, and in official records of various kinds. The fullest accounts are those descriptions of the great masques and processionals of the period such as the reports made by Jonson, Campion, and Dekker. It is unfortunate that equally accurate accounts are unknown for the less spectacular dramatic performances of the time for, although the masques and processionals exerted a great influence on Elizabethan public drama, they were too extravagant to be considered representative of that drama. The value of such accounts for the purposes of this study is hence not great.

Early in my investigation it appeared that Elizabethan stage music faithfully reflected the part played by music in the society of the period. It therefore seemed important to consider the many references to music made in representative selections from the nondramatic literature of the Elizabethans.

With some understanding of the subject thus gained from contemporary evidence, I then turned to secondary studies treating the use of stage music by Shakespeare and his fellow playwrights. The bulk of the secondary material is scattered among books of a nonscholarly nature, periodical articles on isolated aspects of the subject, and editorial footnotes. Despite the lack of scholarship evident in much of this material, the facts, suggestions, and conjectures contained therein have been valuable and welcome. Although I have had to disagree with some statements made in secondary works, I have found that others, including some made without supporting citations, are verified by my own study of the contemporary evidence.

At this point I turned from a consideration of the use of music on the Elizabethan stage to an examination of the music itself. In general, the method of investigation outlined above was followed. There are only about a hundred songs performed in all the plays falling within the years covered by this inquiry whose music has survived; out of this number only a handful of songs are believed to have been written specifically for stage performance. Instrumental scores written for the stage before 1610 are yet to be found. This scarcity of contemporary stage music is informative, however, for it indicates that a large portion of the music used in the playhouses must have been drawn from the popular music of the time.

With this indication in mind, I turned first to the collections of music which appeared within the seventy-five years following 1590. The greater latitude in chronology, as compared to that used for the plays, was adopted on the assumption that popular music, especially folk music, is long-lived; that is, much of the music popular during Shakespeare's time would also be popular for many years afterward. This assumption did not seem applicable to the more artistic and intellectual music of the period; this music I restricted by narrower chronological limits. Fortunately, the type of artistic music most prevalent in the Elizabethan playhouses— the lutenist's "ayre"—emerged and flourished between the years 1580 and 1620; and a large amount of this music is available in Edmund H. Fellowes' monumental edition, *The English School of Lutenist Song Writers.* Most of the popular music I examined, however, was found in later collections and secondary works on Elizabethan music.

The knowledge gained from this examination of songs, dance music, and instrumental scores provided some insight into the actual sound of the music and an index to Elizabethan taste in matters musical. My findings were not at all startling. The most popular Elizabethan tunes, judging from their frequent appearances in collections of the period, are those having marked rhythms and simple, though tuneful, melodies. It is the presence of these two elements that determines the popularity of a piece of music in any age.

The methodology just outlined was used to acquire a minimum foundation for the study of Shakespeare's use of music. But apart from its use for the background studies, it also proved suitable for an examination of the Shakespeare comedies.

In essence, the treatment of each comedy followed the same pattern. First the play was placed in time and sequence, and its generally accepted sources were examined. The internal evidence was then studied in relation to the dramatic and musical conventions of the period. This was followed by an assessment of secondary studies bearing on special problems. Finally, authentic or appropriate musical illustrations were selected from the music of the Elizabethan or early Restoration periods.

The illustrations of music were chosen with the producer in mind and with the belief that contemporary music is an important part of any production of Shakespeare's plays. Most producers, it seems logical to suppose, would use this music if it were available. To this end I have supplied authentic or appropriate musical scores for almost every episode wherein the performance of music is called for. In most cases only the melody is furnished for each selection, but the sources containing the complete scores have been identified wherever possible.

Time alone has limited the number of comedies treated by this study. Most of the time and effort involved was spent on the acquisition of a fund of knowledge and understanding of the general use of music on the Elizabethan stage. In view of the few Shakespeare comedies considered by this inquiry, the conclusions reached regarding Shakespeare's use of music must hence be tentative until all his plays have been studied. It should be noted, however, that the background acquired for this study is appropriate for similar studies directed at Elizabethan drama in general.

I have been fortunate in the aid given me by many people too numerous to be listed. Their anonymity here cannot lessen my gratitude. To Dr. T. Walter Herbert of the University of Florida I am indebted for the care and cautious enthusiasm with which he read the original drafts of the book. His close attention will probably never be duplicated. I am also grateful for the help I received from the directors and staffs of the Folger Shakespeare Library, the Library of Congress, the Library of the University of Florida, the Huntington Library, and the New York Public Library.

ONE

The Songs in Elizabethan Drama

HE ELIZABETHAN AGE IS OFTEN REFERRED TO AS the golden age of English song. Vocal music pervaded the life of that time to an extent which we hardly realize. The songs of the period reflect the manners and tastes of all stations of its society and the range of emotions of its people. There we find the complex polyphony of the madrigals and motets, and the crudity of the tinker's catch; we find the exalted measures of the *Te Deum* or the *Gloria,* and the conviviality of the drinking song; the artistry of the lutenist's song and the enthusiasm of the street cries. We could find no more appropriate place to begin our survey of the dramatic music of the Elizabethan theaters, therefore, than with the songs and their singers.

Most of the scholarship on the dramatic music of the period has dealt with the songs.[1] None of this scholarship, however, has been gathered together and applied to the dramatic works of Shakespeare, play by play, so far as I know. To aid the understanding of Shakespeare's practice the following summary of the music lore he knew is presented.

The songs used on the Elizabethan stage may be divided into four major groups: the folk songs, the street songs, the "ayres," and the madrigals and canzonets.[2] We shall be concerned only with the first three types; the madrigal, seldom used except in private performances such as masques, need not concern us here.[3] Likewise, the church music of the period is used so seldom in the plays that only the most general conclusions can be drawn from a study of it.

In general, the folk tunes were marked by strong rhythms, simple melodies, and the crudeness often associated with popular art. They were danced, as well as sung, to a simple instrumental accom-

paniment such as the pipe and tabor, cittern, or fiddle.[4] The tunes
were anonymous, stemming from the folk, and one tune might
serve for any number of different lyrics.[5] Most folk songs were
either ballads, three-man songs—songs set in simple three-part
harmony—or catches. The catches were short rounds; that is, songs
having only a melody which, begun at intervals by each singer,
automatically produced a three- or four-part canon. The familiar
nursery tune, "Three Blind Mice," is a catch.[6]

The street song differed from the folk song in that its lyrics
were usually composed by a known writer who set them to folk
tunes, usually for only one voice. The subject matter of these songs
varies; generally the broadside ballads described some curious
event such as an unusually spectacular execution, the confession
of a notorious criminal, or the birth of a monster, or presented
amorous and lewd lyrics, or advertised the wares of itinerant vendors. The ballad, to which type the street song (excepting the
vendors' cries) belongs, was generally peddled about the streets
by ballad singers such as Autolycus in *The Winter's Tale*. The
broadside ballads of Deloney and Edgerton are examples of this
urban street song.[7]

In contrast to the folk song, the ayre was what we now call an
art song. It was written by a literate composer who, in addition
to writing the melody for a specific lyric, also wrote his accompaniment for particular instruments. In musical construction the ayres
varied from simple, folklike tunes set to a cittern accompaniment,
to complicated contrapuntal works set to an elaborate instrumental
accompaniment.[8] The ayres had more complex rhythms than the
folk songs, for, while the latter had their rhythms limited by
their use for dance purposes, the former were generally written
to be played or sung. Syncopations and frequent shifts in rhythmic
patterns were often employed. The ayres were also written for a
set number of voices—from one to five.[9]

Many of the foremost composers wrote ayres which were used
on the stage. Several of these composers, for example Robert Johnson, John Wilson, John Hilton, Alphonso Ferrabosco, Thomas
Ravenscroft, and perhaps Thomas Morley, wrote ayres specifically

for stage productions. In the plays of John Fletcher five composers are represented: two songs were set by John Wilson, one by Robert Johnson, and one each by Edmund Chilmead, Stephen Mace, and John Hilton.[10] In the works of Ben Jonson the ayre "Come, my Celia, let us prove" was set by Alphonso Ferrabosco (who wrote much of the music for Jonson's masques), and another ayre has a setting usually ascribed to Robert Johnson.[11]

Songs in the plays were usually assigned to secondary characters, although songs were sometimes sung "within" or from the music room by singers not included in the cast. Clowns sang, rustics sang, tradesmen sang, but characters of exalted stations seldom sang. The stage thus reflected the customs and attitudes of the time. The etiquette of the period forbade a gentleman to perform musically in public; to do so would have been as unmannerly as to sell one's sonnets to a printer.[12] Accordingly, noble characters seldom sang unless when portrayed among very intimate groups of friends or family.

The customary practices of the period also governed the types of song which a particular character might sing. Rustic characters sang the folk songs and ballads of the countryside. In Peele's *The Arraignment of Paris* (1584) a shepherdess sings "an old song called 'The Wooing of Colman.'" In his *The Old Wives Tale* (1595), Scene i, three rustics sing a three-man song, "Whenas the rye reach to the chin." Lower-class townsmen were assigned to sing the popular street ballads. In *Eastward Ho!* (1605), V, v, Quicksilver sings an autobiographical ballad set to the tune "I wail in woe, I plunge in pain," and in Jonson's *Volpone* (1607), II, ii, Nano sings two songs in praise of Volpone's patent medicine.

The folk songs and street songs were convenient for theatrical purposes because they required neither highly trained singers nor instrumentalists for their performance. They could be sung by any actor, with only a cittern or pipe and tabor for accompaniment. These songs were particularly suitable to the public playhouses because they were popular both with the sophisticated playgoer and with the groundling unfamiliar with the more formal music of the time.

The ayres, however, posed a problem for the playwright. Their performance called for trained singers and instrumentalists who could not always be drawn from the ranks of the actors. How could these nonacting musicians be introduced into a play without damage to verisimilitude? Quite often they were simply hauled in by the scruff of the neck, along with a few words of explanation for their presence. Most often the singers were boys who represented pages; the music of the instrumentalists, who generally were hidden from the audience, was ascribed to "the musicke of the house," the "town consort," or some other convenient fiction. *The Silent Woman* (1609) thus opens: "*Cler.* Ha' you got the song yet perfect, I ga' you, boy? *Boy.* Yes, sir." The boy, after some conversation, sings a song. In *The Beggars' Bush* (1622), III, i, the following stage direction appears: "*Enter Gerrard like a blind aquavitae man, and a Boy singing the Song.*" As ensuing lines reveal, the boy leads Gerrard onto the stage and there sings "Bring out your conyskins, fair maids, to me." He takes practically no part in the action or conversation following the song.

The problem raised by the necessity for introducing nonactors into plays occurred most frequently in the productions written for performance in the public playhouses; it hardly existed in the productions of private plays. The use of the ayre was largely popularized by the children of the chapels, who, though primarily musicians, also made up the acting companies for the earlier indoor theaters. These youngsters could be called upon to sing or to play musical instruments with the assurance that their performance would be competent and well received. There was thus no necessity for the introduction of extradramatic performers onto their stage.

Ayres were also sometimes sung by adult actors, many of whom had served an apprenticeship as musicians before joining the players.[13] Volpone sings the ayre "Come, my Celia, let us prove," and Orgilus sings an ayre, "Comforts lasting, loves increasing," in Ford's *The Broken Heart* (1633).

Let us see now how the songs were performed on the stage. Practices varied between presentations of the children's companies

and presentations of the public players; so it may be well if we
note the differences.

The members of the children's companies—the Children of
Paul's, the Children of the Chapel (Blackfriars), the Children of
the Queen's Revels, and the Children of Windsor—were boys ap-
proximately between the ages of nine and thirteen.[14] These boys
were well-trained vocalists and instrumentalists whose primary
function was to provide music for the great churches and the
Court;[15] they were only secondarily, and as an afterthought, actors.
Their dramatic productions consequently exploited the musical
talents of the groups. The plays in which the children took part
were marked by the use of involved polyphonic music including
songs for one, two, or three voices, and songs for full choirs, many
of which were accompanied by ornate instrumental combinations.
The stage directions in Peele's *The Arraignment of Paris* (1584),
presented by the Children of the Chapel, may give some idea of
the rich musical fare offered by the singing boys:[16]

ACT. I. SCENA III

Pom. Hark, Flora, Faunus! here is melody,
  A charm of birds, and more than ordinary.

> *An artificial charm of birds being heard*
> *within, Pan speaks.*

Pan. The silly birds make mirth; then should we do them wrong,
  Pomona, if we nill bestow an echo to their song.

> *An echo to their song.*
> *The Song. A quire within and without.*

In this scene an echo song is sung by two choirs, one composed of
Pan's followers, onstage, and the other made up of a group of boys
hidden "within."[17] The first part of the song is performed by the
hidden choir, which represents the birds, and an antiphonal "echo"
(the second part of the song) is given by Pan and his entourage.

  ACT. I. SCENA IV *Pallas, Juno, and Venus enter, Rhanis leading the way. Pan alone sings. The Song.* [Text omitted here.] *The
birds sing. The Song being done, Juno speaks.* [Pan apparently

sings his song with a background of mechanical bird calls.][18]

ACT. I. SCENA V *et ultima They* [Œnone and Paris] *sing; and while Œnone singeth, he pipeth.* [This song is a lengthy duet. Œnone and Paris sing alternately at first, then together for the last chorus. While Paris is not singing he accompanies Œnone with a flute or recorder.]

ACT. II. SCENA II . . . *Pallas' Show. Hereupon did enter Nine Knights in armour, treading a warlike almain, by drum and fife . . . Venus' Show. Here Helen entereth . . . : she singeth as followeth.* "Se Diana nel cielo è una stella," [etc.].

ACT. III. SCENA I *Colin, th'enamoured shepherd, singeth his passion of love.*

ACT. III. [SCENA IV] . . . *Œnone singeth as she sits. Œnone's Complaint. . . .*

ACT. III. SCENA V *The Shepherds bring in Colin's hearse, singing . . . A foul crooked Churl enters, and Thestylis, a fair lass, wooeth him. She singeth an old song called, "The Wooing of Colman. . . ."*

ACT. V. *et ultimi,* SCENA I . . . *The Music sound, and the Nymphs within sing or solfa with voices and instruments awhile. Then enter Clotho, Lachesis, and Atropos, singing as followeth: the state being in place. . . . The Song.*

The extensive use of music in this scene is exceeded only by its use in some of the masques. An instrumental consort is combined with a choir, and, after the scene has been set, three soloists sing, apparently with the instruments, the tribute to Queen Elizabeth which closes the play.

As is evident, the songs in *The Arraignment of Paris* were lavishly presented. They include two antiphonal ayres—one set for two choirs and the other for soloist and choir; a duet accompanied by a recorder; six solos—an ayre accompanied by bird whistles, an ayre sung in Italian, an ayre in the form of a lament, an ayre sung alternately by three voices; a folk song for soloist; an ayre (a dirge) for choir; and a "solfa" sung by a choir with the accompaniment of a consort of instruments.

The public players seldom attempted to match the quantity and quality of the music used in *The Arraignment of Paris*; at least, not until the public playhouses began to interpolate masques and other elaborate musical fare into their plays, a practice that did not become general until about 1610. The use of a large number of professional musicians entailed increased costs of production—a factor which the shareholders and actors of the playhouses were not likely to overlook. Also, the audience to which the public players appealed was not so musically literate as the more select groups which frequented the private theaters. The public players, therefore, used songs more sparingly and introduced them in a simpler manner. For their songs they turned to popular tunes and occasional ayres which required few professional musicians for their presentation. The group songs, such as three-man songs and catches, were sung by only three or four voices.[19] *The Shoemaker's Holiday* (1600) contains two three-man songs (III, v, and V, iv) and a drinking song (II, iii) for soloist. *Volpone* contains four songs, one of them sung by Nano and Castrone (I, ii), two sung by Nano (II, ii), and the fourth sung by Volpone (III, vii). *Bartholomew Fair* (1614) presents only two, both popular songs sung by a ballad singer (II, ii, and III, v). One of the early public plays in which a masque was introduced, *The Maid's Tragedy* (1609-1611), contains an unusual number of songs, most of them in the masque. Three ayres are assigned to a choir (I, ii), and two ayres are sung by soloists (II, i). But even this production cannot be compared with *The Arraignment of Paris* so far as the use of music is concerned.

The singers in the theaters did not always sing from the outer stage. The question of the location of the singers, therefore, becomes an important consideration in evaluating dramatic practices. The outer stage was used, of course, when the singers took part in the action of the plays; but the vocalists were placed at many other points, depending upon the dramatic purpose for which their songs were introduced.[20] Songs were sung within the tiring house, in the music room, in the balconies, or even under the stage. In Anthony Munday's *John a Kent and John a Cumber* (1594), IV, i, for example, a "song to the music within" is called for.[21] In Marston's *The Malcontent* (1604), Scene ii, a song is heard in Malevole's chamber, which is seemingly placed in the balcony above the inner stage. The anonymous *Fedele and Fortunio* (*ca.* 1584) has the following stage direction: "*Victoria setteth open the casement of her window and with her lute in her hand playeth, and singeth this ditty.*"[22] In the play by Munday mentioned above, the third "Antique" sings from under the stage.[23] Only one restriction of a musical nature seems to have limited the placement of the singers: when accompanied by a group of instrumentalists, they had to remain near the consort.

So far we have noted the songs in relation to their musical types, and the location of the singers in relation to the playhouse. For the purpose of this study, however, the songs are most important when related to the dramatists and to their use of the songs in the plays. The playwrights of the time were forced by the physical limitations of their stage to exploit all available dramatic devices to the utmost. Music was one of these available devices, and, as we shall see, it was not overlooked.

The dramatic functions of the songs in Elizabethan and Jacobean plays were many and diverse. Songs were used to portray character, to establish settings, to foreshadow and to forward action, and to solve various mechanical problems such as indicating a lapse of time, creating an illusion of action taking place offstage, or covering exits and entrances. The following examples are representative and do not constitute a complete survey; but from this sampling we shall observe that the Elizabethan dramatists borrowed many of their musical devices from a common fund, and that Shakespeare was not the only one, nor even the first, to use music in many of the ways we shall later find it used in his plays.

Malevole's character is announced not only by the discordant music which opens *The Malcontent*, but also by the song which is sung from within his chamber (I, ii). Volpone casts his argument in support of his offer to seduce Celia into an ayre: "Tis no sin love's fruits to steal,/ But the sweet thefts to reveal:/ To be taken, to be seen,/ These have crimes accounted been."/[24] Merrythought, in *The Knight of the Burning Pestle,* shows his incorrigible optimism by bursting into song on the slightest occason.

In the songs sung by Volpone and Merrythought we find two extreme levels of dramatic song. In the case of Merrythought the songs are used in a general way. When a man sings, it is because he is happy. Hence, to show optimism, Merrythought sings. In the case of Volpone, however, the words of the song are actually lines from the play set to music, as in opera. Much of the dramatic impact of the song arises from the contrast between the greedy lust of Volpone and the loveliness of the song which he employs.

The use of song to establish settings and atmosphere was common. The rural atmosphere of the opening scene in *The Old Wives Tale* is largely achieved by the three-man song sung therein. The scene was seemingly acted on a bare platform, for when Clunch, the smith, leads Frolic, Antic, and Fantastic to his cottage, their approach to the house is indicated by the bark of a dog. At the command of Clunch, his wife admits them to the house. The change of setting is indicated by the stage direction "Enter old woman [Madge]." A few lines later, Fantastic remarks: "This smith leads a life as merry as a king with Madge his wife. Sirrah Frolic, I am sure thou art not without some round or other; no doubt but Clunch can bear his part. *Fro.* Else think you me ill brought up; so set to it when you will. *They sing. Song.* 'Whenas the rye reach to the chin,' " etc.[25]

Marlowe's *Dr. Faustus* contains a scene (vii) in which Faustus plays a joke on the pope, the comedy being increased by a burlesque curse sung by the attendant friars in retaliation for the sacrilege. Quicksilver's song of repentance in *Eastward Ho!* is a part of the prison setting of the last scene.[26] Quicksilver is following the custom of ballad makers, who delighted to make songs out of the confessions of criminals.

As a device for foreshadowing the approach of death, songs were particularly in demand. The death of the Duchess in *The Duchess of Malfi* is forecast by a madman who, in his song, likens his fellow madmen to ". . . ravens, screech-owls, bulls and bears" as bringers of ill omens. The death of Aspatia in *The Maid's*

Tragedy is predicted, without much subtlety, when she sings "Lay a garland on my hearse."[27]

In order to forward the action of plays, the dramatists often used songs not only as a part of action but to indicate off-stage action as well. J. Lyly used a song to put Corsites to sleep; earlier, Samias, Dares, and Epiton had disposed of the Watch, an action which occurred during the course of a song.[28] The madman's song in *The Duchess of Malfi* is a part of the psychological torture inflicted upon the unfortunate woman by her brother. John Ford indicates the death of Penthea, off-stage, by the singing of a dirge "within."[29]

Several mechanical problems incident to play production and staging were solved by the use of songs. A lapse of time was often indicated by the insertion of a song which broke the flow of action. A good example of this usage may be found in Udall's *Ralph Roister Doister* (*ca.* 1540). Tib, An, and Marjorie begin work on a piece of sewing: "*Tib. Talk.* So, sirrha, nowe this geare beginneth for to frame." After a few lines of conversation, the three sing several stanzas of a three-man song, "Pipe, mery Annot," at the conclusion of which a stage direction states: "*Lette hir caste downe hir worke.*" Then follows: "*Tib. Talk.* There it lieth! The worste is but a curried cote."[30] A song also fills an interval of time in *The Beggars' Bush,* II, i. The interval falls between the time Snap is posted as a sentinel and his return to report his discovery of Hubert and Hemskirk: "*Fer.* Set a sentinel out first. *Snap.* The word? *Hig.* 'A cove comes,' and 'fumbumbis' to it. *Strike.* [Exit Snap.] *The Song.* [Text omitted here.] *Enter Snap, Hubert and Hemskirk.*"[31]

Exits and entrances were often accompanied by songs. The practice was so common that we need only glance at a sampling of Renaissance English drama to make the point:

The Play of the Wether (1533), the conclusion: [*While they sing, Jupyter withdraws.*]

Ralph Roister Doister, (*ca.* 1540), I, i: *He entreth singing.*

Cambises (1569): *Sing and exeunt.*[32]

The Arraignment of Paris (1584), I, iv: *Pallas, Juno and Venus enter, Rhanis leading the way. Pan alone sings.*

The Malcontent (1604), II, v: *Whilst the song is singing, enter Mendoza.*

There was a conscious attempt made by the playwrights of the time to maintain a flow of sound throughout their plays. Music was often called for when a break occurred in the actors' speech, either for an exit or for other necessary stage business. The music sounded until speech began again. Webster used a song not only to cover an exit but also to contribute to setting and atmosphere and to keep a flow of sound during the course of a dumb show. The following scene is in *The Duchess of Malfi*, III, iv:

> *Here the ceremony of the Cardinal's instalment in the habit of a soldier: perform'd in delivering up his cross, hat, robes, and ring at the shrine, and investing him with sword, helmet, shield and spurs. Then Antonio, the Duchess and their children, having presented themselves at the shrine, are (by a form of banishment in dumb show expressed towards them by the Cardinal and the state of Ancona) banished. During all which ceremony, this ditty is sung, to very solemn music, by divers churchmen; and then exeunt.[33]*

Extraneous songs, those inserted by the dramatist or the players for the sheer amusement of the audience, are scattered throughout the plays of the period. These songs were more prevalent in the academic and court plays than in the productions of the public theaters, possibly because the latter had neither the time nor the singers necessary for songs which served no dramatic or mechanical functions in the plays.[34] Often these irrelevant songs were offered at the beginning or ending of acts and scenes. Act II of *Gammer Gurton's Needle* (1575), for example, is preceded by: "*Fyrste a song:* 'Back and syde, go bare, go bare,' " etc.[35]

It is, of course, often difficult to prove a song to be completely extraneous, particularly one which is performed in the midst of action. In my opinion, though, the songs "Old browne bread crustes," "Who so to marry a minion wife," "A thing very fitte," and "I mun be maried a Sunday"—all from *Ralph Roister Doister* —as well as "Awake, ye woful wights" from *Damon and Pithias*

and "Cupid and my Campaspe" and "O for a bowle of fatt canary"
from *Campaspe*, are suitable examples of extraneous songs in the
early Elizabethan drama. From the later dramas of the period
such songs as "Cold's the wind, and wet's the rain," in *The Shoe-
makers' Holiday*, "Fond fables tell of old" from *Eastward Ho!*
and "Tis mirth that fills the veins with blood" from *The Knight
of the Burning Pestle* seem to serve no dramatic functions.

A brief review of our examination of songs used on the Elizabethan stage reveals that three types were most frequently employed; the folk song, the street song, and the ayre. The folk and
street songs appeared more often than the ayres in the public playhouses because they required no highly skilled musicians for their
performance and because they were more attractive to the general
public than were the ayres. The latter, on the other hand, were widely used in private and court performances, as excellent musicians
could be conveniently found. Practically all the singers of all kinds
of songs were represented as characters of lower or middle class
ranks. Clowns, knaves, rustics, and tradesmen sang the popular
songs, whereas the ayres were sung by pages or similar characters
who might normally be expected to have skill in music. Both men
and boys sang ayres, but the children predominated, especially in
the private theaters.

The presentation of the songs varied from the use of elaborate
and complex contrapuntal arrangements set to large instrumental
accompaniments, as found in the private theaters, to a simple ballad
sung to a cittern, as often occurred among the common players. The
vocalists were placed at any point "within" or "without" the acting
area which a sense of realism might require. The songs were directed toward the delineation of character, the clarification of
settings, the promotion of action, the solution of problems of
production, and pure entertainment.

Notes

1. See the annotated bibliography.
2. E. S. Lindsey ("The Music in Ben Jonson's Plays," *MLN*, XLIV, 86, 87)
suggests three classifications, namely, the ballad tune, the "ayre," and the

madrigal. No arbitrary method of classification can be completely satisfactory; in this case the term "ballad tune" seems too inclusive. The terms "folk songs" and "street songs" are therefore used in order to distinguish between a widespread body of music close to the folk, both rural and urban, and a more localized, urban type of song which cannot always be defined as folk music.

3. *Ibid.* Ben Jonson used three canzonets by Henry Youle in *Cynthia's Revels* (1601), but madrigals and canzonets were, as a rule, neither flexible nor popular enough for dramatic use.

4. Cf. *The Scornful Lady* (1616), II, ii; *A Looking Glass for London* (1591), IV, v; *Orlando Furioso* (1594), IV, ii; *Edward I* (1599), ii, xi. T. Arbeau, *Orchesography* (1588), gives the lyrics to one of the dance tunes which he uses as an illustration (p. 65) and also names his tunes from the lyrics to which they are set; thus, "Basse Dance called 'I will give you joy'" (p. 67), "The Galliard called 'Because of the Traitor I die'" (p. 99). Cf. W. Chappell, *Popular Music of the Olden Time*, I, 70.

5. E. B. Reed (*Songs from the British Drama*, pp. 15-17) gives these stage directions preceding songs from *A New Interlude of Vice, Containing the History of Horestes* (1567): "Haltersick entereth and singeth this song to the tune of 'Have over the water to Floride' or 'Selengers round'"; "Enter Ægisthus and Clytemnestra, singing this song to the tune of 'King Solomon'"; "Enter the Vice, singing this song to the tune of 'The Painter.'" The tunes "Sellingers Round," "Rogero," and "Dargason" were frequently used in this manner, as Chappell shows in his *Popular Music* (I, 64, 69, 70, 93, 94).

6. According to Lindsey ("The Original Music for Beaumont's Play 'The Knight of the Burning Pestle,'" *SP*, XXVI, 427), the catch is printed in Ravenscroft's *Pammelia* (1609).

7. Thomas Mace (*ca.* 1650) probably refers to the street song in the following quotation: "*Common Tunes* (so called) are Commonly known by the Boys, and Common People, Singing them in the Streets, and are of either sort of Time, of which there are many, very Excellent, and well Contriv'd Pieces, Neat and Spruce Ayres." (Quoted by Arnold Dolmetsch, *The Interpretation of the Music of the XVII and XVIII Centuries Revealed by Contemporary Evidence*, p. 49.) The street cries, or vendors' songs, were also occasionally used in dramatic productions. For example, in *King Lear* Edgar's refrain, "Poor Tom's acold," is part of a begging song sung by the Bedlam inmates. (See Sir F. Bridge, "The Musical Cries of London in Shakespeare's Time," *Proceedings of the Musical Association*, December, 1919, pp. 15, 16.)

8. Among the title pages reprinted in Edmund H. Fellowes' *The English School of Lutenist Song Writers*, the following excerpts will illustrate the point: Morley, "The First Booke of Ayres . . . to sing and play to the lute, with the base viole" (1600); Pilkington, "The First Booke of Songs of 4 parts: with Tableture for the Lute or Orpherian, with the Violl de Gamba"; Dowland, "The Second Booke of Songs or Ayres of 2. 4. and 5. parts. With Tableture for the Lute or Orpherian, with the Violl de Gamba" (1600).

9. See note 8.

10. Lindsey, "The Music of the Songs in Fletcher's Plays," *SP*, XXI, 2 ff.

11. Lindsey, "The Music in Ben Jonson's Plays," *MLN*, XLIV, 86 ff.

12. T. Elyot, in *The Gouernor* (1531), p. 27, wrote: "Kynge Philip, whan he harde that his sonne Alexander dyd singe swetely and properly, he rebuked him gentilly, saynge, But, Alexander, be ye nat ashamed that ye can singe so well and connyngly? whereby he mente that the open profession of that

crafte was but of a base estimation. And that it suffised a noble man, hauynge therein knowledge, either to use it secretely, for the refreshynge of his witte, . . . orels, only hearynge the contention of noble musiciens, to gyue iugement in the excellencie of their counnynges." Later, H. Peacham in his *Compleat Gentleman* (1634), p. 100, stated: "I desire no more in you than to sing your part sure, and at the first sight, withall, to play the same upon your Violl, or the exercise of the Lute, privately to your selfe."

13. Samuel Gilborne and James Sands were apprenticed in music to Augustine Phillips, a member of the King's Men (E. K. Chambers, *William Shakespeare: A Study of Facts and Problems*, II, 73, 74.)

14. See note 15.

15. The boys were taken into the choirs at about the age of nine, and were taught by professional instructors to sing and to play instruments. They stayed with the choirs until their voices broke—probably about five years. There were three principal companies of children that presented plays around 1600: the Chapel Children of Blackfriars (later called the Children of His Majesty's Revels), the Children of Whitefriars, and the Children of Paul's (C. W. Wallace, "The Children of Blackfriars, 1597-1603," *University Studies*, University of Nebraska, VIII). For an account of the choirboys before 1585, see G. E. P. Arkwright, "Elizabethan Choirboy Plays and Their Music," *Proceedings of the Musical Association*, April, 1914, pp. 117-138.

16. C. F. T. Brooke and N. B. Paradise (eds.), *English Drama, 1580-1642*, pp. 3-21.

17. The "echo" songs were evidently popular; see Campion's *Gray's Inn Masque, at Court* (1594) in Reed, *Songs from the British Drama*, p. 284.

18. W. J. Lawrence (*Pre-Restoration Stage Studies*, p. 203) cites a passage from Bacon's *Sylva Silvarum* which suggests one method used to produce bird calls. "In regalls [small organs], (where they have a pipe they call the Nightingale-pipe, which containeth water) the sound hath a continual trembling." The choirboy companies frequently used some such device. See T. Middleton's *Blurt, Master Constable*, IV, iii; and J. Marston's *The Dutch Courtezan*, II, i.

19. The three-man songs were folk songs having a crude form of three-part harmony. They were frequently drinking songs. Although Morley does not mention them by name, he speaks of "drinking songs . . . if they may be call'd musicke" (*A Plaine and Easie Introduction to Practicall Musicke . . . 1597*, p. 179.) Evidently no great skill in singing was thought necessary in order to "take a part" in a three-man song. An example of this song type is "Oft Have I Ridden Upon My Grey Nag," one of the songs in Ravenscroft's *Pammelia* (1609). Chappell has reprinted it in *Popular Music*, I, 63. Cf. G. H. Cowling, *Music on the Shakespearean Stage*, pp. 85, 86; E. W. Naylor, *Shakespeare and Music*, pp. 82-84.

20. All the following plays contain scenes employing music "within": T. Dekker, *The Laws of Candy* (1619-1622), III, iii; *Old Fortunatus* (1600), Vol. I, pp. 140, 141; *Westward Ho!* (1607), Vol. II, p. 335; Marston, *Sophonisba* (1606), IV, i; Middleton, *Blurt, Master Constable* (1602), IV, iii; Nathaniel Field, *A Woman is a Weathercock* (1612), II, i. Cowling cites additional plays, pp. 36, 37.

21. Cowling, p. 37, mentions Middleton's *A Chaste Maid in Cheapside*, V, iv; and, on p. 39, Beaumont's *The Knight of the Burning Pestle*, III, v; his *Monsieur Thomas*, III, iii; and Fletcher's *The Captain*, II, ii.

22. Reed, *Songs from the British Drama*, p. 27.

23. Also, in Marston's *Antonio and Mellida,* Part 2 (1602), V, ii, Balurdo sings under the stage.

24. *Volpone,* III, vii. The song was set to music by Alfonso Ferrabosco, the Younger, and was published in his *Ayres* (1609).

25. Brooke and Paradise, p. 26.

26. Act V, v. Speaking of the ballad, Quicksilver says: "I writ it when my spirits were opressed. *Pet.* Ay, I'll be sworn for you, Francis! *Quick.* It is an imitation of Mannington's: he that was hanged at Cambridge, that cut off the horse's head at a blow. *Friend.* So, sir! *Quick.* To the tune of 'I wail in woe, I plunge in pain.'" Security also sings a song of repentence in the same scene, "O Master Touchstone, my heart is full of woe!"

27. See also Massinger's *The Emperor of the East* (1632), V, iii.

28. *Endymion* (1591), IV, ii and iii.

29. *The Broken Heart* (1633), IV, iv.

30. J. Q. Adams, *Chief Pre-Shakespearean Dramas,* pp. 430, 431. Other examples of this usage may be found in Marston's *The Insatiate Countess* (1613), III, iv, and the anonymous *Wily Beguiled* (1606), ll. 2180-2182. The dramatically awkward period of time during which a character falls asleep was, in many instances, happily bridged by soft music played or sung expressly to lull him to sleep. See Dekker, *Old Fortunatus,* Vol. 1, pp. 138-141; *Wily Beguiled,* ll. 1286-1310; R. Wilson, *The Coblers Prophesie* (1594), ll. 992-1028.

31. Brooke and Paradise, p. 846.

32. Adams, p. 664, l. 1132.

33. Brooke and Paradise, p. 668.

34. See L. B. Wright, "Extraneous Song in Elizabethan Drama after the Advent of Shakespeare," *SP,* XXIV, 261-274, and John R. Moore, "The Songs of the Public Theaters in the Time of Shakespeare," *JEGP,* XXVIII, 166-202.

35. See Reed, *Songs from the British Drama,* pp. 263, 266, 267, 276, 299: Jonson, *Cynthia's Revels* (1601), II, v, and V, vi; *The Poetaster* (1602), IV, v; *Sejanus,* I, II, III; and the anonymous *Ram Alley* (1611) at the end of the play.

TWO

Instrumental Music in Elizabethan Drama

ROM THE SONGS WE NOW TURN TO THE INSTRU-
mental music of the Elizabethans and its use
for dramatic purposes. This subject has received little attention from students of the
drama; it is not hard to see why.[1] Instrumental
music, as a class by itself, was just at the point
of divorce from the song and the dance in the sixteenth century;
consequently there was little apparent standardization either in
the construction and classification of instruments or in the various
combinations of instruments for group performance. In only a
few instances was music written primarily for the purpose of being
played and not sung.[2]

It is impossible, therefore, to produce a complete description
of the instrumental music in the drama of the time. The best we
can do is to see what the dramatists did with the instruments at
their disposal, where such information is available, and to study
the instruments themselves in order that we may determine if they
were or were not capable of being used under varying circumstances. As a result of this procedure several patterns will emerge
which can generally be applied to different dramatic situations
as they appear in the comedies of Shakespeare, with one proviso:
that such applications rest upon only two supports—the nature of
the instruments, and the customary usage of those instruments,
both supports being subject to exceptions.

In examining the musical instruments of the period, we shall
restrict ourselves to those which were most frequently used in the
plays, as evidenced by interior references. Such instruments include
lutes, citterns, viols, rebecs, violins, shawms (also called waits,
curtals, and hautboys), recorders, flutes, fifes, cornets, sackbuts,
trumpets, drums, and regals. Bells, birdcalls, and other devices
were also used in the theaters, but since these are not, strictly
speaking, musical instruments, we need not consider them here.[3]

The Lutes

The lute was a stringed instrument which was plucked like a guitar or a mandolin. In shape it resembled one half of a pear, cut lengthwise, having a fretted finger-board which extended from the smaller end and over which the strings were placed along the flat side. There were several types of lutes, which differed in size, number of strings, and method of tuning. During the reign of Elizabeth the most common type was the treble lute with eleven gut strings.[4] The strings included five pairs, tuned sympathetically and used to produce chords. The eleventh, and highest, string was most suitable for playing melodies, and for this reason was given the name "chanterelle." Because the treble lute was small and because it had a melody string, it could be used as a solo instrument or as an accompaniment for songs. Another type, slightly larger, was called the theorboe, or tenor lute; this had a lower range than the treble lute.[5] A third member of the family was the bass lute, or arch-lute as it was often called. This lute was the largest of the group, measuring about six feet in height.[6] Both the theorboe and arch-lute were largely restricted to the production of chordal accompaniments, either for songs or in instrumental ensembles.[7]

The lutes were popular because the treble could be played solo, and all forms of the lute could be played with singers and other instruments. In instrumental groups the lutes supplied much of the volume of sound and the percussive quality which the piano now furnishes in small orchestras. In fact, the three types of lutes, when played together, apparently sounded much like a harpsichord.

The social standing of the lutes was high. Music for the lute, and songs with lute accompaniment, were written by the most prominent musicians of the age.[8] The notation used was in a form peculiar to the music written for the lute and its cousins. This system was called "tablature" and resembles, to some extent, the guitar symbols placed on popular song sheets of today.[9] Other instruments were so meagerly supplied with written music that the strings of viols, for instance, were sometimes tuned in the same manner as those of lutes, so that violists might play from the lute tablature. Musicians called this practice "playing Lyra-way."[10]

The Cittern[11]

The cittern, or cithern, resembled the lute in frontal outline, but, unlike the lute, had a flat back. It was strung with four single wire strings, or four pairs, which were often played with a plectrum or with the fingernails.[12] The notation used by the performers on this instrument was written in lute tablature.[13]

The cittern was played mostly among the lower-class Elizabethans because it was easy to master and, I suspect, because its simpler construction made it much less expensive.[14] Ill-adapted to producing melodies, its primary function was to furnish chords for song accompaniments and for instrumental groups. In comparison with the sparkling quality of the lute tones, the music of the cittern was softer and less resonant.[15]

The Viols[16]

The viols were bowed string instruments. Two types were in use during the late English Renaissance, the *viol da gamba* and the *viol da braccia*. The dominant type in sixteenth- and seventeenth-century England was the gamba, or "leg" viol. The viols da gamba varied slightly in shape, but they were generally marked by sloping shoulders, flat backs, thick ribs, and wide, fretted finger-boards.[17] They were strung with six, sometimes seven, gut strings.[18] The bridge of the viol was only slightly rounded, a feature which caused difficulty in playing on a single string, but which made the production of chords or double stops easy.[19] The tonal volume of this instrument was not so great as that of the modern violin, nor did it have the brilliance of the violin family. Its tone was distinguished, however, by a mellowness and a clear, singing quality. The latter feature owed much to the frets on the finger-board; when the finger pressed a string against a fret, the tonal result was similar to that produced by an open violin string. Unlike the tonal quality of the violin, this quality was uniform on all the notes of the viol.[20]

The family of gamba viols included a small treble viol, an alto viol, a tenor viol, and bass viols of several sizes. The bass viols were the most popular of the group; we find them mentioned most often as solo instruments, as accompaniments for songs, and in consorts of instruments.[21] The treble, alto, and tenor viols were used with groupings of other instruments, but only rarely do they appear as solo instruments. The "chests" of viols so frequently mentioned in accounts of the period, refer to the viol family when used in a "set" similar to a violin quartet, or when grouped together in a chest or case. A set, or "consort," of viols included five or six instruments—usually one treble, one alto, one tenor, and two bass viols.[22] Such a consort occupied the same position in the musical life of the period as the modern string quartet does among musicians today; it supplied private recreation and pleasure to persons having an uncommon degree of musical literacy, but lacked popularity with the casual listener. Groups of viols were played in public entertainments, but not often in the classic six-viol combination described above.[23]

In performance the gamba viols were held downward—the bass viols between the knees, and the smaller viols resting on the knees.[24] Music written especially for the viols was scarce. The "fancies" and dances written for viol consorts were just becoming generally familiar at the beginning of the seventeenth century, and of the two types of music, the dances were much more popular than the intricate and artistic, or "artificial," polyphony which delighted the composer and performer of the fancies.[25] For the most part, the musicians playing viols for public entertainments relied either upon their memories or upon song music and tablature to fill the need for written music.

The Rebec[26]

The rebec was a country cousin of the viols. In shape it resembled an elongated lute, though generally the rebec was smaller. By the middle of the sixteenth century it was considered by many to be a rustic instrument.[27] It generally had three strings, was played with a short, arched bow, and was held against the shoulder of the player. The fiddle, as writers of the period often termed it, was apparently played by ear; I know of no music written for it.

The Violins

The violins and the other members of the family—the viola and

the bass violin (an instrument which we now call the violoncello) —
belong to the *viol da braccia,* or "arm viol," side of the viol instruments. In contrast to the gamba viols, the tone of the violins was
brilliant, loud, and harsh.[28] The members of the violin family were
late in being accepted in England; not until the Restoration did
they come into general use.[29] During the reigns of Elizabeth and
James there is only occasional mention of the instruments, and in
most cases only the treble violin is specified.[30] They seem to have
been used primarily by itinerant musicians and country fiddlers
until the middle of the seventeenth century when, though generally
accepted, they were restricted largely to the performance of dance
music. Thomas Mace suggested in 1676 that "to the Press or chest
of Viols be added a Pair of Violins to be in readiness for any extraordinary Jolly or Jocund Consort-Occasion."[31]

The Shawms

The name "shawm" here includes the hautboys, waits, curtals,
and bombards. These instruments were all of the wood-wind-with-
double-reed variety similar to the modern oboe, English horn, and
bassoon. Accounts of the shawms toss terminology about with great
inconsistency, but it appears that the term "hautboy" was used
most often for the treble and alto shawms, that the tenor shawm
was called a "shawm," and that the bass shawm was called a
"curtal."[32] The double-bass shawm, an unwieldy monster, was
called a "bombard," but I have found no evidence that it was used
in the theaters.

The volume of sound produced by a shawm was almost as great
as that of a trumpet.[33] Its tone quality was harsher than the
tones produced by modern double-reed instruments; when several
shawms were played together, the result was a skirling sound
similar to that produced by a band of bagpipes.[34] The loud and
piercing quality of their music caused them to be restricted to large
halls or to the open air and made them inappropriate for private
indoor theatrical performances.[35] Most English communities of any
size maintained a municipal band of shawms which, in addition to
furnishing music for processions, banquets, and other state occa-

sions, functioned as the city watch.[36] Some of the bands, it has been suggested, were also employed in the public playhouses.

The Citizen, in the Prologue to *The Knight of the Burning Pestle*, tries to replace a consort of fiddles by one of shawms:

Cit. What stately music have you? You have shawms?

Prol. Shawms? No.

Cit. No! . . . Ralph plays a stately part, and he must needs have shawms. I'll be at the charge of them myself. . . .

Prol. So you are like to be.

Cit. Why, and so I will be: there's two shillings;—let's have the waits of Southwark; they are as rare fellows as any are in England; and that will fetch them all o'er the water with a vengeance, as if they were mad.

The practice of using municipal consorts in plays had appeared before the construction of the Theater and the Rose.[37]

The Recorders

The recorders were vertical flutes, having a mouthpiece in the end rather than on the side as is the case with the modern cross flute. The recorder mouthpiece also contained a fipple, the device found in penny whistles and organ pipes which produces the musical tone. There were many sizes of these instruments, especially in the higher tonal ranges. The usual division of voices, however, was into treble, tenor, and bass.[38] The treble and bass recorders were pitched an octave apart; the compass of each of the three was two chromatic octaves.[39] The smaller pipes resembled the present clarinet in size and shape; the bass recorder had a narrow brass tube between its body and its mouth aperture, which caused it to resemble a bassoon.[40] The fingering of the shawms and the recorders was identical; both had six finger holes in front and one in the rear.[41] It would, therefore, be relatively easy for one musician to double on both instruments. The recorders were often referred to as pipes or flutes.

The music produced by these instruments was soft and woody. Arnold Dolmetsch describes it as "sweet, full, profound, yet clear, with a touch of reediness."[42] A warbling effect could be achieved, as Bacon tells us, by moistening the inside of the pipe with saliva.[43] Evidently the sound of recorders was considered rather mournful, for consorts of them were often used in funeral processions, both actual and dramatic.[44]

The recorders and viols were sometimes substituted for one another in instrumental combinations.[45]

The Flutes

The flute (cross flute, or German flute), used in England during the sixteenth and seventeenth centuries, was an early version of the present flute. It was found in several forms, although the variations were slight.[46] Its cousin, the fife, was pitched an octave higher than the flute.[47] The fife was generally used, with a drum, in military formations.

The Pipe

The pipe, or three-hole recorder, was played with one hand. It was actually a member of the recorder family in that it was a vertical flute with fipple. But since it was set apart, both by the level of society to which it appealed and by its peculiar technique of performance, we may consider it separately. Although it was considered a vulgar instrument by the upper-class Elizabethan, it was, at the same time, quite versatile. [48] Along with the tabor it accompanied songs, dances, and jigs, and was in fact the poor man's orchestra.[49] Its versatility was derived from two qualities: it was easy to carry about, and it had a surprising range. The way in which the pipe achieved such a great range is clearly explained by Arbeau:

The mouthpiece [of the pipe] is held in the player's mouth and the lower end rests between the little finger and the third finger, besides which, in order that it should not slip through the player's hand, there is a little cord at the end of the flute through which the third finger is passed to support and hold it. It has only three holes, two in front and one behind, and it is admirably fashioned as with the index and middle fingers touching the two holes in front and the thumb touching the one behind the notes of the scale are easily found. . . . You must know that pipes which are tall and long with a flat narrow mouthpiece like the flute in question will easily and naturally blow a fifth, and if one sound them harder still they will reach the octave. Suppose the long flute is blown gently and all the holes are stopped, it sounds G, then if one opens the first hole, which was stopped by the middle finger, it will sound A, and if one opens the second hole, stopped by the index finger, it will sound B and if one opens the third hole, which is behind and stopped by the thumb, it will sound C. After which with all holes entirely stopped and blowing a little harder, it jumps a fifth above and sounds D. With the same breath, if the middle finger be lifted, it will sound E, and F if the index finger be lifted. This done, by raising the thumb it will sound G, and continuing thus to lift the fingers and give it the appropriate blast, one can find many steps in the scale.[50]

The Cornets

Early cornets, unlike the modern brass instruments, were tapered tubes made of horn, ivory, or wood covered with leather. They had simple cup mouthpieces, very much like those of trumpets, and the tube was pierced with seven finger-holes—six in front and one behind, as was the case with the recorders and shawms. The family, or "nest," of cornets included three sizes: the high treble cornet, the treble cornet (the most popular), which was a fifth lower in pitch than the preceding size, and the tenor cornet, which was pitched an octave below the treble.[51]

The cornets were often curved in shape—the tenor cornet in the shape of a letter S. A variation of the cornets was the muted cornet, which was made in the same sizes as the ordinary cornets. In order to produce a muted tone, the mouthpiece cup was countersunk into the body of the tube instead of being attached to the exterior of the tube, as was the case with the standard cornets.

These instruments were unusually difficult to play well because they required very strong lungs and a high degree of lip control.[52] In spite of this difficulty, when they were played correctly their music was delicate, pleasant, and imitative of the human voice.[53] Their early function was to accompany large choirs, but, with the increasing secularization of music, they became musical jacks-of-all-trades. Their ability to produce dance music, song accompaniments, and imitations of other instruments, made them popular, particularly in the private theaters.[54]

The Racket

The racket was a peculiar, shawmlike instrument of bass pitch. It consisted of a tube bent back and forth eight times, pushed together, and then enclosed by a cylinder. Both the mouthpiece, with its double reed, and the terminal end of the tube projected from the top of the cylinder. The cylinder itself was short and was pierced by a complicated system of finger holes. The tonal quality of this musical platypus was muffled and reedy; it was sometimes used in place of the curtal.[55]

The Sackbuts

Having examined the string and woodwind instruments, we find ourselves on more familiar ground when we meet the brass instruments, beginning first with the sackbuts. Sackbuts are now called trombones, and despite the passage of time there is very little difference between the old and the new.[56] The Elizabethan sackbuts were made in the usual three pitches—treble, tenor, and bass; but since the treble sackbut actually produced notes in normal alto range, the treble cornet was often added to the consort of sackbuts in order to attain a complete tonal range within the group.[57]

Like the cornets, sackbuts were usually employed with choral groups, although they were also popular with the waits, or watchmen.[58] The suitability of these early trombones for either indoor or outdoor use is explained by Mersene: "It [the sackbut] should be blown by a skilfull musician, so that it may not imitate the sounds of the Trumpet but rather assimilate itself to the sweetness of the human voice, lest it should emit a warlike, rather than a peaceful sound."[59] In comparison with the modern trombone the sackbut had a softer tone, which made it suitable for small ensembles.

The Trumpet

The trumpet was the nobleman of sixteenth- and seventeenth-century instruments. Trumpeters belonged to a special guild and did not play in combination with other instruments.[60] This was probably no great loss to the consort music of the period, for the trumpet had no valves and was normally restricted to those notes usually employed in the bugle calls of our time.[61] In shape the Elizabethan trumpet resembled the modern trumpet and was about four feet long. The tone produced from it was softer than that of the modern trumpet because of its thicker metal and narrower bell.[62] There was no family or set of trumpets.

The functions of the trumpet were, in England, apparently limited to the presentation of flourishes, fanfares, and military signals. By reason of its use in royal households, it was commonly associated with scenes of stately pomp and ceremony.

The Horn

Like the trumpet, the horn was not made in sets, although it varied slightly in shape and size. In its larger form the horn had the appearance of a French horn without valves. Also, like the trumpet, the horn was reserved for signals and flourishes, usually in connection with hunting. Its tone was probably strident, as the practice of rounding the tone did not prevail until about the beginning of the eighteenth century.[63]

The Drums

Of the several varieties of drums used in Elizabethan England, three kinds were common. The kettledrums, shaped and constructed almost like their modern counterparts, were used in military formations and in processions.[64] In military formations the usual procedure was to mount two kettledrums on a horse—a drum over each foreleg. The drums were then played by the rider. In processions usually only one drum was used, and it was carried on the back of a boy. Apparently the kettledrums were seldom used in consort with other instruments.[65]

A smaller and more common drum, made of wood, was the tabor. The tabor was a barrel-shaped instrument of various depths, having a skin cover at each end.[66] In its larger forms the tabor was used by foot soldiers; in its smaller forms it was the almost inseparable companion of the three-hole pipe. According to Arbeau, the small drum was two feet deep and one foot in diameter.[67] The big drums, he tells us, were also used with a consort of hautboys. The pipe and tabor was a combination frequently present at weddings, morris dances, and other revels.[68]

A third type of drum was the timbrel, or tambourine—a small hoop of wood covered with skin on one side only—whose principal purpose was to accentuate the rhythm of dance music.[69]

The Regal

The regal was a small portable organ.[70] The keyboard, pipes, and two bellows were sometimes so disposed on a hinged frame that the instrument could be split in half and folded together. When thus closed, it resembled a large book; the source of a common name applied to it, the "Bible regal," is thus explained.[71] There was a stationary organ called the regal, but when the smaller organ is referred to it is generally spoken of as "regals," "a pair of regals," or "a pair of organs."[72] The regals were distinctive also for their use of reed, rather than metal, stops.[73]

The regals were generally used with vocal choirs. Their tone was similar to that of our clarinet, though harsher.[74]

Very little music was written for most of the instruments we have examined. In general, no music was written for specific instruments other than for the lute and its cousins, for the virginals, and for the organ.[75] Instrumental music was not yet emancipated from theories of vocal composition. The lute and its variants were played from tablature, as we have seen; the virginals and organ had their own system of piano-like notation, but the other instruments were not so recognized. Composers of the time usually wrote their works in several parts—cantus, altus, mean and bassus (treble, alto, tenor, and bass). The music could then be played by any instruments having sufficient range for each part. In this man-

ner one score could be used by either vocalists or instrumentalists
—or by combinations of the two.[76] A comparable practice is that
of informal ensembles of today which often play from only a
piano score.

Ayres were usually written in lute tablature with sometimes
a part for bass viol in the usual notation. If a consort of viols was
desired as an accompaniment for ayres, the violists often tuned
their viols in lute fashion and played their parts from the lute
tablature. A viol so tuned was called a "lyra-viol although it also used its
special tablature. [77] No tempo or dynamic marks were included in the music; the tempo of the ayres was determined, apparently, by the sentiments
expressed by the lyrics; the tempo of dance music was derived from the
various dance forms—pavane, galliard, coranto, or whatever. The tempo of
each dance was a matter of common knowledge.[78]

During the reign of Elizabeth the orchestra achieved the status
of a persisting physical unit for the first time. The various instrumental choirs existed, as we saw when we examined the families
of instruments; but only infrequently were combinations of these
choirs made. Even then the choirs could not be said to have divided
the portions of a harmony between them or to have taken different
voices in a single polyphonic rendition; they usually "echoed"
one another.[79] There were two obstacles to a union of the several
choirs; one was a preference on the part of the musicians of the
day for perceived variety in tonal textures, as opposed to the tonal
quality of masses of instruments;[80] the other was an inability to
combine some of the instruments because the volume of sounds
they produced was not compatible.[81] As a result, consorts were often
composed of the instruments of only one choir—for example, a
consort of viols, a consort of recorders, or a consort of hautboys.
This type of consort was called a "whole consort."

The headmaster of the English College of St. Omers, Pas de
Calais (1600-1617), in describing the musical activities of the
school, wrote to his superiors:

1. The music of the "whole consort," as it is called, of viols is
highly to be esteemed, and the students are to be carefully trained
in this.

2. The "broken consort" is much more delightful, however, for the reception of guests and persons of distinction, especially if the selections are well-chosen and pleasant.

3. In the "broken consort" the following instruments are best: the bass viol, or viol da gamba; the lute, or wanting this, the orpharion;[82] the treble viol; the cither; the flute; add the tenor violin and the bassoon for effectiveness and charm.

4. The music of wind instruments is full of majesty, especially for church services, for the reception of persons of high rank, and for the theater. Such instruments are the hautbois, which does not overtax young performers, and the recorder; but the former is more majestic.

5. Other wind instruments require more lung-power, e.g., the sackbut and the cornett.[83]

As the headmaster suggests, the broken consort became increasingly popular at the end of the sixteenth century, and thereafter gradually supplanted the whole consort except for the purpose of chamber music. It will be noted that the broken consort was composed of several instruments of different families—hence the name. Meyer believes the instruments used in the broken consorts were, at first, casual combinations of any instruments available at any particular time, subject only to the restriction of equable dynamics.[84] By 1600, however, the broken consort had assumed a standard form. The evolution may be followed, to a certain extent, by reference to various records of the era.

A woodcut in the 1579 edition of Spenser's *Shepheardes Calender* portrays a broken consort consisting of a bass viol, a harp, a lute, and a cross flute. In 1597 Anthony Holborne published *Preludes, Pavans, and Galliards* for a cittern and viols.[85] Two years later Morley's *First Booke of Consort Lessons* appeared: his music called for a treble lute, pandora [mandore], cittern, bass viol, treble viol, and flute.[86] The broken consort which played for the wedding of Sir Henry Unton *ca.* 1600 was made up of the same instrumentation as called for by Morley's *Consort Lessons,* except for the treble viol, which was replaced by a treble violin.[87] We may note also that the instrumentation listed by the headmaster of St. Omers is almost the same as that listed by Morley; the only difference is that the former omits the pandora.[88] In 1609, Philip Rosseter's *Lessons for Consort* appeared with the same instrumental grouping called for in Morley's work. Praetorius, in his *Syntagma Musicum*, III, 5 (1619), thus describes an English consort: ". . . several persons with all sorts of instruments such as clavicymbal or large spinett, large lyra, double harp, lute, theorbo, bandora, penorcon, cittern, viol da gamba, a small descant fiddle, a traverse flute or recorder, sometimes also a quiet sackbut or racket, sound together in one company . . . ever so quietly, tenderly and lovely, and agree with each other in a graceful symphony."[89] An ensemble of violins, consort viols, and cornets is called for in John Adson's *Courtly Masquing Ayres* . . . (1621).[90] Finally, Walter Porter's collection of ayres and madrigals (1632) lists: "Toccatos, Sinfonias and Ritornellos, after the manner of Consort Musique. To be performed with the Harpsechord, Lutes, Theorbos, Base Viall, and two Violins or two Viols.[91]

While there were variations in the composition of the broken consorts, it will be noticed that, in nearly all examples described above, the instruments used were strings (plucked and bowed) and woodwinds (flute or recorder). It will also be noted that in four of the examples the instrumentation is practically the same. We may be justified, therefore, in concluding that the broken consort during the productive period of Shakespeare was composed of strings and flutes or recorders, and that its classic form was that called for by Morley and Rosseter.

The broken consorts mentioned so far are "quiet" consorts; that is, they contain no instruments with powerful voices. There exists, however, a record of at least one "loud" consort, that used in *Silenus* (1613), which contained a pipe, a tabor, a treble violin, two bass violins ('celli), two sackbuts, a mandore, and a tenor cornet.[92] We might also reasonably believe that, in a play having stage directions calling for both "Soft Musick" and "Loud Musick," sometimes a soft broken consort and a loud broken consort were both employed.

Since I have used the term "Musick," and since that single,

bare word is the only stage direction which introduces the instrumental music in many of the plays of the period, a few words on its significance are necessary. The term might refer either to a broken or to a whole consort; the context usually contains indications of the type of consort referred to. For example, a stage direction in the play *Westward Ho!*[93] calls for "Musick within" and then adds "the Fidlers." The latter part of the direction refers to a consort of viols or similar bowed instruments. In the case of stage directions such as "The recorders play" or "Cornets sound," however, we may agree with Arnold Dolmetsch that the directions refer only to a whole consort of the instruments mentioned.[94]

The great age of the Elizabethan theater, which is the focus of our study, found such an array of musical instruments, and such a condition of rapid development in their use, as we have now observed. The men of the theater were quick to adapt the instruments, the music, the musicians, and the various types of instrumental combinations to the physical and dramatic requirements of their own art. In general, instrumental music served two purposes in the theaters; it provided entertainment of a purely musical nature before and after the plays and sometimes between the acts, and it was used for several purposes, some dramatic and some mechanical, during the course of the performance of the plays. Before considering these general functions in detail, however, we would do well to become acquainted with the musicians, the music they played, the location of the music room, and the probable organization of the theater orchestras.

The musicians of the playhouses were drawn from two primary sources: from the ranks of the actors and from the ranks of professional musicians. In the instance of the private theaters, with the possible exception of the cornet players,[95] the musicians were also the actors. The choirboys who performed in Blackfriars were taught to play instruments as well as to sing and act.[96] The musicians of the public playhouses at first may have been drawn from the companies of players, many of which contained actors who were formerly professional musicians.[97] After about 1590, however, the public players seem to have restricted their talents to acting, and, though they still frequently sang songs, they turned to the professional musicians for their instrumental music. The instrumentalists were paid by the actors, not by the housekeepers, and were numbered along with the gatherers, tiring men, and mechanics among the hired men of the playhouse.[98]

The instrumental scores used in the theaters were almost exclusively those written for dancing or as accompaniments for songs. The "In Nomines" and "fancies"—the only pure consort forms of the period—were generally too involved and technical to have popular appeal.[99] When scores were used, they were likely to be the music for dances, such as the pavane or coranto, or the music set to a popular ayre. The folk music and street songs were probably played from memory; at least I have found few contemporary settings of these songs and dances for the instruments commonly used in the playhouses.[100]

The theater consorts were usually stationed in special boxes called "music rooms" or "music houses." The location of these rooms within the various theaters is a debatable question and, no doubt, was not the same in every theater. In describing the public playhouses Cowling states that the music rooms were always situated above and to the side of the outer stage. This may be true of the Swan, as he claims, inconclusive though his evidence most certainly is;[101] however, the music room of the Globe and that of the Fortune were, as J. C. Adams has clearly demonstrated, located within the third level of the tiring house, and they opened at the center of the outer stage.[102]

In the private theaters also the location of the music room varied from house to house. In Blackfriars the musicians were apparently placed above the stage, either in the center or to the side.[103] The place occupied by the music room at Whitefriars is unknown, although there is no doubt that there was one.[104] The theater used by the Children of Paul's had two music houses, but their exact location is also unknown.[105] The King's Masquing House at Whitehall contained a music room at the side and to the front of the stage, apparently on the floor level.[106]

Fortunately for the study of music in the Shakespearean drama, serious and productive study has been devoted to the construction of the Globe playhouse. The music room occupied a rectangular space measuring eight by twelve feet, and was twenty-three feet above the stage platform.[107] The open side of the room, facing the audience, was crossed by a railing and was screened by a thin curtain which was usually closed while the musicians performed in the music room. The area of the room was large enough to accommodate six or eight men with their instruments. The room would thus hold the number of men mentioned by Malone as his conjecture concerning the size of the early theater consorts.[108] It should be noted also that the consort for which Morley and Rosseter wrote their scores would fit nicely into the Globe music room.

We must remember, however, that the size of the music room did not necessarily limit the number of instruments or players used in any particular playhouse. The musicians were not restricted in location to the music room; they moved from one place to another as the effective presentation of their music and the exigencies of a particular play production might require. Musicians played from the outer stage, from the inner stage, from the tiring house, and from the balconies above the stages.[109]

I find it impossible to give a complete and detailed account of the organization and personnel of any specific theater consort, for I know of no direct evidence of a permanent, well-defined musical group being maintained by any playing company of the time. But we can, despite the lack of direct evidence, draw some inferences from material at hand. Suppose we consider first the consorts of the private theaters.

As we have seen, the choirboys were trained to play instruments as well as to sing; therefore no distinction can be made (with one exception) between the actors and the musicians. The exception is the apparent distinction between the boy-musicians of Blackfriars and the cornetists who performed so frequently in the Blackfriars plays. I believe that, in the case of this company, a consort of cornets composed of adult musicians was used to augment the music provided by the boys. This slight distinction has been made by no other students of the subject, so far as I know, and its significance should be explained.

There has been an unconscious assumption by students of the choirboy companies and their plays that the cornets were played by the boys as a regular part of their activities. The nature of the instrument makes this assumption questionable. The accounts I have seen describing the cornets and their music agree that they were difficult to play, that they required strong lungs and precise lip control, and that they were either played very well or played very badly. The extensive use of cornets in the private theaters suggests that they were popular with a discriminating audience, and the versatility which characterized their use also indicates a high degree of skill on the part of the cornetists. While it is possible that such skill could have been acquired by the choirboys during the six or eight years they were part of the company, it is unlikely that any of them possessed the lung power required by the instruments and the types of music used in the plays, as the ages of the boys ranged from about six to fourteen years.[110] I have found no evidence that the Blackfriars boys, or any other group of choirboys, actually played cornets for plays.[111]

The use of cornets in the production of *The Malcontent* by the King's Men is a part of the question. The play, written by Marston for the Blackfriars Children, was acquired by the King's Men after it had been acted several times, possibly as a result of the reorganization of the Children of Blackfriars incident to the death of Elizabeth in 1603. The King's Men added an induction, reduced the amount of music in the play, and produced it in 1604.

Apparently, cornets were not used in the public playhouses prior to about 1609.[112] The presence of stage directions calling for cornets in the modified play of the King's Men is unusual. An explanation is possible if we assume that the cornetists were professional musicians and not boys of the company. When the Children of the Chapel were reorganized in 1603, the professional cornetists may have taken temporary employment with the public playhouses, thus supplying the music for the 1604 production of *The Malcontent*. The successor to the Children of Blackfriars, the Blackfriars

Children of His Majesties Revels, again employed cornets until 1608 when, apparently, the King's Men acquired the services of the cornetists of Blackfriars along with the Blackfriars theater.

It seems, therefore, that the consort of cornetists employed at Blackfriars was composed of adult musicians more or less permanently attached to that theater. The cornet consort, I imagine, included from four to six players.

It is difficult to find evidence of a well-defined musical establishment permanently attached to any particular theater. The fact is that consorts varied so widely from play to play in the repertories of all the theaters, that variations among the practices of the theaters themselves do not emerge clearly from the stage directions at our command. Henslowe, in his account book, in 1598 listed the musical instruments in possession of the Admiral's Men, of the Rose playhouse, as three trumpets, one drum, one treble viol, one bass viol, one pandore, one cittern, one sackbut, a chime of bells, and three timbrels.[113] He also listed two rackets, but there is no indication that these were musical instruments and not tennis rackets.[114] Later on, Henslowe's company acquired another sackbut, another bass viol, and "othere enstrumentes."[115] This list of instruments, in itself, sheds more darkness than light on the problem. For example, the list tells us nothing of the uses to which the instruments were put, and that is what we would like to know; the possible conjectures have been exhaustively treated by Cowling.[116] We may note, though, that the list would provide for a broken consort composed of treble viol, bass viol, pandora, cittern, and timbrels; the three trumpets and drum could have supplied flourishes and marches, and the sackbut could have been muted and added to the broken consort for solemn music such as was used in the Admiral's Men's production of *King Edward the Fourth* (*ca.* 1600).[117] But this is still purely a matter of conjecture; for clearer light we must turn to interior evidence provided by the plays of the period.

As we have previously noted, the public players used less music than the private companies. Often drums and trumpets supplied all the noise required. Yet several scripts used by the public players between 1590 and 1615 call for fairly large groups of instruments. Of the plays which can with reasonable assurance be assigned to public companies Dekker's *Old Fortunatus* (1600), *Satiro-mastix* (1602), *The Whore of Babylon* (1607), *The Roaring Girl* (1611), and Greene's *If It Be Not Good* (1612), and Peele's *The Old Wives Tale* (1595) show evidence of the use of several instruments other than the drum and trumpet.[118]

Old Fortunatus calls for "Musicke" for a lute and for trumpets. That the term "musicke" did not refer to the trumpets may be inferred from the stage direction: *"Trumpets sound: Enter Athelstane . . . Musicke sounds within."*[119] The general nature of the "musicke" in this scene may be inferred from its use to accompany singing, which would require a degree of softness foreign to the trumpets. Further information is provided by the comments of Shadow, who enters the stage while Andelocia is being charmed asleep, under Agripine's spell, with the aid of a lullaby played by the "Musicke": *"Musicke still: Enter Shaddow. . . Shad. . . .* Musicke? O delicate warble . . . O delicious strings: these heauenly wyre-drawers. . . ."[120] Shadow's use of the noun "warble" is a common one during the period when the music of wind instruments of the flute family is mentioned, particularly the music of a flute or recorder. "Strings" may refer to bowed or struck stringed instruments. Apparently, in addition to the trumpets, a broken consort composed of viols, lute, and flute, or, possibly, viols and recorder, was employed in the play.[121]

The stage directions in *Satiro-mastix* call for "Musicke" (for dancing), trumpets, "Lowde musicke," "Soft Musicke" (for a marriage masque), and a "bolde Drum."[122] I have found no evidence of trumpets being used for dancing at any time, although viols or fiddles were often used. The term "Soft Musicke" also is applied most often to the music of viols or recorders. Since recorders would have been a bit mournful for a wedding masque, a consort of viols, or a broken consort of strings, is indicated.

Hautboys play during two dumb shows in *The Whore of Babylon*.[123] In *The Roaring Girl* a song is accompanied by a bass viol.[124] The command "Strike, strike your silver strings, . . ." which precedes a dance in *If It Be Not Good,* is apparently given to a string consort.[125] Drums and trumpets were also used in the play.[126] *The Old Wives Tale* contains the stage direction: *"Enter the Hostess and Jack, setting meat on the table; and Fiddlers come to play. . . ."*[127]

There are many other examples of the use of instrumental music by players other than the choirboys, but the companies performing the plays cannot be firmly established as being public players.[128] We may safely conclude, however, that the public players used consorts, both broken and whole, in some of their plays, and that the term "Musicke" was used to indicate both the broken and the whole consorts.

To judge from the examples cited, it would appear that the number of instruments used in a particular play might vary from a trumpet and drum to an orchestra composed of a five- or six-piece consort augmented by about three trumpets and one or two drums—a hypothetical total of between ten and twelve pieces. The number of musicians hired by the actors in the playhouses cannot be ascertained. In some instances doubling was probably practiced: a lutenist might also play the cittern, orpharion, penorcon, pandurina, bandore, and archlute; the violist might play all the other members of the same family, the hautboist might double on the recorder.

The use of instrumental music in the "act time" of Elizabethan plays was an accepted custom in both the private and public theaters, although the former laid greater stress on the practice than did the latter.[129] Mr. J. R. Moore suggests that the lack of extensive entr'acte music in the public playhouses was one result of the shorter playing time permitted by open air performances, as compared to the longer playing time possible in the artificially lighted indoor theaters.[130] This was, no doubt, one factor considered by the players, but the presence of many skillful musicians among the choirboys is enough explanation for the emphasis placed on music in the private theater plays.

Instrumental music served many dramatic purposes on the stage; it was used to suggest settings, to portray character, to forward the action, and to heighten the emotional impact of passages and scenes.

Settings were often emphasized by the employment of instruments associated by the audience with the particular scenes suggested. In most cases the choice of instruments reflected the actual usages of the period. In Elizabethan England hautboys and trumpets were frequently used on state occasions. Hautboys usually supplied processional music which was interspersed with trumpet flourishes and fanfares. During the course of banquets hautboys also played; the trumpets sounded at the beginning and ending of the feast. For example, a contemporary account states: "[The] Banquet being taken away with sound of Musicke, there, ready for the purpose, his Maiestie made his entrance into this his Court Royall: . . . (The Wayts & Haultboyes of London)."[131] Correspondingly, in Heywood's *If You Know Not Me,* Part II (1606) hautboys are used to set the stage for the entrance of the queen. "*Sir Tho.* The Queene hath din'd: the trumpets sound already, . . . Bid the waits and Hoboyes to be ready at an instant. *Enter, at one door, the Queen.*"[132]

Another type of solemnity, that which marked scenes of a funereal or mournful pomp, was accompanied by music played on instruments capable of producing grave, subdued tones—most often recorders, sackbuts, or drums. In Marston's *Antonio and Mellida,* Part I, V (1602), occurs the stage direction: "*The still Flutes sound a mournful Cynet.*[133] *Enter a Cofin.*" And in his play, *Sophonisba, V, iv* (1606): "*Organ and recorders play to a single voice. Enter in the meantime the mournful solemnity of Massinissa's presenting Sophonisba's body.*" The use of sackbuts and drums in solemn scenes is indicated by a stage direction in Beaumont and Fletcher's *The Mad Lover* (ca. 1618), III, iv: "*A dead march within of drums and sackbuts.*"[134]

Musical instruments contributed to the creation of an atmosphere of mystery in scenes portraying supernatural events. Fortunatus is charmed to sleep by music in *Old Fortunatus,* as is Amurack in *Alphonsus, King of Aragon* (1599), and Mars in *The Coblers Prophesie* (1594).[135] In *Sophonisba,* IV, i, "*Infernal music plays softly whilst Erictho enters, . . .*" and in *If It Be Not Good* this direction appears: "*Enter (at the sound of hellish musick,) Pluto and Charon.*"[136]

We would naturally expect music to accompany scenes of revelry. Banquets, wedding festivities, and masques, when presented on the Elizabethan stage, were generally accompanied by appropriate music. The music for banquets was provided by hautboys, or string consorts, as a rule. In *Westward Ho!* (1607) a consort of fiddles provides dinner music; hautboys play for a banquet in *The Maid's Tragedy*, (1609-1611), IV, ii.

Music usually suggested the festive spirit of a marriage or of an approaching marriage. Dancing and singing often accompanied the instruments, and in many instances a short masque was performed on the stage. A few examples: *The Scornful Lady*, IV, ii (1616): "*A Street. Music. Enter Young Loveless and Widow going to be married.*" *Satiro-mastix* (1602): "*Soft Musicke, chaire is set under a Canopie. Kin.* Sound Musicke . . . Musicke shall spend this hour. . . ." [The king's remark introduces a nuptial masque].[137] *James the Fourth*, V, ii, (1594): "*After a solemne service, enter from the widdowes house, a service, musical songs of marriages, or a maske, or what prettie triumph you list.*"[138]

Instruments associated with rustic life were frequently employed as a part of rural settings. Stage directions do not often name the specific instruments, but we know that bucolic life was commonly linked with the pipe, bagpipe, tabor, rebec, crowd, and tongs and bones—the latter a crude rhythm device.[139] For example, in *Edward I* (1599), Scene ii, a direction states: "*Enter [Jack] the Novice and his company, to give the Queen music at her tent. Jack.* Come, fellows, cast yourselves even round in a string—a ring I would say: . . . set your crowds. . . ."

Elizabethan poets found many similes and metaphors in the relationship between musical structure and the harmonious structure of human character. According to the Pythagorean concept of the universe then current, the planets were kept in their orbits by the "music of the spheres" which, by harmonic law, held them in place.[140] The earth and its inhabitants were also influenced by this divine music. The "good" nature of man was a nature in tune with the celestial music; the "evil" nature of man was one out of tune with the universe.[141]

Considered in the light of this concept, the impact of the music which opens Marston's *The Malcontent* may be judged more accurately. The initial stage direction, I, ii, states: "*The vilest out-of-tune music being heard.*" Duke Pietro enters shortly and asks: "Where breathes that music? *Bil.* The dischord rather than the music is heard from the malcontent Malevole's chamber." Thus, even before the appearance of Malevole, his character has been well defined by the music.

The physical limitations of the Elizabethan stage threw much of the burden of indicating off-stage action on the musicians. The use of trumpets and drums to indicate battles, triumphal processions, and the off-stage arrival of important characters is so familiar that it needs no further discussion here. Likewise the use of horns "within" to suggest a distant hunting party is well known. A more subtle use of music, however, was its use to portray the effects of charms and spells upon characters. In Greene's *Alphonsus, King of Aragon*, III, ii, the fact that Amurack is enchanted, and that his subsequent actions are performed while he is under a magical spell, is indicated by the use of music. "*Sound musicke, hearken* Amurack, *and fall a sleepe.*" When he is asleep, Medea enters and enchants him. Then: "*Sound Instruments within:* Amurack *as it were in a dreame, say. . . . Sound Instruments a while within, and then* Amuracke *say. . . .* "[142]

A consort is used for a symbolic purpose in Robert Wilson's *The Coblers Prophesie* (1594), line 994, where the inharmonious nature of Folly is illustrated by the music of a fife, an instrument too shrill for normal consort purposes. The excerpt I give is, I believe, self-explanatory:

Venus: Bid Nicenes, Newfangle, Dalliance and the rest bring forth their Musicke Mars intends to sleepe.
Follie: I will forsooth.   *Exit* Follie.
Mars: I thinke in deede that I shall quickly sleepe,
Especially with Musicke and with song.
Enter Follie *with a Fife,* Nicenes, Newfangle, Dalliance, *and* Iealozie *with Instruments, they play while* Venus *sings. . .*
Enter Contempt, and kisse Venus.

*   *   *   *   *   *   *   *   *   *   *

Venus: Hold on your Musicke, Follie leaue thy play,
Come hither lay his head vpon thy knee. . . .
Come my Content [Contempt], lets daunce about the place,
And mocke God Mars vnto his sleepie face.
   Con: Venus agreed, play vs a Galliard.
         Musicke plaies, they daunce. . . .
  Mars. Why sings not Venus? hir loue I to heare,
Sweet let the Fife be further from mine eare.
        Follie *holds still the Fife.*
Nay let the Fife play, els the Musicke failes.
       Follie plaies againe.
What still so nere my eare, sweet, Venus sing. . . .[143]

In this example, the fife enters directly into the action of the scene.

Music was commonly employed to create a background for lyrical speeches or to heighten the emotional intensity of scenes. Such usage would naturally require a consort of instruments which could be played softly, in order that the speaker might be clearly understood. Normally, a stringed group would be suitable, but sometimes recorders, cornets, or even hautboys might be used if they could be placed some distance away from the stage, or if they were otherwise muted.

The use of background music is excellently illustrated by a speech in Rowley's *When You See Me You Know Me* (Q 1613), which apparently employs two consorts, one of strings and the other of woodwinds, to reflect the thoughts of the speaker.

Tye. Tis ready for your Grace, giue breath to your loud tun'd instruments.
         Loud Musicke.
Prince. Tis well, me thinks in this sound I prooue a compleat age,
As Musicke, So is man gouern'd by stops,
Aw'd by diuiding notes, sometimes aloft,
Sometimes below, and when he hath attained,
His high and loftie pitch, breathed his sharpest and most
Shrillest ayre, yet at length tis gone,
And fals downe flat to his conclusion,   *(Soft Musicke.)*

Another sweetnesse, and harmonious sound,
A milder straine, another kind agreement,
Yet among'st these many strings, be one vntun'd
Or iarreth low, or higher than his course,
Not keeping steddie meane among'st the rest,
Corrupts them all, so doth bad men the best.[144]

In the first part of this passage Tye calls for wind instruments, to whose music the Prince begins his speech. After the stage direction *"Soft Musicke,"* the Prince refers to "these many strings"—an apparent reference to another consort producing the gentler strains.

Several more or less mechanical problems of staging were frequently solved by the use of the theater musicians. The noise produced by the machinery of lifts and other stage devices was often covered by the sound of music. The solemn strains which accompanied the appearance of gods and spirits not only lifted the hearer out of the world of actuality but also served a prosaic purpose as well. Ben Jonson mentions this practice in his account of the production of *The Masque of Queens* (1609): "Here the throne . . . sodaynely chang'd, and in the place of it appeared Fama bona . . . She, after the musique had done, wch wayted on the turning of the machine, call'd from thence to Vertue. . . ."[145]

A similar practice was the use of the consort to sustain the aural interest of the spectators while a bit of stage business or a dumb show took place. Dekker's *The Whore of Babylon* (1607) contains this stage direction: *"The hault-boyes sounding, Titania in dumb shew. . . ."*[146] In *Westward Ho!* we find: *Musicke. Whilst the song is heard, The Earle drawes a Curten, and sets forth a Banquet. . . .*[147]

The performance of instrumental music before the plays and occasionally between the acts was an established custom, although there is some debate about the extent to which the practice was followed by the public players.[148] It would be reasonable to suppose that the private theaters were foremost in adopting extraneous musical entertainment, and the evidence amply supports the supposition. The point is illustrated by the directions in Marston's *Antonio and Mellida*, Part 2 (1602): *"Alb.* . . . Sound lowder musick: let my breath exact,/ You strike sad Tones vnto this dismall act. ACT *ACT II. SCEN. I. The Cornets sound a cynet . . . The Cornets sounde for the Acte* (V) . . .".[149] The playing of entr'acte music, however, sometimes occurred in public playhouse performances, as, for example, apparently in *Sejanus*.[150]

The use of music on the stage of the period gave rise to several minor conventions. For instance, the theater consort, unless it appeared on the outer stage, was usually hidden by being placed either "within," or behind the curtains of the music room.[151] This custom left the playwright free to indicate, by means of explanatory remarks from his characters, the purpose served by the music, and its supposed source. Likewise, when the musicians appeared in view, the dramatist was again usually careful to identify the musicians through the lips of his characters and to inform his audience why they were present.[152]

The necessity for giving cues to the musicians led to the development of another set of conventions. The simplest method was for an actor to call for music whenever it was needed. When the distance between actor and consort made this procedure impractical, the actor used some gesture as a signal to the musicians. We would expect the prompter to cue in the music and, when the musicians performed near him, he often did so. But when the musicians occupied the music room, which was usually above and behind the normal station of the prompter, the musicians apparently found it easier to take their cues directly from the actors. One of the simpler directions supplied by actors occurs in *The Scornful Lady* (1616), II, ii: "*Enter Young Loveless and his Comrades, with Wenches and two Fiddlers.*" In subsequent lines, Loveless directs the musicians: "Strike up you merry varlets. . . . Lead on a march, you michers. . . . Strike him a hornpipe, squeakers!" Cues given by actors to musicians in the music room were subtler. In Jonson's *Cynthia's Revels* (1601), a singer on the outer stage is accompanied by a consort hidden in the music room. The cue for the consort to play is provided by the remark of another actor, also on the outer stage: "*Mer.* . . . The humorous aire shall mixe her solemne tunes/ With thy sad words: strike musicque from the spheares. . . ."

In concluding our survey of music in the drama of Elizabethan England, we must realize that the conventions we have observed do not, by any means, exhaust the body of practices actually employed by the dramatists of the time. Our examination is limited to those practices capable of proof. Nor do the categories of dramatic conventions here arbitrarily assigned provide a complete picture of the uses to which the music was put; for example, the playing of one piece of music might serve several simultaneous functions in the production of a play. Perhaps the most significant point is this: The most casual glance at the majority of Elizabethan plays employing music will reveal that the music is usually not incidental, but is an integral part of the plays. In other words, the dramatists wrote their plays using music as one of their tools; music, or even a particular piece or type of music, was in the mind of the dramatist when he wrote scenes employing that art. Hence, by a serious study of the music used by the dramatist, we may be able to obtain a glimpse of the creative process at work, to follow a concept from its genesis in the mind of the dramatist on through to its actual presentation upon the stage. The following chapters will present such a study of seven comedies of William Shakespeare.

II

Notes

1. The subject receives a very general treatment in Naylor, *Shakespeare and Music*, and Cowling, *Music on the Shakespearean Stage*. More details may be found in several essays by W. J. Lawrence: "The English Theatre Orchestra. . . ." *The Musical Quarterly*, III, 9 ff.; "Music and Song in the Elizabethan Theatre," in *The Elizabethan Playhouse and Other Studies*; and "Music in the Elizabethan Theater," in *Shakespeare Jahrbuch*, XLIV, 36-50. See also H. M. Fitzgibbon, "Instruments and Their Music in the Elizabethan Drama," *Musical Quarterly*, XVII, 319 ff.

2. There were three independent instrumental forms at the beginning of the seventeenth century, the "In Nomine," the "Fancy" or "Fantasy," and the "Browning." The "In Nomine" was a theme and variations, not necessarily religious in nature, although the theme was usually a plain song. The form appeared in the middle of the sixteenth century and was used by Taverner (1495-1545) and many later composers. The "Fancy" differed from the "In Nomine" in that the composer of the former was free to invent his own theme as well as his variations. Morley (*A Plaine and Easie Introduction . . . 1597*, p. 162) remarks: "But such [fantasies] they seldome compose, except it either bee to shewe their varietie at some odde time to see what may be done vpon a point without a dittie, or at the request of some friend, to shew the diuersitie

of sundrie mens vaines vpon one subiect." The "Browning" was a 'folk tune which had been given an artistic arrangement, usually variations of several kinds. A more detailed discussion of these three instrumental forms may be found in E. H. Meyer, *English Chamber Music*, pp. 83-112.

3. A discussion of the use of sound effects in the plays of the period may be found in Lawrence, *Pre-Restoration Stage Studies*, pp. 199-208, and W. W. Wood, "A Comparison between Shakespeare and His Contemporaries in Their Use of Music and Sound Effects," *Summaries of Doctoral Dissertations*, Northwestern University, XII, 33-38.

4. This is the opinion expressed by C. Sachs (*The History of Musical Instruments*, p. 344); K. Geiringer (*Musical Instruments*, p. 70); and F. W. Galpin (*Old English Instruments of Music*, p. 42). Arnold Dolmetsch (*The Interpretation of the Music . . .*, pp. 437, 438) believes that at the end of the sixteenth century the lute with thirteen strings was the most popular.

5. Geiringer, p. 70; Sachs, p. 344.

6. Galpin, p. 43.

7. *Ibid.*; A. Dolmetsch, p. 443.

8. The composers and their music are well represented in Fellowes, *The English School of Lutenist Song Writers*.

9. An excellent discussion of lute tablature may be found in A. Dolmetsch, pp. 439-441.

10. J. Playford (*A Brief Introduction to the Skill of Musick . . . 1667*, p. 75) mentions "the Lyra Viol, which is [played] by Letters or Tablature," and (p. 82) "A bass viol to play 'Lyraway' which is by Tablature must be less than the former two."

11. For more detailed treatments of the cittern, see Sachs, pp. 345-347; Geiringer, pp. 91, 92; Galpin, pp. 29-34; and A. Dolmetsch, pp. 443-444.

12. Sachs (p. 346) and Geiringer (p. 91) state that some citterns had more than eight strings.

13. Galpin, p. 30.

14. *Ibid.*, pp. 29, 30. Naylor (p. 17) cites the passage from Jonson's *Silent Woman* in which Morose exclaims, "That cursed barber! I have married his cittern that is common to all men."

15. Galpin, p. 33.

16. For more extensive treatment of the viols, see Sachs, pp. 347-350; Galpin, pp. 85-96; A. Dolmetsch, pp. 444-453; and G. R. Hayes, *Musical Instruments and Their Music, 1500-1750*, II, "Viols and Violins."

17. Sachs, p. 347; Hayes, p. 26 ff.; Galpin, Plate 17.

18. Sachs, p. 348.

19. The slight arch on the viol bridges permitted the violists to play music containing double, triple, or quadruple stops with ease compared to the difficulty which modern violinists find in playing similar music, such as the Bach "Chaconne." The flattened bridge also permitted the violist to play chords usually written for the lute or similar instruments, as we have seen. The additional voices or parts which one viol could contribute to a consort increased its value for consort purposes as well as for solo performance. The sound produced by a viol da gamba playing chords is suggested by a piece of program music in Tobias Hume's *Musicall Humors* (1605) which, he states, was written in "the imitation of Church Music, singing to the organs, but here you must use the Viol de Gambo for the organ." (Quoted by P. Warlock, *The English Ayre*, p. 83.)

20. A. Dolmetsch, p. 446.

21. For example, the title-page of William Corkine's *First Book of Airs* (1600) reads, in part: "Ayres, to Sing and Play to the Lute and Basse Violl. With Pavins, Galliards, Almaines, and Corantos for the Lyra Violl." The Lyra viol was one of the smaller bass viols (Sachs, p. 348.)

22. According to Hayes (p. 16), this combination was the prevalent consort at the end of the sixteenth century.

23. E. H. Meyer, p. 140.

24. Hayes, pp. 30-34. The viol da braccia and rebec, however, were held against the shoulder (Geiringer, pp. 87, 88).

25. E. H. Meyer, pp. 97-103. See note 21, above.

26. Sachs, pp. 276-278; Geiringer, p. 91.

27. Sachs, p. 278; Geiringer, p. 85.

28. Naylor, pp. 11, 12.

29. *Ibid.*, pp. 47, 48.

30. See below.

31. Sachs, p. 359.

32. *Ibid.*, pp. 314-317; Geiringer, pp. 100-102.

33. Arbeau, *Orchesography*, p. 50; C. V. Stanford and C. Forsyth, *A History of Music*, p. 185.

34. Stanford and Forsyth, p. 184. See Arbeau, p. 50.

35. I have found no instance in which the hautboys or shawms were used in the private theaters or in intimate instrumental groupings. The avoidance of the trumpet by the boy actors of the private theaters, as noted by Lawrence (*Shakespeare's Workshop*, pp. 53, 54), seems to have been also extended to the shawms and hautboys.

36. These municipal bands were generally known as "waits." Dekker mentions the "Waytes and Haultboyes of London" in his account, *The King's Entertainment Through the City of London* (1603). See Dekker, *Works*, I, 280. A description of the municipal duties and dramatic activities of the "waits" may be found in "Players at Ipswich," *Malone Society Collections*, II, Part 3, pp. 265, 266, 275, 276, 280. See also Galpin, p. 162.

37. Brooke and Paradise, *English Drama, 1580-1642*, pp. 690, 691, and "Cambridge Dramatic Records," *Malone Society Collections*, II, Part 2, pp. 207, 208.

38. Sachs, p. 310; Galpin, p. 141; Cowling, p. 56.

39. A. Dolmetsch, p. 457.

40. An illustration of the bass recorder may be found in Naylor, facing p. 48.

41. Sachs, p. 314.

42. *Op. cit.*, p. 457.

43. Bacon, *Works*, I, Cent. II, par. 170, and Cent. III, par. 230.

44. See Ford, *The Broken Heart* (1633), V, iii; Marston, *Sophonisba* (1606), V, iv; Galpin, p. 152; Fitzgibbon, pp. 320, 321.

45. E. H. Meyer, p. 131.

46. Galpin, p. 154.

47. *Ibid.*

48. Naylor, pp. 79, 80.

49. Arbeau, p. 51. It is significant, I believe, that although the pipe and tabor are often alluded to in plays, I have found little evidence in the stage directions of the use of the pipe and tabor in non-Shakespearean dramas produced or published between 1590 and 1620. In general, the dramatists used the fiddle, crowd, or harp, when common music was needed.

50. *Op. cit.*, pp. 48, 49.

51. Galpin, pp. 193, 194; Sachs, p. 324.

52. Cf. p. 28; also Sachs, p. 324, and Stanford and Forsyth, p. 188.

53. Yet Marston, in *Antonio and Mellida*, Part 2 (1602), I, i, describes the tone of the cornet: *"One windes a Cornet within. Ant. . . .* Harke Madam, how yon Cornet ierketh vp/ His straind shrill accents, in the capering ayre: . . ." Cf. Galpin, p. 192. The tone quality of the cornet probably resembled that of a cow horn, though, of course, the cornet was easier to control and was, in all respects, a true musical instrument. Its popularity lasted a long time; the tenor cornet, or "serpent," was used in many bands as late as the first quarter of the nineteenth century.

54. The versatility of the cornets may be observed in their uses in Marston's plays, *Antonio and Mellida* (1602), *Sophonisba* (1606), *The Faun* (1606), and *The Malcontent* (1604).

55. Sachs, pp. 319, 320; Geiringer, p. 102.

56. Galpin, Plate 42; Sachs, pp. 325-327; Geiringer, p. 109.

57. Galpin, p. 211.

58. *Ibid.*, p. 209.

59. Quoted by Galpin, p. 212.

60. *Ibid.*, pp. 204, 207.

61. I have found no evidence of the use in English plays of the slide, or chromatic, trumpet described by Sachs, "Chromatic Trumpets in the Renaissance," *Musical Quarterly*, XXXVI, 62-66.

62. Sachs, *History*, p. 328.

63. For a full account of the horn, see Galpin, pp. 184-189; Geiringer, p. 81.

64. Galpin, pp. 251, 252.

65. They were used with trumpets, however. Dekker, in his account, *The King's Entertainment Through the City of London* (1603), wrote: ". . . to delight the Queene with her owne country Musicke, nine Trumpets, and a Kettle Drum, did very sprightly & actiuely sound the 'Danish march': . . ." (Dekker, *Works*, I, 295.)

66. Galpin, Plates 28, 30.

67. *Op. cit.*, p. 50. The English tabor was smaller than the tabor described by Arbeau. (Galpin, p. 149, Plate 30.)

68. Arbeau, pp. 50, 51.

69. Galpin, pp. 240, 241.

70. *Ibid.*, p. 230; Sachs, p. 308; Geiringer, pp. 105, 106.

71. Sachs, *History*, p. 309; Geiringer, p. 106.

72. Galpin, pp. 227, 228, 231.

73. Sachs, *History*, p. 308; Geiringer, p. 106.

74. Galpin, p. 234.

75. E. H. Meyer, pp. 83-96.

76. A reproduction of the complete score of Dowland's "Lachrimae," arranged for four voices, viol da gamba, and lute, may be found in Cowling, Plate VIII.

77. See note 10, p. 17.

78. Morley, pp. 181, 182; A. Dolmetsch, p. 33. Some of the earliest expression marks, or directions for interpretation, appear in Tobias Hume's *Musicall Humors* (1605): "Play this pashenat," "Play this as it stands," "Drum this with the back of the bow." (Cited by Warlock, p. 84.)

79. In *The Description of a Maske presented before the Kinges Maiestie. at White Hall, on twelft night last, in honour of the Lord HAYES, and his*

Bride, . . . (1607), Campion describes the placing of the various instrumental groups as follows: "The great Hall (wherein the Maske was presented) receiued this diuision, and order: The vpper part where the cloth and chaire of State were plac't, had scaffoldes and seates on eyther side continued to the skreene; right before it was made a partition for the dauncing place; on the right hand whereof were consorted ten Musitions, with Basse and Meane lutes, a Bandora, a double Sack-bott, and an Harpsicord, with two treble Violins; on the other side, somewhat neerer the skreene were plac't 9 Violins and three Lutes, and to answere both the Consorts (as it were in a triangle) six Cornets, and sixe Chappell voyces, were seated almost right against them, in a place raised higher in respect of the pearcing sound of those Instruments. . . . Behind the [scenery] toward the window was a small descent, with an other spreading hill that climed vp to the toppe of the window, with many trees on the height of it, whereby those that played on the Hoboyes at the Kings entrance into the hall were shadowed. . . ." (P. Vivian, ed., *Campion's Works*, pp. 62, 63.)

80. E. H. Meyer, p. 131.
81. *Ibid.*
82. An English instrument different in shape from the lute and which used wire strings, but which was tuned and played in the same manner as the lute. (A. Dolmetsch, p. 443.)
83. W. H. McCabe, "Music and Dance on a 17th Century College Stage," *Musical Quarterly*, XXIV, 314. I question the use of the term, "bassoon," in paragraph 3. Mr. McCabe probably translated a descriptive Latin term by using the word "bassoon." The bass recorder, similar in appearance to the bassoon, would have been more appropriate to the consort described.
84. *Op. cit.*, 131, 132.
85. *Ibid.*, 130.
86. *Ibid.*
87. E. H. Meyer, p. 128; A. Dolmetsch, p. 463.
88. The pandora (bandora, mandore) was closely related to the lute and orpharion.
89. Cited by E. H. Meyer, pp. 130, 131.
90. *Ibid.*, p. 130.
91. *Ibid.*
92. *Ibid.*, p. 132.
93. Dekker, *Works*, II, 351.
94. A. Dolmetsch, p. 462.
95. The cornetists were probably adult professional musicians. See pp. 33, 34.
96. C. W. Wallace, *The Children of the Chapel at Blackfriars, 1597-1603*, pp. 9, 116; also p. 106, fn. 1.
97. Augustine Phillips, William Kemp, George Brian, Thomas Pope, Richard Cowley, John Sinkler, Thomas Vincent, Robert Pallant, William Toyer, and Thomas Mason were all musicians connected with Shakespeare's company. See T. W. Baldwin, *The Organization and Personnel of the Shakespearean Company*, pp. 80, 81, 120, 134, 233, 281; W. W. Greg, ed., *Henslowe's Diary*, II, p. 69; Greg, ed., *The Henslowe Papers*, p. 152; Chambers, *William Shakespeare*, I, 40, and II, 73, 74.
98. *Malone Society Collections*, II, Part 3, p. 365.
99. Morley, p. 162; E. H. Meyer, pp. 94-96, 140.
100. The *Fitzwilliam Virginal Book* contains settings of folk music ("Sellingers Round," for example) by Byrd. These were probably "Brownings" or folk

tunes used as themes for variations. (E. H. Meyer, p. 112.) The virginals were not used to any extent in the playhouses, probably because of their feeble volume.

101. Cowling, pp. 24-29.

102. *The Globe Playhouse*, pp. 298-301; Lawrence, *The Physical Conditions of the Elizabethan Public Playhouse*, p. 5.

103. Marston's play, *Sophonisba*, which was presented at Blackfriars in 1606, has the stage direction, IV, i, "A short song to soft music above." Cf. Lawrence, *The Physical Conditions*, p. 91; Malone, *The Works of Shakespeare*, III (Prologomena), 112, fn. 5.

104. Cowling, p. 28.

105. Marston, *Antonio and Mellida*, Part 2, V, v.

106. Shakespeare Society, *Revels at Court*, pp. 214, 215, 221.

107. *The Globe Playhouse*, pp. 301, 309.

108. Malone, III, 111, 112.

109. As in Wilson, *The Coblers Prophesie*, ll. 992-1028; Marston, *Sophonisba*, IV, i; Greene, *James the Fourth*, I, i; and Marston, *The Malcontent*, I, i, respectively. Cf. Malone, III, 112, fn. 5; Cowling, pp. 29-41; Lawrence, "The English Theatre Orchestra," *Musical Quarterly*, III, 9 ff.

110. See pp. 23, 24, 28; Galpin, pp. 192, 193.

111. The stage directions pertaining to the cornets afford only negative information on this point. The usual direction is impersonal, for example, "Cornets sound a flourish" or "Cornets play." In Marston's *Antonio and Mellida*, Part 2, I, Antonio directs: "Boy, winde thy Cornet. . . ." The boy leaves the stage, and shortly the cornet is heard. The direction for the actual sounding of the cornet, however, is "One windes a Cornet within."

112. Lawrence, *Shakespeare's Workshop*, pp. 48-74.

113. Greg, ed., *The Henslowe Papers*, pp. 115, 116, 118.

114. *Ibid.*, p. 118.

115. Greg, ed., *Henslowe's Diary*, I, 98, 100, 110.

116. *Op. cit.*, 82, 83.

117. T. Heywood, *Works*, I, 154.

118. *The Malcontent*, which was publicly performed by the King's Men, has been previously discussed, see p. 33. The extent to which music was used in the public playhouses has been the subject for much debate. See Malone, III, 111, fns. 3, 4; Cowling, pp. 24-41; Moore, "The Songs of the Public Theaters," *JEGP*, XXVIII, 155-202; T. S. Graves, "The 'Act Time' in Elizabethan Theatres," *SP*, XII, 103-134.

119. Dekker, *Works*, I, 134 (Q 1600).

120. *Ibid.*, I, 138-141.

121. There is some evidence that the Q 1600 text is that used for a court performance in which one of the choirboy groups may have participated. The Epilogue in the text opens with the lines: "With Hymnes sung to thy name, and praiers that we/ May once a year so oft enjoy this sight,/ Til these young boyes change their curld locks to white, . . ." (*Ibid.*, 175.)

122. *Ibid.*, 206, 207, 253 (Q 1607).

123. *Ibid.*, II, 204, 227 (Q 1607).

124. *Ibid.*, III, 197 (Q 1611).

125. *Ibid.*, 332, 333.

126. *Ibid.*, 279.

127. L. 850.

128. For example, *The Honest Whore* (1604); *Alphonsus, King of Aragon* (1599); *Orlando Furioso* (1594); *James the Fourth* (1598); *If You Know Not Me*, Part II (1606); *Edward I* (1599); *David and Bethsabe* (1599); *The Wit of a Woman* (1604); *Wily Beguiled* (1606); *The Coblers Prophesie* (1594); *The Atheist's Tragedy* (1611); *Love and Fortune* (1589); *Fidele and Fortunio* (1584).

129. Graves, 103-134.

130. Moore, "The Songs of the Public Theaters," *JEGP*, XXVIII, 173.

131. Dekker, *Works*, I, 280.

132. Heywood, *Works*, I, 316, 317. Cf., n. 79, above.

133. Galpin, p. 64, suggests that the "still pipes" called for in *Tancred and Gismonda* (1568) and *Jocasta* (1566) were a type of muted shawm called the "cromorne." Cowling, p. 63, has noted that, in the plays mentioned, the sound of the still-pipes is described as "sweet" and "mournful," which, together with Marston's name, "still-flute," causes him to infer that both "still-pipe" and "still-flute" signified recorders. The "Cynet," or "sennet," was an extended fanfare.

134. Cf. *A larum for London* (1602), ll. 260, 319; *The Spanish Tragedy* (1602), IV, v; *Antonio and Mellida*, Part 2, II, i; *Sophonisba*, III, i.

135. Dekker, *Works*, I, 92; Greene, III, ii; Wilson, ll. 992-1028; respectively.

136. Dekker, *Works*, III, 265.

137. *Ibid.*, I, 253.

138. Cf. *The Scornful Lady* (1616), II, ii; *Westward Ho!* (1607) in Dekker, *Works*, II, 349; *Northward Ho!* (1607), *ibid.*, III, 65; *The Christmas Prince* (1608), p. 46; *A Woman Kilde with Kindnesse*, in Heywood, *Works*, II, 97, 98; Middleton, *Blurt, Master Constable* (1602), II, ii; Middleton, *A Mad World, My Masters* (1608), II, i; G. Peele, *David and Bethsabe* (1599), Sc. vi; *Wily Beguiled* (1606), ll. 687-689; *Ram Alley* (1611), V, i; Field, *A Woman is a Weathercock*, II, i, III, ii, and V, i.

139. It is difficult to distinguish, by the stage directions of the plays, between rustic musical instruments and their more urban cousins. Stage writers of the period used very general terms in referring to country music; "pipe" and "fiddle" are the usual names encountered. As can be seen, "pipe" could refer to a pipe and tabor, to a bagpipe, or to any of the several varieties of flute and recorder. Likewise, "fiddle" might be the name applied to a viol, violin, rebec, crowd, humstrum, or hurdy-gurdy. Other than the "pipe" and "fiddle," rustic instruments included the pan-pipe, drum, clashpan (cymbal), and tymbyr (tambourine). (Stanford and Forsyth, pp. 182, 183.) The costume sketches for Inigo Jones' *King's Masque* (1637) show five anti-maskers, one playing a rebec, who is called a "scraper," another playing a gridiron, another singing a ballad, another playing the "knackers," or bones, and another playing the "tongs and key." (P. Cunningham, *Inigo Jones and Ben Jonson*, Plates 12 and 14.)

140. Naylor, *Shakespeare and Music*, pp. 147-153; B. Pattison, *Music and Poetry*, pp. 1, 2.

141. Cf. Shakespeare, *Richard II*, V, v: "*King Richard.* Music do I hear? Ha, ha! keep time. —How sour sweet music is,/ When time is broke and no proportion kept;/ So is it in the music of men's lives."

142. See also *Old Fortunatus* (1600), Dekker, *Works*, I, 92, 123, 138-141; *If It Be Not Good* (1612), *ibid.*, III, 332, 333; *Orlando Furioso* (1594), IV, ii; *Wily Beguiled*, ll. 1286-1310.

143. Ll. 992-1028.
144. As quoted by Moore, "The Songs of the Public Theaters," *JEGP*, XXVIII, 199, 200.
145. Cunningham, p. 88.
146. *Works*, II, 204, 227.
147. *Ibid.*, 335. Cf. *ibid.*, I, 105, 222; *ibid.*, II, 25; Greene, *James the Fourth*, IV, iv; Heywood, *Works*, I, 297; Marston, *Antonio and Mellida*, Part 2, III, i, and V, i; *Sophonisba*, III, i, and V, iv; Middleton, *Blurt, Master Constable*, II, ii, and III, iii; *A Mad World, My Masters*, II, i; C. Tourneur, *The Revengers Tragedie*, V, iii; Field, *A Woman is a Weathercock*, V, i.
148. Graves, "The 'Act Time' in Elizabethan Theatres," *SP*, XII, 103-134.
149. Cf. *Gorboduc*; *Cynthia's Revels* (1601); *Sophonisba* (1606); *Tancred and Gismonda* (1592); *Love and Fortune* (1589); *The Dumbe Knight* (Q 1608); *Fidele and Fortunio* (1584).
150. C. H. Herford and P. Simpson, eds., *Ben Jonson*. It is stated in the Jonson Folio of 1616 that this version of the play was acted by the King's Men in 1605. The Q 1605 version of the play includes stage directions calling for a "chorus—of musicians" at the end of each of the first three acts.
151. Lawrence, "The English Theatre Orchestra." *Musical Quarterly*, III, 9 ff.
152. In *Westward Ho!* (1607) occurs a humorous example of such information within the lines. It was a common custom for music to accompany amorous assignations. Such a meeting takes place in the play, much against the wishes of the couple concerned. *"Musick within: the Fidlers. Goz.* . . . cannot sinne be set a shore once in a raigne upon your Country quarters, but it must have fidling? what set of Villaines are you, you perpetuall Ragamuffins? *Fid.* The Towne Consort Sir." The fiddlers then come on the outer stage and play the accompaniment for a song. (Dekker, *Works*, II, 351, 352.)

THREE

The Two Gentlemen of Verona

F WE COULD CALL BACK SHAKESPEARE'S GHOST, like Macbeth's specters, for questioning, probably the most important questions we could ask would concern his motives for doing many of the things he did. Regarding *The Two Gentlemen of Verona* and its music, we would first wish to know why he used the music called for in Act IV, ii of the play. As we do not have our souls in pawn to the forces of evil, we must seek the answer to our question elsewhere. That answer emerges almost as clearly as if Shakespeare had spoken it when we turn to the old Spanish romance from which the dramatist drew his plot, for there, at the same point in Montemayor's story, we find a very close parallel in the music as well as in the plot. The differences are slight but significant. One reason, then, why Shakespeare employed music in the play is that he found the music in his source. Here we have a key which will unlock several tempting doors.

Before pursuing the subject further, however, we should consider the preceding, first play by Shakespeare, *The Comedy of Errors*. It contains no music and hence seems to fall outside the province of our study. Yet, when we consider that it is one of the very few Shakespearean plays that omit music, the lack of music in itself becomes significant. By noting the possible reasons why the playwright did not use music in the Plautean farce we may glimpse his shaping hands at work.

Several reasons immediately present themselves. *The Comedy of Errors* is a farce—a comedy of situation. It follows closely its Plautean source: the setting is simple and fitted for a simple stage; there is relatively little character delineation; the language is often prosaic, seldom rising above the artistic level of word play; the action is largely governed by the classic situation. Thus, both the dramatic elements of the play and the mechanics of its stage production offer little scope for those functions usually performed by music in the drama of the period. Any music introduced into the play would be extraneous. Chambers has noted that it is the briefest of Shakespeare's dramas, and suggests that it was written to precede a masque, jig, or other afterpiece.[1] However that may be, all the equipment needed for its production consists of actors, a platform, doors, and, possibly, an upper stage.[2]

Shakespeare possibly used no music in *The Comedy of Errors*, then, because there was no dramatic purpose to be served by music. He could have inserted an extraneous song or two, as was often done in the plays of the period, but he did not choose to do so.[3] When he began work on *The Two Gentlemen of Verona*, however, he was given an opportunity to employ music. As we shall see, he made the most of it.

To us it will be interesting to note these well-known matters: The only authoritative text of *The Two Gentlemen* is that of the 1623 Folio. The date of its composition is unknown but, on the basis of internal evidence, editors suggest dates ranging between 1590 and 1595.[4] The conjecture which I accept is that of Neilson, who assigns the probable date of 1592.[5] No contemporary performance of the play is on record. Its source is generally considered to be Montemayor's *Diana Enamorada*, a pastoral romance.

Act IV, ii, of the play is devoted almost entirely to the serenade which Protheus, Thurio, and a consort of musicians offer to Silvia, and during which Julia discovers the perfidy of Protheus. The action of the scene is anticipated in III, ii, lines 82-94, where Protheus, while talking to the Duke and Thurio, offers to aid the latter, a bumbling suitor to Silvia, in winning the heart of his lady-love:

> *Pro.* . . . After your dire-lamenting Elegies,
> Visit by night your Ladies chamber-window
> With some sweet Consort; To their Instruments
> Tune a deploring dumpe[6]: the nights dead silence
> Will well become such sweet complaining grieuance:
> This, or else nothing, will inherit her.
>   *Du.* This discipline, showes thou hast bin in loue.

Th. And thy aduice, this night, ile put in practise:
Therefore, sweet *Protheus*, my direction-giuer,
Let vs into the City presently
To sort some Gentlemen, well-skil'd in Musicke.
I haue a Sonnet, that will serue the turne
To giue the on-set to thy good aduise.[7]

The action in the scene containing the promised serenade hinges on the way the serenade is performed. Since the Folio text includes no stage directions other than a list of characters appearing in the scene, a fresh analysis of the scene is necessary to determine, as nearly as possible, the disposition of the actors and the music in the space available to them. Richmond Noble has made one analysis. It would be pleasant to base this study upon his work, but his conclusions, I think, are not always built upon a solid foundation of evidence. Hence a fresh approach seems necessary.[8]

In describing the scene containing the serenade, Reed and Quiller-Couch[9] correctly note that, after the song is ended, the musicians play while the Host and Julia speak some sixteen lines—the lines containing Julia's references to Protheus as "the Musitian."

The conversation of Julia and the Host, as the text indicates, hence takes place against a background of instrumental music. But this creates a problem of production. The nature of the word play forbids any other occupants of the stage from distracting the audience, either visually or aurally. A group of instrumentalists playing there would interfere with the effective presentation of the lines following the song. Yet the lines require a musical accompaniment. The distinct delivery of the word play thus becomes the urgent problem of the scene, since, as we shall see, its dramatic focus is on these particular lines.

The most likely solution to the problem raised by the necessity for background music would be for the musicians to play off-stage—possibly within the tiring house. The music would in this way be supplied, but in an unobtrusive manner. If we accept this solution, however, we shall be at variance with the staging of the scene as suggested by the stage directions of Shakespearean editors. To

test the validity of my solution, I propose to use it as a definite
point of reference for our understanding of the stage action and,
upon the hypothesis that the instrumentalists are off-stage, to make
a reconstruction of the action in the scene, which, though based
on deductions, is kept in strict conformity to all the requirements
laid down by the text we have, and in conformity to the dramatic
conventions of the period. The scene, I believe, was staged in the
following manner:

THE STAGE: [A platform backed by a wall having three doors
equally spaced across the stage.][10]
THE SETTING: [Near Silvia's apartment in the Duke's palace.
The left door represents a corner of Silvia's residence and also the
path leading to the city and to the Host's inn. The center door
represents an entrance to Silvia's apartment. The right door represents another corner of the residence and also a path leading to
another side of the apartment.][11]
THE TIME: [Near midnight.]
[Protheus enters through the left door as though coming from the
city. Carrying a lute, he advances to the center of the stage.][12]
"*Pro.* . . . But here comes *Thurio*; now must we to her window,/
And giue some euening Musique to her eare."
[Thurio and three or four musicians enter from the left door as
though also coming from the city.][13]

>   *Th.* How now, sir *Protheus*, are you crept before vs?
>   *Pro.* I gentle *Thurio*, for you know that loue
> Will creepe in seruice, where it cannot goe.
>   *Th.* I, but I hope, Sir, that you loue not here.
>   *Pro.* Sir, but I doe: or else I would be hence.
>   *Th.* Who, *Siluia?*
>   *Pro.* I, *Siluia*, for your sake.
>   *Th.* I thanke you for your owne: . . .

[Protheus, Thurio and the musicians begin leaving the stage.
Thurio continues speaking as they withdraw through the right
door.][14]

>   . . . Now Gentlemen

Let's tune: and too it lustily a while.
[As the serenaders disappear, the Host and Julia enter from the

left door as though coming from the city. Julia is disguised as a boy.]

    Ho. Now, my yong guest; me thinks your 'allycholly; I pray you why is it?

    Iu. Marry (mine *Host*) because I cannot be merry.

    Ho. Come, we'll haue you merry: ile bring you where you shall heare Musique, and see the Gentleman that you ask'd for.

    Iu. But shall I heare him speake.

    Ho. I that you shall.

    Iu. That will be Musique.

[The Host and Julia walk across the stage while they talk. As they near the right door, they hear the sound of instruments being tuned off-stage.][15] "*Ho.* Harke, harke." [Julia and the Host move across the right door and stand at the side as though looking through the door.][16] "*Iu.* Is he among these?/ *Ho.* I: but peace, let's heare'm." [Protheus alone sings the song accompanied by the instrumental music of the consort.][17]

> *Song. Who is Siluia? what is she?*
> *That all our Swaines commend her?*
> *Holy, faire, and wise is she,*
> *The heauen such grace did lend her,*
>   *that she might admired be.*
> *Is she kinde as she is faire?*
> *For beauty liues with kindness:*
> *Loue doth to her eyes repaire,*
> *To helpe him of his blindnesse:*
>   *And being help'd, inhabits there.*
> *Then to Siluia, let us sing.*
> *That Siluia is excelling;*
> *She excels each mortall thing*
> *Vpon the dull earth dwelling.*
>   *To her let us Garlands bring.*

[As the song is performed, Julia displays signs of great grief. At the end of the song the musicians stop playing for a brief interval.][18]

    Ho. How now? are you sadder then you were before; How doe you, man? the Musicke likes you not.

Iu. You mistake: the Musitian likes me not.

Ho. Why, my pretty youth?

Iu. He plaies false (father.)

Ho. How, out of tune on the strings.

Iu. Not so: but yet

So false that he grieues my very heart-strings.

[Here the musicians begin playing a brisk dance tune.][19] [See Plate I.] "*Ho.* You haue a quick eare./ *Iu.* I, I would I were deafe: it makes me haue a slow heart./ *Ho.* I perceiue you delight not in Musique./ *Iu.* Not a whit, when it iars so." [The Host notices the change in the type of music.]

Ho. Harke, what fine change is in the Musique.

Iu. I: that change is the spight.

Ho. You would haue them alwaies play but one thing.

Iu. I would alwaies haue one play but one thing.

But *Host,* doth this Sir *Protheus,* that we talke on,

Often resort vnto this Gentlewoman?

Ho. I tell you what *Launce* his man told me,

He lou'd her out of all nicke.

Iu. Where is *Launce?*

[The instrumental music ceases at this point.][20] "*Ho.* Gone to seeke his dog, which to morrow, by his/ Masters command, hee must carry for a present to his/ Lady./ *Iu.* Peace, stand aside, the company parts." [Julia and the Host move back against the wall at one side of the right door. The serenaders enter through the same door, seemingly in the midst of conversation.] "*Pro.* Sir *Thurio,* feare not you, I will so pleade,/ That you shall say, my cun-

PLATE I.—*The Galliard called "Because of the Traitor I Die."* This galliard appears in Arbeau's *Orchesography* (1588), p. 99. Earlier, p. 78, he remarks, "The galliard is so called because one must be gay and nimble to dance it, as, even when performed reasonably slowly, the movements are light-hearted."

ning drift excels./ *Th.* Where meete we?/ *Pro.* At Saint *Gregories* well./ *Th.* Farewell." [As Thurio leaves the stage through the left door, Silvia appears at the center door. She does not advance farther onto the stage.]²¹ "*Pro.* Madam: good eu'n to your Ladiship./ *Sil.* I thanke you for your Musique (Gentlemen)/ Who is that that spake?" [After bowing to Silvia, the musicians depart through the left door. Protheus remains.]²²

"*Pro.* One (Lady) if you knew his pure hearts truth,/ You would quickly learne to know him by his voice. . . . *Sil.* . . . And so, good rest. *Pro.* As wretches haue ore-night/ That wait for execution in the morne." [Here Silvia withdraws from the center door; Protheus departs through the left door.]²³ "*Iu. Host,* will you go?/ *Ho.* By my hallidome, I was fast asleepe." [The Host and Julia leave the stage through the left door. The stage is now bare for the next scene.]

I believe this construction of the scene in question is not only feasible, but that it closely approximates the contemporary staging as suggested by the Folio text and by the dramatic practices of the time.

Mr. Noble, in his discussion of the scene, remarks: "Cut out the serenade and it is obvious that considerable revision of the play would be necessary to achieve the dramatic end in view. It is this essential character of the song that Shakespeare was from the very commencement of his career original in its use."²⁴ Here it can be seen that Mr. Noble equates the song with the whole serenade, overlooking the fact that instrumental music was certainly performed, and by doing so reaches a conclusion of dubious validity. It is true that music, possibly even vocal music, is essential to the action of the play in that it provides the opportunity for Julia to discover the infidelity of Protheus. But it does not necessarily follow that this particular song containing these sentiments is essential to the play. It is true that a song was often part of a serenade and, in this instance, a song provides a method by which Protheus may be distinguished from the other musicians so that Julia's following remarks will have a well-defined target. But the song used by Shakespeare contains no specific references to the

action of the play; the lyric as such is therefore not at all essential
to the scene.

If the thought of the song is examined, it will be found rather
conventional. The only apparent connection the lines have with
the scene is their use of Silvia's name; Delia, Chloe, or the name
of some other pastoral figure would be equally appropriate to the
type and sentiment of the song. Noble believes it is a caricature
of a love song aimed at the poetic attempts of the clumsy Thurio
who had written a sonnet to be used for the senerade.[25] But this
suggested touch of Shakespeare's, even if authentic, seems incidental when we compare it with the closely knit matching of
dialogue and background music following the song.

The structure and sentiment of the song indicate that it is an
ayre. It could hardly be set to a folk tune; most folk tunes of the
period were set to eight- or ten-line stanzas, whereas "Who Is
Silvia?" contains fifteen lines. In fact, any musical setting of the
song would require some juggling of either the words or the
music—the insertion of rests in the music, or the repetition of
words or phrases in the lines. Such juggling is seldom found in folk
music, but it is common in the works of the Elizabethan song
writers. The original music for "Who Is Silvia?" has been lost,
but the example in Plate II may suggest the flavor of the music
used for the song in the early productions of the play.

What caused Shakespeare to use a scene employing music?
And what caused him to shift the emphasis in his serenade from
the song, where it would normally fall, to the word play? It is in
seeking the answers to these questions that we will observe his
creative process in action.

The primary source of the play generally recognized is the
Diana Enamorada of Montemayor (1559-1560). The work was not
"Englished" until 1582, when Bartholomew Yonge translated it
in manuscript. The manuscript was not published until 1598. A
French translation, made by Nicolas Colin, was published in 1578,
1582, and 1587. A lost play, *Felix and Philiomena*, acted in Greenwich in 1584, is also considered a possible source.[26]

If Shakespeare used the original Spanish version or a close

translation of the original, the account of the discovery of the unfaithful lover would, paraphrased, have struck his eye as follows: Felismena, arriving in the city in search of her lover, takes lodging at an inn. Late that night she is awakened by the innkeeper, who tells her of a serenade to be performed in the street before the inn. She opens her window and sees a group of musicians below. She recognizes the voice of Fabio, her lover's manservant. The music begins with a consort lesson played by three cornets and a sackbut. After the consort plays, a voice which she recognizes as that of Don Felis, her lover, sings a "romance" setting forth the well-worn plight of a slighted lover. The song is sung to the accompaniment of a "dulcayna" and a harp. The initial pleasure of Felismena changes to despairing grief when she realizes that Don Felis is singing not to her but to another lady. Don Felis, after singing the "romance," sings a "soneto" or short song.

Any attempt to retrace a mental process is admittedly hazardous. In the instance of Shakespeare's composition of IV, ii, of *The Two Gentlemen of Verona*, we have to guide us only a probable source and the completed work. Shakespeare had only the source; his progress toward the scene as we find it may have involved many turns and detours. But, from our vantage point, we can look back to the source and, between the two points, discern a series of trail markers which apparently fall into a straight line.

PLATE II.—*She Whose Matchless Beauty*. From Robert Jones's *First Booke of Songes and Ayres* (1600), as transcribed by Edmund Fellowes in *The English School of Lutenist Song Writers*, 2nd Series, No. 4.

In the source appears a situation. Felismena, while watching a serenade by musicians, discovers the singer is Don Felis, her lover, and that his song is directed at another lady. It is this situation that is the point of dramatic focus in the scene. Shakespeare, no doubt, realized that adherence to his source would involve the use of music. Yet the dramatic focus of the scene is not upon the music, but upon the discovery of Felis by Felismena. As we have seen, the dramatists of the time were not averse to using music if it served their purpose. Shakespeare's purpose, as a dramatist, was to accent by all possible means the importance of Felismena's discovery. Since music is called for by the serenade, and since it would please the audience to have music, how could the music be disposed to afford full dramatic advantage and, at the same time, to avoid distracting attention from the point of the scene—the discovery?

Turning to his source, Shakespeare perhaps noted that the Host would serve as a means by which Julia could reveal her discovery and to whom she could express her grief. Yet she must remain unrecognized; hence the meaning behind her words must not be intelligible to the Host, but must be understood by the audience. Shakespeare, at this point of his dramatic career, used puns and word play to a great extent. In fact, earlier in the play he had written a nineteen-line passage (I, ii, lines 79-98) for Julia and Lucetta, in which they discuss a love letter from Protheus in terms of music.

If a similar play on words could be used between Julia and the Host—one meaning for the Host, another for the audience—the problem of by-passing the Host would be solved. And, if terms of music be again employed, an ironic parallel would be constructed between Julia's reactions when she receives Protheus' letter in Act I and her reaction to her discovery of Protheus' infidelity in Act IV. Why not? The actual music was available for motivating the word play; the instrumental piece which precedes Montemayor's song is not necessary for the dramatic version. If it should be shifted to follow the song, and if the performance of all the music takes place off-stage, the consort piece would unobtrusively supply the motivation and direction of the play on words. Furthermore, if the music symbolizes Protheus, and if the consort plays a light-hearted piece of music in the midst of Julia's grief, Protheus' callousness and the gulf it creates between him and Julia would be emphasized.

The total dramatic effect of this disposition of language, action, and music is to throw a triple emphasis on the most important passage of the scene. The discovery is stated first by Julia's grief when she recognizes Protheus; the effect of the discovery on Julia is emphasized by the play on words which follows the discovery; and the immediate result of the discovery is graphically portrayed by the background music which accompanies the word play.

The conclusion seems clear. Shakespeare used music in *The Two Gentlemen of Verona* primarily to further his dramatic ends. His interest was first on the dramatic points he wished to make, second, on language as a means to achieve those ends, and third, on music as an intensifier of language. Where music could not be used in this way, he made it as unobtrusive as possible or dispensed with it entirely as in *The Comedy of Errors*. His use of music in this play also indicates that he wrote the scene with two contrasting pieces of music in mind, the graceful song and the gay consort piece, and that the staging of IV, ii, is governed by the disposition of music and musicians for the performance of those two pieces of music.

Notes

1. *William Shakespeare*, I, 307.
2. Sir A. Quiller-Couch and J. Dover Wilson (New Cambridge edition), p. 81, state: "Evidently the play was to be acted upon a simple platform with three doors at the back, and no inner stage . . . the bare dais of a hall, with three doors at the back would serve . . . there is an obvious necessity for an upper stage in III, i."
3. If the play had been composed for performance by the Chamberlain's Men, Shakespeare's decision would not have been dictated by a lack of available musicians. During the period of time covered by the suggested dates for the writing of *The Comedy of Errors*, the Chamberlain's Men had as members several actor-musicians, among them William Kemp, Thomas Pope, Augustine Phillips, and George Bryan. See Baldwin, *The Organization and Personnel of the Shakespearean Company*, pp. 72-74; Chambers, *William Shakespeare*, I, 40, and II, 73, 74.

4. R. W. Bond, the editor of the Arden edition (XXXVI, x-xvi) guesses that the play was written about 1590 and revised in 1595. His conjecture is based on a reference to the play in Francis Meres' *Palladis Tamia* (1598), on metrical evidence, and a seeming influence of Lyly on the style. Quiller-Couch and Dover Wilson, p. vii, from internal tests of craftsmanship and versification place the date "somewhere near the threshold of Shakespeare's dramatic career." Chambers (*William Shakespeare*, I, 330-331) finds close resemblances between it and *The Comedy of Errors, Romeo and Juliet*, and *The Merchant of Venice*, and hence suggests the date 1594-1595. Hardin Craig (*The Complete Works of Shakespeare*, p. 94) surmises only that, because of its greater romantic interest, the play appeared later than *The Comedy of Errors* and *Love's Labour's Lost*.

5. *Op. cit.*, p. 26. ". . . the gap between its undeniable immaturity and the mastery exhibited in the later plays makes it injudicious to assign it a date later than 1592."

6. The "dumpe" was a slow, mournful dance. See *NED* and Naylor, *Shakespeare and Music*, p. 23.

7. The text is that of the Folio of 1623; the line numbers are those of the Globe edition. This will be true of all quotations from the play made in this study.

8. According to Richmond Noble (*Shakespeare's Use of Song*, p. 44), Thurio and the consort come on the stage after Protheus' soliloquy which opens the scene. The musicians tune their instruments while the Host and Julia speak their opening lines. The serenaders then perform the song, "Who Is Sylvia?" Noble also implies that during the course of the song the word play between the Host and Julia takes place, and that the "change in the Musique" referred to by the Host occurs during the final portion of the song. This analysis of the action seems erroneous to me. The stage presentation of a song accompanied by musical instruments and simultaneous delivery of lines which must be clearly understood in order to be effective is manifestly impossible. Both Reed and Quiller-Couch disagree with Noble. As will be seen, I follow these scholars and build on their foundation.

9. Reed, *Songs from the British Drama*, p. 280; Quiller-Couch and Dover Wilson, p. 56.

10. "THE STAGE" Since so little is known of the stages of The Theatre, The Curtain, and The Rose playhouses, in one of which the play was possibly performed, I suggest this arrangement as a common denominator of the three possible stages. This arrangement also agrees with the stage as seen by Quiller-Couch and Dover Wilson, if we omit the balcony they suggest. In I, i, of the play, they insert the stage direction, "Verona: a street near Julia's house; . . ." In this instance, the two end doors represent the visible ends of the street, the center door, the entrance to Julia's house. In I, ii, for which they suggest the same setting, they insert the direction: "A door opens: Julia and Lucetta come forth." Later, a similar setting is used by them for II, v: "Milan: a street near the quay; an alehouse hard by." Here the two end doors would serve as extremes of the street; the center door the entrance to the alehouse.

11. "THE SETTING" For the setting of the scene, Quiller-Couch and Dover Wilson suggest the following: "A wall, with a postern, behind the Duke's palace: inside a strip of garden dividing the wall from a lofty turret; outside, a narrow lane with bushes: a moonlit night." And, later, "A window opens in the turret; Silvia appears on the balcony." The Folio text does not call for a balcony, nor does it contain any indication that Silvia appears at a window. Protheus states that the serenade will be performed under Silvia's window,

but if the serenade is performed off-stage, the window would be imaginary.
12. "Protheus . . ." Protheus enters through the left door as though coming from the city where, according to the text, III, ii, he had gone with Thurio to obtain musicians. He carries a lute, I believe, because it would be in character for him to sing the song rather than Thurio who, also in character, would be as incompetent in the musical portion of courtship as he is in other gallantries. Also, in her word play Julia clearly refers to Protheus when she employs the singular noun, "the Musitian," and follows it with the statement, "he plaies false." Protheus hence must be the principal musician of the consort. In this role, he would most likely carry a treble lute, the instrument commonly used by gentlemen of the period for song accompaniments and also for consort purposes. See Chapter II, p. 17.
13. "Thurio . . ." In III, ii, Thurio states that the musicians will be obtained in the city. The musicians who arrive with him were probably, though not necessarily, professionals. The instruments they played is a matter of guesswork. The Host, 60, mentions strings, and string instruments would be appropriate for the occasion. I would guess that the consort was composed of a treble lute, a theorboe, a bass viol, and a treble recorder. This combination would provide two treble voices, a tenor, and a bass voice. This is a larger group than would be needed to accompany a song; it would, however, be almost a minimum grouping for the consort "lesson," or instrumental piece, which follows the song.
14. "Protheus, Thurio . . ." Their departure through the right door would indicate that they were proceeding to another part of Silvia's apartment for the performance of the serenade. I do not think the musicians tuned their instruments while on the stage. Such activity would interfere with the opening lines of Julia and the Host, which explain their presence at the palace. The serenaders have no dialogue assigned them until about forty-eight lines after this point.
15. "The Host . . ." It seems likely that the sound of tuning should be heard after the serenaders reach off-stage their supposed station under Silvia's window and that the Host's exclamation, "Harke, harke," should refer to the sound of the tuning.
16. "Julia . . ." This would indicate to the audience that the serenaders were visible to the Host and Julia but not *vice versa*.
17. "Protheus alone . . ." The song is sung following the Host's remark, "but, peace, let's heare'm." In this way the song would not be interrupted by the remarks of Julia and the Host. In Montemayor's *Diana* . . . Don Felis alone sings the song which Felismena overhears. He is accompanied by a consort of musicians. Naylor, *Shakespeare and Music*, p. 97, and Noble, *Shakespeare's Use of Song*, p. 43, believe the song was sung by all of the musicians. The only support I can find for their supposition is the use of the plural pronouns in the lines of the song, for example: "Then to Siluia let us sing." Since the lines occur within the song, the use of plural pronouns may well be a figure of speech such as "Goodnight, ladies, we'll have to leave you now." As we have seen, it would be in character for Protheus to sing the song. See note 12, above.
18. "As the song . . ." A brief interval of time should elapse between the end of the song and the beginning of the consort piece. The Host's remark on the change in the music does not occur until several lines later; the music should not be played too long before he notices the change.

19. "Here the musicians . . ." A contrast should be made between the music of the song and that of the consort piece in order to give point to the Host's remark, "Harke, what fine change is in the Musique." Since the musical setting for the song was probably lyrical in nature, a galliard, coranto, or lavolta tune would provide the necessary contrast (see Plate I).

20. "The instrumental music . . ." The music obviously should end just before Julia remarks, "Peace . . . the company parts."

21. "As Thurio leaves . . ." On their way back to the city, the serenading party would cross the stage moving toward the left door through which they came. Silvia would have ample time to leave her imaginary window and to reach the entrance of her apartment at which she appears. Propriety would not permit her to leave her apartment in order to thank the musicians, but she could converse from the door or from a balcony.

22. "After bowing . . ." Silvia's thanks are directed at all of the remaining musicians. Her question shifts attention to Protheus, at which point the other musicians would probably bow and slip quietly away. There is no evidence in the text that they are on the stage after this point.

23. "Here Siluia . . ." The Host tells Julia, IV, ii, 137, 138, that Protheus is staying at his inn. We would hence expect Protheus to leave in the direction of the inn.

24. "Shakespeare's Songs and Stage," *Shakespeare and the Theatre*, pp. 124, 125.

25. *Shakespeare's Use of Song*, pp. 39, 42.

26. This theory is rejected by T. P. Harrison, Jr., "Concerning 'Two Gentlemen of Verona' and Monte Mayor's 'Diana,'" *MLN*, XLI, 251, 252.

FOUR

Love's Labour's Lost

THE TITLE PAGE OF THE EARLIEST PRINTING OF THIS comedy describes it as "A Pleasant Conceited Comedie Called, Loves labors lost. As it was presented before her Highnes this last Christmas. Newly corrected and augmented by W. Shakespere. Imprinted at London by W. W. for Cutbert Burby. 1598." From this information we may assume that Shakespeare wrote the play at some earlier date, then revised and polished it for the court performance. Perhaps the play was acted some time before it was presented at court. There may even have been a pirated quarto, now lost, which caused the "newly corrected and augmented" version to be printed.[1] The influence of Lyly apparent in its language and in its subject matter suggests that the comedy was written originally for a highly literate audience. Editors have placed it among the earliest comedies and have suggested dates for its composition ranging from 1588 to 1595.[2] I favor the date 1594, considered "a reasonable guess" by Neilson and Hill.[3] I know of no source for the main plots nor of any established sources for the episodes with which we shall be concerned. The earliest record of the play is the 1598 Quarto, on which most subsequent editions are based.

In the Quarto text, which is the foundation of the present discussion, there are four passages which claim our attention: the first is an exchange of words between the grandiloquent Spaniard, Don Armado alias the Braggart, and his pert page, Moth (I, ii, lines 127-131); the second is another exchange of words between the same two (III, i, lines 1-4); the third is the Mask of the Muscovites (V, ii); the fourth, the songs following the "antic" of the Nine Worthies (V, ii, lines 549-721).

The first passage interests us paradoxically, because it contains no music. Don Armado, after declaring his intention of rewriting the ballad, "The King and the Beggar," as a love song, feels himself so much in love with Jaquenetta that he must have a love song to comfort him. "*Ar.* Sing Boy, My spirit growes heauie in love. *Boy.* And thats great maruaile, louing a light Wench. *Ar.* I say sing. *Boy.* Forbeare till this companie be past."[4] Costard, Dull, and Jaquenetta then enter. After some conversation among the group, Dull leads Jaquenetta off to her punishment and Moth leads Costard away; Moth never sings the requested song.

I do not think Don Armado would have asked twice for a song unless a song was intended to be sung at this point. Also, if the song had been performed it would have fallen between two scenes according to one dramatic practice of the time; for example, the scene containing Don Armado and Moth would have ended with the song and a new scene would have begun upon the entrance of Dull, Costard, and Jaquenetta. A song would not be out of place at this point since songs were often used to denote scene changes in the drama of the period.[5]

We find a similar situation at the beginning of Act III. The 1623 Folio, which has act divisions marked for the play, presents this version of the opening lines of the act: "*Actus Tertius. Enter Broggart* [*sic*] *and Boy. Song. Bra.* Warble childe, make passionate my sense of hearing. *Boy.* Concolinel. *Brag.* Sweete Ayer, go tendernesse of yeares: . . ." The 1598 Quarto, however, gives this version: "*Enter Braggart and his Boy. Bra.* Warble child, make passionate my sense of hearing. *Boy.* Concolinel. *Brag.* Sweete Ayer, go tendernes of yeeres, . . ." Here again Don Armado calls for a song, but in the Quarto version there is no indication in the stage directions that a song was performed. Either the editors of the Folio used a later version of the play now lost, or else they thought the Quarto lines indicated a song was sung at the beginning of Act III and therefore inserted the stage direction to that effect. The song would have been performed beginning where the boy says "Concolinel." The meaning of the word used by Moth has been never satisfactorily explained; nor can I clarify it. The commonly accepted explanation is that the word is the name of a tune or the first word of a song. Another possible omission is indicated here.

If the missing songs were performed in an earlier version of the play, and if the songs denoted divisions within the play, why were the songs omitted in the Q 1598 text? There is a possible explanation. I believe the two songs were sung at the points noted in the court performance before Elizabeth and that, judging from Armado's remarks concerning them, they were two amorous "ayres." If songs of this type were employed in the play at all, we would certainly expect them to be used in a court presentation. Perhaps Shakespeare, in touching up the play for the court, simply made provision for two songs supplied and sung by a court musician during the special performance. When the performance was over, the court singer retained his songs and thus prevented their becoming a part of the printed play.

When we consider the Mask of the Muscovites, the first thing we notice is its simplicity. In contrast to the later Stuart masques, such as those written by Jonson and Campion, the little masque of *Love's Labour's Lost* contains in itself no dramatic element. The entertainment the King and his friends plan to offer the Princess and her ladies is really a masquerade, or masked dance, rather than a masque. It has been suggested that the source of the Mask of the Muscovites is an account by Holinshed of a masked dance given by Henry VIII at Westminister in honor of several foreign ambassadors.[6] Holinshed describes several masked dances given by Henry VIII, all of which resemble, in form, the masked dance of the play. An equally probable source is a masked dance given by English noblemen at the French Court at Ard in 1520. Here is a portion of Holinshed's account of the affair:

A Maske in the French court of English lords. After dinner the ladies dressed them to danse, and certeine yong honourable lords of England, apparelled after the manner of Russland or farre Eastland, whose hosen were of rich gold sattin called aureat sattin, overrolled to the knee with scarlet, and on their feet shooes with little pikes of white nailes after the Estland guise, their dublets of rich crimsin velvet and cloth of gold, with wide sleeves lined with cloth of gold: over this they had clokes of crimsin velvet short [?], lined with cloth of gold, on euerie side of the clokes rings of silver, with laces of Venice gold, and on their heads they had hats made in the town of Danske, and purses of seales skinnes, and girdels of the same: all these yong lords had visards on their faces, and their hats were drawne with like hatbands full of damaske gold.[7]

Holinshed does not mention the music employed for this mask nor for any other masks he describes that might possibly be a source for the dance in the play. We must, therefore, depend almost entirely upon internal evidence for the information we seek. That evidence is found in V, ii, lines 155-158 and 211-221. *"Quee. . . . So shall we stay mocking entended game,/ And they wel mockt depart away with shame./ Sound Trom.*[8] *Boy.* The Trompet soundes, be maskt, the maskers come. *Enter Black-moores with musicke, the Boy with a speach, and the rest of the Lordes disguysed."*

*　*　*　*　*　*　*　*　*　*　*

　　Rosa. Play Musique then: nay you must do it soone.
Not yet no daunce: thus change I like the Moone.
　　Kin. Wil you not daunce? How come you thus estranged?
　　Ro. You tooke the moone at ful, but now shee's changed?
　　King. Yet still she is the Moone, and I the Man.
The musique playes, vouchsafe some motion to it,
　　Rosa. Our eares vouchsafe it.[9]
　　King. But your legges should do it.
　　Rosa. Since you are strangers, and come here by chance
Weele not be nice, take handes, we will not daunce.
　　King. Why take we handes then?
　　Rosa. Onely to part friends.
Curtsie sweete hartes, and so the Measure endes.

We notice first that the music for the dance is furnished by a consort of musicians disguised as Moors. The composition of the consort can only be guessed, but since it is to play dance music, and since string instruments most frequently supplied music for dancing during the period, I would suggest that the consort contained four viols—two trebles, a tenor, and a bass—and a timbrel or drum to accentuate the rhythm of the music. The music played was obviously a dance tune. We cannot know exactly what tune was played, but we can determine the probable type of dance used in the scene, and hence the probable form of the dance tune.

If we examine the conversation between the King and Rosaline quoted above, we note first that Rosaline calls for music. The King apparently makes a gesture as though offering to begin the dance, but Rosaline refuses him. A few lines later, Rosaline offers to begin the dance saying, "Weele not be nice, take handes. . . ." Then, to the discomfiture of the King, she adds, ". . . we will not daunce." After taking the King's hand—a movement apparently followed by the other couples—Rosaline capriciously directs, "Curtsie sweete hartes, and so the Measure endes." Hence it can be seen that the dance should begin with each couple taking hands, and end with a curtsy from the ladies and, no doubt, a bow from the gentlemen.

This is little evidence to work with. When, however, we turn to Arbeau's *Orchesography* (1588), pp. 76, 77, we find in his description of the galliard a dance that seems particularly appropriate to the scene in *Love's Labour's Lost*. He describes it as follows:

In the towns nowadays the galliard is danced regardless of rules, and the dancers are satisfied to perform the five steps and a few passages without any orderly arrangement so long as they keep the rhythm, with the result that many of their best passages go unnoticed and are lost. In earlier days it was danced with more discernment. When the dancer had chosen a damsel and led her to the end of the hall, after making the "révérence," they circled the room once or twice together simply walking. Then the dancer released the damsel and she went dancing away to the other end of the hall and, once there, continued dancing upon the same spot. In the meanwhile, the dancer having followed her presented himself before her to perform a few passages, turning at will now to the right, now to the left. This done the damsel danced her way to the opposite end of the hall and her partner, dancing all the while, pursued her thither in order to execute more passages before her. And thus, continuing these goings and comings, the dancer kept introducing new passages and displaying his skill until the musicians stopped playing. Then, taking the damsel by the hand and thanking her he performed the "révérence" and

returned her to the place from whence he had led her forth to
dance.[10]

According to Arbeau, the galliard begins with the dancer choosing a damsel and leading her to one end of the hall. This would,
I think, involve the taking of the damsel's hand by the dancer.
After the various figures have been performed, the music stops
and the dance, or "measure,"[11] ends with a "révérence," or bow,
by the gentlemen, presumably acknowledged by a curtsy from
the lady.

Of course, the dance is never performed in the play; the King
offers to take Rosaline's hand when the music begins, and is re-
buffed. Later, Rosaline takes the King's hand but refuses to dance.
Just before the music stops the King asks, "Why take we handes
then?" Rosaline explains, "Onely to part friendes." The music
stops; the "Measure" ends; the ladies then curtsy to the bewildered
nobles.

It seems highly probable, therefore, that the dance music played
by the consort was a galliard tune, and, as the tune is completed,
for the purpose of the play, within eleven or twelve lines, it must
have been rather short. Among the tunes used as illustrations by
Arbeau is a galliard called "Love let us Kiss" (see Plate III).
The title of this galliard tune is appropriate to the situation and
the tune is short and simple, though, when repeated, flexible in
length.

If we agree that the scene in which the nobles meet their down-
fall employed a galliard and the music thereto, the question then

PLATE III.—*Melody of the galliard called "Love let us Kiss."* The first line of
this plate is a reproduction of an illustration in Arbeau's *Orchesography*, pp.
102, 103. The second line shows the melody in modern notation.

arises, Why would Shakespeare wish to use this particular dance for the scene? For the answer we must review, briefly, the construction of the play.

The play involves two parallel plots, one high comedy and one low comedy, which are unified by the element of mockery and ridicule that pervades the two. In the high comedy plot, the King of Navarre and his friends make a vow to "fast and study" and to see no women for a period of three years. No sooner is the vow made than the Princess of Aquitaine and her ladies-in-waiting arrive to treat of state matters. The King promptly falls in love with the Princess, and his friends each fall in love with one of the French ladies. The gentlemen, after evading the consequences of their vow by an outrageous bit of logical legerdemain, set out to woo and win the ladies with a dance. The ladies, aware of the broken vow, humiliate the noblemen with a rude reception which is the climax of the high comedy.

The low comedy plot consists largely of ridicule, by Moth and Costard, of the exaggerated mannerisms and sententious language of Don Armado and the quibbling pedantry of Holofernes and Nathaniel. The burlesque "antic" of the Nine Worthies is the climax of the low comedy and, since it is presented before the assembled nobility, now reconciled, it also serves to draw the parallel plots together for the end of the play.

In the context preceding the masque scene, the noblemen determine to disguise themselves and invade the camp of the ladies with dance and revelry as the prologue to their courtship. The ladies, informed by Boyet of the impending visit, decide to take the initiative in order to mock and shame the visiting maskers.

Now, if we examine Arbeau's description of the galliard more closely, we find an interesting parallel in situation and action between the dance and the play. The galliard appears to be a courtship dance—its figures imitate the flight, the pursuit, the repulse, the preening and prancing of the male, and the eventual consent of the female. But in *Love's Labour's Lost* the ladies take the initiative and refuse to dance; when the gentlemen first approach, the ladies turn their backs. At this point, a paragraph following the description of the galliard previously quoted is pertinent. Capriol, the pupil of Arbeau, remarks: "This manner of dancing the galliard seems to me more laudable than the slipshod way in which I usually see it performed because when the dancer all but turns his back to the damsel she retaliates by doing the same thing to him while he is performing the passages."[12]

Since the scene obviously involves a dance, perhaps the turning of the ladies' backs would have suggested the dance figure to a courtly audience. Later, Rosaline commands the musicians to play; the command should have come from the King by whom the musicians were employed. When the King extends his hand for the dance Rosaline refuses it, though later she takes the King's hand. At the end of the measure it is the ladies and not the gentlemen, who curtsy, signaling the end of the dance. It would seem, therefore, that much of the mockery of the King and his party depends on the reversed situation of the noblemen and ladies in respect to the parts they should normally take in dancing the galliard.

If I am correct in my supposition, the answer to our question is this: Shakespeare used the galliard and its accompanying music in the masque scene because it was appropriate to the setting and because, by adding visual and tonal interest to the scene, it helped him to achieve the dramatic climax which he wanted at that point of the play. The galliard was a courtly dance suitable to the situation and to the characters in the scene. Its various figures were probably familiar to the court audience before which the play was performed; hence it could be used as a suggestive parallel without disturbing the unity of dramatic construction. In the event that the parallel, as suggested by the figures alone, might be obscure, the musicians probably played a familiar galliard tune in order to remove all doubt about the type of dance attempted by the noblemen. The music would thus serve as a necessary part of a masked dance, and also serve to identify for the audience the type of dance suggested. Thus the music would help to clarify the significance of the dance to the situation portrayed by the scene.[13]

The climax of the low comedy is the burlesque pageant of the

Nine Worthies, perhaps aimed at the rarefied quality of plays based on mythology, such as Peele's *Arraignment of Paris* or the anonymous *The Triumph of Love and Fortune*. The farce is followed by the two songs which end the play. The text of the songs is given in both Quarto and Folio; directions within their context indicate the way in which they were probably performed. The songs are introduced (V, ii, lines 894-903) in the following manner: "*Brag*. . . . But most esteemed greatnes, will you heare the Dialogue that the two Learned men have compiled, in prayse of the Owle and the Cuckow? it should have followed in the ende of our shew. *King*. Call them foorth quickly, we will do so. *Brag. Holla*, Approch. *Enter all. Brag*. This side is *Hiems*, Winter. This *Ver*, the Spring: the one maynteined by the Owle, th'other by the Cuckow. *B.*[14] *Ver* begin."

The stage direction states, "Enter all," which evidently means all of those members of the cast not already on the stage.[15] At this point of the play the stage contains Armado, the King, his three friends, the Princess, her three ladies, Boyet, and Marcades. If we omit the Forester, whose bit part was probably doubled, the "all" could only refer to Holofernes, Nathaniel, Moth, Costard, Dull, and Jaquenetta. It is apparently the "all" who sing the songs. Armado does not sing, since he performs as master of ceremonies.

According to the text, Armado divides the singers into two groups, one representing Spring, the other, Winter. Apparently the gentlefolk are offered a mixture of a medieval "debat" similar to "The Owl and the Nightingale" and a song contest such as that found in the August Eclogue of Spenser's *Shepheardes Calender*.[16] One side sings the two stanzas of the first song; the other side sings the two stanzas of the second song. Here are the texts of the songs, lines 904-939:

The Song

When Dasies pied, and Violets blew,
And Ladi-smockes all siluer white,
And Cuckow-budds of yellow hew:[17]
Do paint the Meadowes with delight:
The Cuckow then on euerie tree,

Mocks married men; for thus singes hee,
Cuckow.
Cuckow, Cuckow: O word of feare,
Vnpleasing to a married eare.
When Shepheards pipe on Oten Strawes,
And merrie Larkes are Ploughmens Clocks:
When Turtles tread and Rookes and Dawes,
And Maidens bleach their summer smockes:
The Cuckow then on euerie tree,
Mockes married men, for thus singes he,
Cuckow.
Cuckow, cuckow: O word of feare,
Vnpleasing to a married eare.

Winter.

When Isacles hang by the wall,
And Dicke the Sheepheard blowes his naile:
And Thom beares Logges into the hall,
And Milke coms frozen home in paile:
When blood is nipt, and wayes be full,
Then nightly singes the staring Owle
Tu-whit to-who.
     A merrie note,
     While greasie Ione doth keele the pot.
When all aloude the winde doth blow,
And coffing drownes the Parsons saw;
And Birdes sit brooding in the Snow,
And Marrians nose lookes red and raw:
When roasted Crabbs hisse in the bowle,
Then nightly singes the staring Owle,
Tu-whit to-who.
     A merrie note,
     While greasie Ione doth keele the pot.

If the six singers were equally divided, there would be three
voices in each group. This suggests that the voices employed for
each song were a treble, a mean (tenor), and a baritone or bass.
To judge from the language and imagery of the two songs, I would
assign the first to Moth (treble), Nathaniel, and Holofernes, and

the second to Jacquenetta, who was actually a boy (treble), Costard, and Dull. Since the singers represented persons of low social station, we would expect them to perform a type of song in keeping with their parts—perhaps a ballad or a three-man song. The eight-line structure of the stanzas (omitting the single "Cuckow" for the moment and joining the two half lines, "Tu-whit to-who" and "A merrie note") also indicates a folk tune setting which, together with the three-part harmony mentioned above, in turn suggests a three-man song—a type often used, as we have seen, to accompany the wassail bowl.[18]

The tune to which both songs were probably sung is unknown, but I have found one that seems to meet all the requirements— the chronology of the play, its text, the character of the singers, their suggested musical ability, and the situation. The tune, according to Chappell, is printed in *Deuteromelia* (1609), a collection of songs already traditional at the time the collection appeared, where it is set for three voices and is described as "one of King Henry's Mirth or Freemen's Songs."[19] The tune is shown in Plate IV.

Musicians will notice that this song is in the common song form, ABA. The A theme appears twice followed by the B theme once, which is followed by the A theme repeated three times. The tune would be a unified musical structure if it ended with measure 16, omitting the last eight measures. If we shorten the tune in this manner and use the resulting tune as a setting for the songs in the text of *Love's Labour's Lost*, they will fit snugly, as can be seen in Plate V.[20] Without any changes other than those normally made in setting new words to an existing tune, the notes in measures 9 and 10, where the cuckoo is first mentioned, imitate the call of the cuckoo.

I must now justify the regularization of the text of the songs which I suggested earlier. We may safely assume that the songs were performed by the clowns in the play; we know that the musical-dramatic conventions of the time in such cases called for a traditional or popular type of song;[21] and we know that such songs were and are marked by their regularity of rhythm, as opposed to the more artistic, though irregular, rhythms of art songs;

we know that the lyrics of popular songs most often have a four-, eight-, or ten-line structure, whereas the Quarto text of the songs has eight and a fraction lines in the case of the first song, and seven lines and two separated half lines in the case of the second. Clearly, the lines were regular if they were sung to a traditional tune.

Capell saw the need for regularity in the lines and attempted to emend them by inserting a "To-who" in the Owl Song at the same point where the single "Cuckow" appears in the Cuckoo Song.[22] This emendation made the songs alike in metrical count but did not dispose of the line fraction. I believe that Capell was on the right track, but instead of inserting a "To-who" into the text, I would remove the single "Cuckow" from the text and mark

PLATE IV.—*Of All the Birds.* According to Chappell, *Popular Music of the Olden Time,* I, 67, 75, this is one of King Henry's Mirth or Freemen's Songs. There is a setting for three voices in Ravenscroft's *Deuteromelia* (1609).

it as a stage direction, and would supply a similar stage direction in the Owl Song, only this time a "To-who." The emended text would thus appear:

"The Cuckow then on euerie tree,/ Mockes married men, for thus singes hee,/   [*Cuckoo call.*]
Cuckow, cuckow: O word of feare,/ Vnpleasing to a married eare."
And, for the second song: "When nightly singes the staring Owle
                                                    [*Owl call.*]
Tu-whit to-who. [*A merrie note.*] While greasie Ione doth keele the pot."

The single "Cuckow," I believe, is a cue for an imitation bird call, and I also believe that an imitation owl call occurred at the same point in the second song.[23] The inconsistent irregularity of the Quarto text at these points (and the Folio precisely follows the Quarto) would seem to indicate an indecision on the part of the original printer.[24] If the bird calls were used during the songs, they would have sounded without interrupting the rhythm of the singers.

Several students of Shakespeare's songs believe that the two

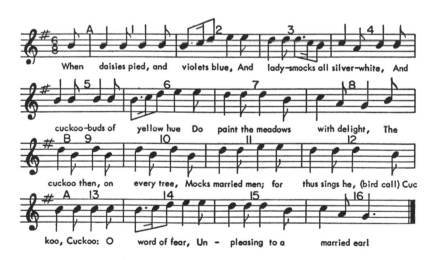

PLATE V.—*When Dasies Pied and Violets Blew.* Here are Shakespeare's lyrics set to a portion of the melody used for the song, "Of All the Birds."

songs are extraneous, that they serve no direct dramatic purpose.[25]
I am not so sure. The introduction preceding the performance of
the songs suggests that Shakespeare considered them an integral
part of the play. Furthermore, if the language and imagery of
the songs are compared with the central theme of the play, that
is, the ridiculing of pastoral conventions and exaggerated scholas-
ticism, an interesting parallel will be observed.

The language of the two stanzas assigned to Spring is marked
by the frequent use of vowel tones and alliteration. When read
aloud it has a light, melodious, and graceful quality. The imagery
makes use of several pastoral subjects—the pied daisies, the shepherds piping on oaten straws, and the larks as ploughmen's clocks.
Yet the refrain lifts the cuckoo out of the pastoral context and
associates him with a common subject for scorn and mockery. The
subject matter of the Spring song is certainly in the courtly tradition and forms a close parallel to the pastoral quality of the
high comedy plot.

In contrast to the Spring stanzas, the language of those assigned
to Winter is marked by the use of strong consonants and a relative
absence of alliteration. The general effect is one of ruggedness.
Also in strong contrast to the imagery of the Spring stanzas, that
of Winter is realistic and, in the refrain, even coarse. We find the
images of the shepherd blowing his nails, Marrian's red and raw
nose, the coughing which drowns out the Parson's sermon, and
greasy Joan stirring the pot. The rustic and homely quality of
the Winter stanzas forms a neat parallel to the realism in the low
comedy plot of the play. It is significant, I think, that the mocking
twist given the Spring stanzas is absent from the Winter song.

The relationship of the songs to the structure of the play thus
appears to be so close that I would hesitate to label them extraneous songs. Their position at the end of the play prevents their
serving to forward the action or to develop characterization, yet
they are a part of the setting and structure of the play. They serve,
I think, for a final statement of the theme of the play and, at the
same time, for as effective a ribbon bow as ever tied up a Christmas
gift for a queen.

The conclusion we may draw concerning Shakespeare's dramatic craftsmanship seems clear. Shakespeare used music and a dance in the masque scene of the play as an auxiliary with which to command increased attention from the audience at a climactic point where attention is necessary for a sure comprehension of the significance of the action. In the instance of the two songs, the music serves to smooth over an unconventional and rather abrupt end to the action of the play. As Berowne says, "Our wooing doth not ende like an olde Play; Iacke hath not Gill. . . ." But, in both cases, Shakespeare took pains to make the music he used an integral part of his dramatic structure: in the first instance, by constructing a parallel between the galliard and the action of the masque scene, and in the second, by using songs as a parallel to, and a reassertion of, the unifying theme of the play.

Notes

1. See T. M. Parrott, *Shakespearean Comedy*, p. 118.
2. Dover Wilson (New Cambridge edition, pp. vii-xxxiv) proposes the date 1593. His conclusion is based on evidence in Meres' *Palladis Tamia* and evidence from several topical allusions and stylistic parallels he finds in the Sonnets. Chambers (*William Shakespeare*, I, 335) refers to the play as the earliest of the lyrical group in which he includes *A Midsummer Night's Dream, Romeo and Juliet*, and *Richard II*. Craig (*Shakespeare*, pp. 89, 90) does not attempt to fix a date but quotes T. S. Baldwin (1588) and J. C. Adams (1592).
3. Riverside Press edition (1942), p. 53.
4. The text of the play quoted in this chapter is that of the Quarto of 1598, as appearing in the photostat copy acquired by the University of Florida Library, unless otherwise noted. The act and scene divisions and line numbers are those of the Globe edition.
5. Neither the Quarto nor the Folio text contains any notation indicating scene divisions; hence the absence of such an indication at this point is not even negatively contrary to our view, supported as it is by strong evidence in the dialogue. For examples of songs denoting scene changes see Peele, *The Arraignment of Paris*, I, iv; III, i: Lyly, *Endymion*, IV, iii: Marston, *The Malcontent*, I, iii; II, v; and V, i: Beaumont, *The Knight of the Burning Pestle*, II, i.
6. Neilson and Hill, eds., *The Complete Plays and Poems of William Shakespeare*, Riverside Press edition, p. 54. Cf. F. Sorensen, " 'The Mask of the Muscovites' in 'Love's Labour's Lost,' " *MLN*, L, 499-501, and Holinshed, *Chronicles* (1587), III, 807.
7. *Op. cit.*, III, 860.
8. The part played by trumpets in the plays is well explained in Naylor, *Shakespeare and Music*, and in L. C. Elson, *Shakespeare in Music*.
9. Corrected by Theobald. Q and F give; *"King*. Yet still she is the Moone, and

I the Man. *Rosa*. The musique playes, vouchsafe some motion to it, Our eares vouchsafe it."

10. Arbeau describes the galliard as it was danced in France, where his book was first published. I see no reason that it should have been danced differently in England. In any event, his is the only extensive contemporary account of the various dances with which I am acquainted.

11. According to the *NED* the term "measure," when applied to a dance of the period concerned, was used either as a general term for any type of dance or as a specialized term meaning a "grave or stately dance." The pavane fits the specialized definition of the word, but I think the galliard is much more appropriate to the scene. Cf. n. 13.

12. Arbeau, *Orchesography*, p. 77.

13. The courtship motif is a common one in dances as are the figures involving bowing and the holding of hands. The galliard, however, combines these and other features which make it, in its gaiety, peculiarly appropriate for the scene.

14. *"Brag."* apparently speaks again after separating the two groups.

15. Quiller-Couch and Wilson, New Cambridge edition, p. 184, N. 886, "S. D. Q. 'Enter all.' That is all the players not on the stage." Noble, *Shakespeare's Use of Song*, p. 37, "Who were the singers of the songs? The stage direction for entrance is 'Enter All', which presumably implies all the actors in attendance and not merely those who have been taking part in the 'show.'"

16. The final two lines of the play closely resemble an emblem like those following each of Spenser's *Eclogues*. For example, the emblem, "there is a god within us," etc., at the end of the "October Eclogue."

17. Corrected by Theobald. Q has "And Cuckow-budds of yellow hew: And ladi-smockes all siluer white. . . ."

18. See Chapter I, n. 19.

19. Chappell, *Popular Music of the Olden Time*, I, 67, 75. Naylor, p. 15, believes the term "Freemen," as used to denote a type of song, is a corruption of "threemen."

20. I feel free to shorten the song tune. One of the marks of a folk tune is the frequent augmentation and diminution which it undergoes in the hands of folk singers who take more liberties than I would dare to take. Although it cannot be proved at this time, I suggest that the tune, as Chappell prints it, is an augmented version of the shorter tune I use for the Shakespearean song.

21. See Chapter I, pp. 3 and 7.

22. "Love's Labour's Lost," *The Works of Shakespeare*, II, p. 92. Noble (p. 38, *Shakespeare's Use of Song*), censures Capell for changing the text, asserting: "*The Owl Song*. Capell added 'tu-who' after the line ending 'staring owl,' his reason being to make the rhythm of the two songs similar and thus to facilitate the same tune being set to both songs, a thing which modern musical practice, with its insistence on strict appropriateness, would forbid. Unfortunately Capell's emendation has survived in many modern texts. The owl's hoot is 'tuwittahoo,' there is no pause and the whole often resembles laughter. In our text the original line arrangement has been restored and its propriety is so obvious that many will marvel that any editor ever printed it otherwise, and yet I know of no modern text which conforms in the matter with the first edition of the play." If I understand Noble correctly, he objects to one tune being used for both songs because such a procedure would not be consistent with modern musical practice, in the sense that the word "modern" is usually under-

stood. The propriety of the original line arrangement mentioned by Noble does not appear obvious to me since it contains the line fragment mentioned above.

23. A description of artificial bird calls and the devices used to produce them in the Elizabethan drama may be found in Lawrence, *Pre-Restoration Stage Studies*, pp. 199-208.

24. Quiller-Couch and Dover Wilson (pp. 100 ff.) call the original compositor of the 1598 Quarto "the veriest tyro of his craft."

25. Noble (*Shakespeare's Use of Song*, p. 34) writes: "The two songs help to clear the stage, and as Epilogues they are used delightfully to sustain even in the end, the laughing character of the comedy . . . to restore the spirit of comedy banished by the news of the death of the Princess' father." A little later (p. 36) he adds: "Both are Elizabethan comic songs, without any serious intentions whatever." Noble notes the ridicule present in the songs, p. 33. Wright ("Extraneous Song in Elizabethan Drama," *SP*, XXIV, 262) says: "The comic epilogue songs in *Love's Labour's Lost* have little relation to the preceding play. The graceful farewells of the King and his party and the Princess serve to clear the stage." H. B. Lathrop ("Shakespeare's Dramatic Use of Songs," *MLN*, XXIII, 2) states: "Of the complete songs a few are mere epilogues." Among the epilogue songs he includes those which close *Love's Labour's Lost*.

FIVE

A Midsummer Night's Dream

"Man is but an ass, if he go about to expound this dream."
—BOTTOM, ACT V.

OTTOM IS QUITE RIGHT. COMPOUNDED OF MOON-beams and shadows, *A Midsummer Night's Dream* is a delicate comedy of earthy humor and fantastic conceits, of fairy pranks and noble sentiments. From beginning to end, as its title suggests, it is pervaded by a dream-like quality, a mixture of sheer fantasy and solid reality, sparkling with some of the most beautiful poetry written by Shakespeare. For all the evanescence of the play, however, its construction reveals a solidity and sureness of technique far above the comedies which preceded it. The artistry of the work is highly complex, composed as it is of a blend of low comedy and high comedy, of the supernatural and the natural, the masque form and the dramatic form, of prose, poetry, and music. Yet these diverse elements, so interfused as to defy complete analysis, achieve a firm dramatic unity.

We need not try "to expound this dream," but we may observe the important part played by the music in the structure and "theatre" of the comedy. A close look will reveal the wealth of melody implied or called for in the play which has inspired musicians and composers such as Mendelssohn to attempt to capture its essence in musical idiom.

Before beginning our examination of the music in the play, we should again take, as our point of departure, that body of facts and conjectures generally accepted by students and editors of the play regarding its date of composition or original performance, the occasion for its composition, and its text.

As usual, several dates have been suggested for the first performance of the play.[1] I think the date 1596 most likely for the

following reasons: Elizabeth Carey, the daughter of ⸢
Carey, Lord Chamberlain, was married to Thomas Berk
Blackfriars home of Sir George Carey on February 19,
would be reasonable to suppose that the Chamberlain's
tributed to the festivity of the occasion; Shakespeare made use
of an unusually large group of musicians in *A Midsummer Night's
Dream*—a group which, in size, he did not use again until *The
Tempest*; Sir George Carey was not only the patron of The Chamberlain's Men, but was also a noted patron of music who maintained a large private musical establishment;[3] there is also a close
affinity between *A Midsummer Night's Dream* and *Love's Labour's
Lost*, as many editors and students of the plays have noted.

The earliest text of the play, that of the Quarto of 1600, shows
several signs of revision. For example, Dover Wilson and Chambers
suspect that Puck's epilogue was an alternate ending used in place
of the fairy dance when the play was performed publicly.[4] There
is strong evidence that the play was revived for a performance
before James in 1604.[5] Chambers has also noted that, in the Folio
text, the act divisions have been superimposed on a text written
for continuous performance; this indicates, to him, a revival of
the play.[6] The title page of the 1600 Quarto contains this information:

A Midsommer nights dreame. As it hath beene sundry times publickely acted, by the Right honourable, the Lord Chamberlaine
his seruants. Written by William Shakespeare. Imprinted at London, for Thomas Fisher, and are to be soulde at his shoppe, at
the Signe of the White Hart, in Fleetestreete. 1600.

On the strength of the evidence before us, we may begin our
study of the play with the following hypotheses in mind:

1. The play was written for a noble wedding.

2. The extra musicians and the fairies were probably drawn
from a musical establishment—perhaps from the household where
the play was first performed.

3. The play was presented publicly several times after its first
performance.

4. The Quarto of 1600 contains the text of the play as it was performed publicly.

5. The play was revived in 1604 for a court performance.

One of the important problems to be solved by Shakespeare was the effective presentation of the fairies; they had to be clearly distinguished from the mortals in the play. Language and costume contributed to the solution of the problem, as did the use of children in suggesting the diminutive size of the fairies. The essential nature of the fairies—their airiness—required a more subtle depiction, however, such as music could most appropriately supply. The first instance of Shakespeare's use of music for this purpose occurs in II, ii, lines 1-26, where Titania's fairy attendants sing her to sleep just before she is enchanted by Oberon: "*Enter Queene of Fairies, with her traine.*[7] *Queen.* Come, now a Roundell, and a Fairy song;/ . . . Sing me now asleepe,/ Then to your offices, and let me rest."

Fairies Sing.
You spotted Snakes with double tongue,
Thorny Hedgehogges be not seene,
Newts and blinde wormes do no wrong,
Come not neere our Fairy Queene.
Philomele with melodie,
Sing in your[8] *sweet Lullaby*
Lulla, lulla, lullaby, lulla, lulla, lullaby,
Neuer harme, nor spell, nor charme,
Come our louely Lady nye,
So good night with Lullaby.
   2. *Fairy.*[9] *Weauing Spiders come not heere,*
Hence you long leg'd Spinners, hence:
Beetles blacke approach not neere;
Worme nor Snayle doe no offence.
Philomele with melody, &c.
   1. *Fairy.*[10] *Hence away, now all is well;*
One aloofe, stand Centinell.   *Shee sleepes.*[11]

Enter Oberon.

It is not difficult to determine the actions taken by the performers of the song. Titania calls for a roundel, which is a circular dance.[12] The fairy attendants, probably about six in number, apparently join hands and dance around Titania as they sing the song. The song itself is an ayre in the form of a lullaby, a type of song quite popular during the period.[13] The language, the subject matter, and the eleven-line structure of the roundel all suggest an art song, as opposed to a folk form.[14] In structure, the song consists of two quatrains to which is joined a seven-line refrain.

I have set the lyric to an Elizabethan lullaby published in 1599 (see Plate VI). If one had only Q 1600 to proceed upon, he would assume that the first stanza and refrain of the song are sung by all the fairies in both texts;[15] the second stanza is sung by a soloist, with the rest of the fairies joining in the second refrain. But though both texts give the stanza to a soloist, they do not agree on which fairy sings. In the Quarto text, the soloist is called "1. Fai."; in the Folio text he is called "2. Fairy." In the Quarto text, the final couplet of the song is assigned to "2. Fai."; in the Folio text, to "1. Fairy." If we accept the Folio version of the song, we would normally expect the "1. Fairy" to appear in the text before the "2. Fairy." He does not do so; but modern editors, noting that the second stanza of the song is sung solo and the first stanza is not, have assigned the first stanza to the "1. Fairy," the second stanza to the "2. Fairy," and have marked the refrains as choruses for all of the fairies.[16] This solution of the problem has the force of logic behind it, and for that reason I accept it, though with some hesitation. The Quarto text may be correct; the vocal arrangements of ayres were not always made in a logical manner. The final couplet of the Folio version of the song probably serves the same function that the "coda" serves in modern musical compositions, namely, to mark the conclusion of a piece containing frequent repetitions in its structure. The same device is used later in the final fairy masque of the play.

The appropriateness of the song to the situation and the close affinity of its structure to the art song suggest that Shakespeare wrote the song to be set to music especially composed for the play. We know little about the music to which the song was originally

PLATE VI.—*Lullabie.* The fairy lullaby sung to Titania is here set to a lullaby found in Anthony Holborne's *Pavans, galliards, almains, and other short aeirs . . . 1599.* The first edition of this collection was printed in 1597. The vocal part is a slightly altered version of Holborne's melody. The cantus and bassus parts are in their original form.

set, and we have no certain knowledge about its composer. However, we may speculate. If the wedding for which the play was written was performed at the home of Sir George Carey, Lord Chamberlain, there is a good chance that some of the music for the play was composed by John Dowland, the famous lutenist and song writer, who was apparently employed in Sir George Carey's musical establishment at that time.[17]

Titania's lullaby was probably accompanied by instruments. It belongs to a type of song usually set to a specific instrumental accompaniment. Though there is no cue for an instrumental accompaniment for the song in either the Quarto or the Folio text, an instrumental consort was available as we know from a stage direction appearing later, IV, i, line 87, in both Quarto and Folio texts. The probable instrumentation of the consort is, of course, a matter of conjecture. Under the circumstances a rather large grouping would be indicated; the classic broken consort—a lute, a mandore, a treble viol, a bass viol, a cittern, and a flute or treble recorder would have been appropriate. While the fairies sang, the musicians were apparently hidden from the audience, as indeed they probably were throughout the play. In every instance where their music is called for, it represents supernatural melodies evoked from the air at the request of Titania or Oberon. Such an illusion

was most easily created and maintained by having the music
originate from an unseen source, that is, by hiding the musicians
from the audience. As we know, this practice was a common one
in the public playhouses of the time.[18]

There are several reasons why Shakespeare placed a fairy
dance and song at this point of the play. It is necessary for Titania
to fall asleep in order that Oberon may cast his spell over her.
The song, as the text shows, was composed for the purpose of
lulling Titania to sleep.

But why should Titania be so honored when the lovers fell
asleep without music? As we have noted, music and the portrayal
of the supernatural were closely allied in the Elizabethan drama.[19]
On a stage with limited mechanical devices, music often served
to achieve the sense of unreality demanded by scenes containing
ghostly characters and actions. The fairies with which Shakespeare
peopled this play are airy sprites defying time and space, con-
stantly in motion. Even a lullaby is sung to dancing feet. Shakespeare joined music with some of his most delicate poetry in order
to set his fairies apart from the gross mortals of the play; it is
hardly a coincidence that, throughout the play, music is reserved
completely for those episodes involving the fairies or the rustics
in contrast to the fairies. Even when Titania falls so far from
fairy grace as to become enamored of an ass, the depth of her dis-
grace is suggested by the contrast between the lovely song to which
she falls asleep and the earthy song of Bottom to which she awakes.

After Titania's lullaby the next appearance in the play of
music—of a sort—is that by Bottom as an ass in his scene with
Titania, III, i, lines 121-141:

Enter Peter Quince.[20]

Pet.[21] Blesse thee *Bottome,* blesse thee; thou art translated.
                                                              Exit.
   Bot. I see their knauery; this is to make an asse of me,
to fright me if they could; but I will not stirre from
this place, do what they can. I will walk vp and downe
here, and I will sing that they shall heare I am not afraid.

The Woosel cocke, so blacke of hew,
With Orenge-tawny bill.
The Throstle, with his note so true,
The Wren and[22] little quill..
    Tyta. What Angell wakes me from my flowry bed?
    Bot. The Finch, the Sparrow, and the Larke,
The plainsong Cuckow gray;
Whose note full many a man doth marke,
And dares not answere, nay.
For indeede, who would set his wit to so foolish a bird?
Who would giue a bird the lye, though he cry Cuckow,
neuer so?
    Tyta. I pray thee gentle mortall, sing againe,
Mine eare is much enamored of thy note; . . .

There seems little doubt that here Bottom sings two fragments
of a song. The completion of the song, to judge from the text, was
probably a refrain. The song resembles a folk type such as would
be appropriate for Bottom. The performance of the song was
probably as crude as could be sung with any resemblance to music,
since the humor of the situation is derived partly from the dainty
Titania's delight in what was, no doubt, a far-from-angelic voice.
No instrumental accompaniment is indicated nor does any seem
necessary.

The tune of Bottom's song is unknown. The subject matter
set forth is similar to that of the Cuckoo Song in *Love's Labour's
Lost*. But Bottom sang a different tune; even the meters of the two
songs differ. For the purpose of illustration, I have set the words
of Bottom's song to a ballad tune which was popular when the
play was originally performed (see Plate VII).

Bottom's taste in music is evidenced again in IV, i, lines 28-32,
wherein Titania and her fairy attendants are shown ministering
to Bottom's whims: "*Tita.* What, wilt thou heare some musicke,
my sweet loue. *Clow.* I haue a reasonable good eare in musicke.
Let vs[23] haue the tongs and the bones. *Musicke Tongs, Rurall Musicke.*[24] *Tita.* Or say sweete Loue, what thou desirest to eat."

Here we have a conflict which I find difficult to resolve. The

Q 1600 text has no stage direction at this point to indicate music performed at Bottom's request. On the other hand, the Folio text, which I quote, contains directions for the performance of music. A choice must be made between the two texts.

The validity of the Quarto text, it seems to me, rests upon three arguments:

1. There is no stage direction for the performance of music in the Quarto text.

2. There is no apparent dramatic necessity for music at this point; Bottom's reference to tongs and bones is alone sufficient to emphasize his taste in music.

3. The stage directions in the Folio text were possibly inserted by the players and may not have reflected Shakespeare's intention for the scene.[25]

Indeed, the Folio stage directions are omitted in modern editions of the play. But several arguments may be advanced in favor of the Folio text:

1. The Quarto text is notably bare of stage directions; there is no direction for the performance of Bottom's song, though we know from Titania's comment—"Sing again, Mine eare is much enamored of thy note"—that he sang it.

The Woosell cock so black of hue, With orange-tawny bill, The

throstle with his note so true, The wren with little quill,

PLATE VII.— *The Woosel Cock, so Black of Hewe.* This tune is found in the *Fitzwilliam Virginal Book* (c. 1600) with the title "Rowland," and in Robinson's *School of Music* (1603), with the name "Lord Willoughby." The illustration above is taken from Chappell's *Popular Music of the Olden Time,* I, 114, 115. Bottom sings only the verse of his song: the refrain which he omits probably followed much like the melody of the refrain included above.

2. If the play was written originally for a private performance, the insertion of such music would not be unusual. Inigo Jones used rural music of the type indicated by the Folio stage direction in his *King's Masque* (1637).[26] In view of the festive occasion dominating the original performance of the play, the mention of the tongs and bones might have been sufficient excuse for inserting the crude music called for in the Folio text.

3. We are interested in the play as it was actually performed, as well as in Shakespeare's conception of its performance.

4. Unless there is evidence to the contrary, Heming and Condell may be presumed to be closer to Shakespeare's intentions than subsequent students.

On the basis of the above analysis, I believe the argument in favor of the Folio text is the stronger. As far as direct evidence is concerned, the Quarto version is obscure. The Folio, however, provides a definite statement on the question. It is this direct statement, I think, that should be decisive.

If we accept the Folio version as authoritative, what kind of music is described by the term "Rurall"? The reference to tongs and bones indicates that it was quite crude. Also, since the purpose of the scene is to draw humor from the contrast between the airy Titania and the earthy Bottom, we would expect the music he likes to partake of his nature. The "instruments" used by the performers in Inigo Jones's masque would also have been appropriate for this scene. They include a rebec, a gridiron, "knackers" (bones), and "tongs and key."[27] The rebec played the tune, and the other devices supplied a rhythmic accompaniment. As the music is performed at the command of Titania, we may suppose that it originated from a supernatural source. The musicians were hence probably hidden from the view of the audience.

We have seen music used to depict the ethereal nature of the fairies in Titania's lullaby and music used in Bottom's song to stress the contrast between the fairies and the clowns. We now find (IV, i, lines 81-87) music used to emphasize the fairy-gentle-folk relationship in the play. Titania, Oberon, and Puck remove their enchantments from Bottom and from the sleeping lovers:

"*Tita.* How came these things to passe?/ Oh, how mine eyes doth[28] loath this visage now!/ *Ob.* Silence a while. *Robin* take off his head:/ *Titania*, musick call, and strike more dead/ Then common sleepe; of all these, fine the sense./ *Tita.* Musicke, ho musicke, such as charmeth sleepe./ *Musick still.*[29] *Rob.* When[30] thou wak'st, with thine owne fooles eies peepe."

The cue for the musicians to begin playing is given by Titania. The music played is described in the same line— ". . . such as charmeth sleepe." It is the function of the music to restore the sleeping mortals to their senses. At the conclusion of the consort piece, Puck describes the future result of the magical music on the mortals: "When thou wak'st, with thine owne fooles eies peepe." Other than the general nature of the music, which was probably soft and soothing, we know nothing positive. Probably, however, it was of the kind that would be produced by an instrumental arrangement of such an ayre as "Sleep, Wayward Thoughts," by John Dowland (see Plate VIII). The original music was probably played by the same consort that accompanied the first fairy song.

PLATE VIII.—*Sleep, Wayward Thoughts.* The melody and lyric here reproduced may be found in John Dowland's *First Book of Airs* (1597), as reprinted in Fellowes, *The English School of Lutenist Song Writers.*

The passage involving the sleep-inducing song contains three interesting aspects of Shakespeare's dramatic art; in it may be perceived his use of music to suggest the magical powers of the fairies, his adaptation of a common Elizabethan belief in the curative powers of music for human ills, both mental and physical,[31] and his use of music, as in *The Two Gentlemen of Verona*, to underscore the turning point of the play.

The relationship of the music to the turning point of the play requires some explanation. It will be remembered that the confusions which beset the mortals in the play are results of the quarrel between Titania and Oberon. The inference made by Shakespeare is that when discord occurs in the fairy world human affairs also become out of tune. We would hence expect that the resolution of the quarrel between Oberon and Titania would be quickly followed by a harmonious adjustment in mortal relationships. As we have seen, the music evoked by Titania was for the purpose of resolving the mortal discord. From the sleep disenchantment episode to the end of the play, all difficulties disappear and joy reigns throughout Athens. The end of the fairy strife and the disenchantment of the mortals clearly mark the turning point of the comedy.

Lest the significance of the passage just discussed be possibly overlooked by his audience, Shakespeare apparently restated the point, again with language, action, and music. Immediately following the sleep-disenchantment episode occurs a passage which Dover Wilson and Quiller-Couch have, I think, correctly interpreted.[32] For Oberon again calls for music, a cue which a mere casual glance at either text would lead us falsely to associate with the preceding passage:

> *Rob.* When thou wak'st, with thine owne fooles eies peepe.
> *Ob.* Sound musick; come my Queen, take hands with me
> And rocke[33] the ground whereon these sleepers be.
> Now thou and I are new in amity,
> And will to morrow midnight, solemnly
> Dance in Duke *Theseus* house triumphantly,
> And blesse it to all faire posterity,[34]

There shall the paires of faithfull Louers be
Wedded, with *Theseus,* all in iollity.

Puck's line, however, appears to mark the close of the "musicke
such as charmeth sleepe"; hence, Oberon's call for music must be
the prelude to another episode. After his command for music,
Oberon says, ". . . come, my Queen, take hands with me, . . ."
which suggests a dance, especially when Oberon adds, ". . . And
rocke the ground whereon these sleepers be." Evidently Oberon
and Titania here perform a dance to the music of the hidden
consort. After the dance is ended, Oberon announces, "Now thou
and I are new in amity, . . ." The music and dance symbolizes
the concord re-established between Oberon and Titania. But, more
than that, it also apparently symbolizes the harmony restored in
the relationship of the mortals. This Oberon indicates by antici-
pating the events of the following act with the lines: "There shall
the paires of faithfull Louers be/ Wedded, with *Theseus,* all in
iollity." The two passages we have just examined, then, should
be considered as having one primary dramatic purpose, though
they also have several secondary overtones. Titania's music marks
the end of all conflict and, hence, the turning point of the play.
Oberon's music symbolizes the new amity between the fairy king
and queen, and, together with the dialogue, foreshadows the concord to be reached by the mortals. The music throughout the two
episodes also aids the illusion of magic and enchantment.

The music to which Oberon and Titania danced was probably
a pavane, which was the most stately of the dances performed in
the courtly circles of the period. Oberon and Titania, though they
are fairy monarchs, are every inch a king and queen. Both their
language and actions bear the stamp of empire. The pavane is
appropriate to them. The example of the dance given in Plate IX
is the melody of a pavane from John Adson's *Courtly Masquing
Ayres* (1621).[35]

Upon the exit of Oberon, Titania, and Puck, we are brought
back to reality by the hoarse clamor of a hunting horn, the herald
of a new day. Theseus, Hippolyta, and their attendants, while

hunting discover the lovers asleep in the woods. The lovers are awakened, and in a very interesting manner. We would expect the Duke or one of his attendants to awaken the lovers by speaking to them or by shaking them. Such is not the case; the Duke commands, IV, i, line 142: *"The.* Goe bid the hunts-men wake them with their hornes. *Hornes and they wake. Shout within, they all start up.*[36] *Thes.* Good morrow friends: Saint *Valentine* is past,/ Begin these wood birds but to couple now?"

Why would Shakespeare have wanted the lovers awakened in such a complicated fashion? One dramatic consequence we may at least observe: the music of the horns is closely related to Titania's "musicke, such as charmeth sleepe." Her music marks the curative spell under which the lovers sleep; it is fairy music. The hunting horns end the spell and return the lovers to a world of reality. Fairy music charms; mortal music awakes. So it is with the lulling and awakening of the lovers, and so it was with the lulling and awakening of Titania.

The remainder of the music is in the festive spirit of the last act. The clowns perform their "tedious brief tragedy" and offer an epilogue at its conclusion. The Duke refuses the epilogue, choosing instead to be entertained by a Bergamask dance performed, probably, by Moon and Lion (V, i, lines 357-371). *"Bot.*[37] No, I assure you, the wall is downe, that parted their Fathers. Will it please you to see the Epilogue, or to heare a Bergomask

PLATE IX.—*Pavane.* Reprinted here is the melody of a pavane from Adson's *Courtly Masquing Ayres* . . . (1621). The above illustration was taken from a transcription in the New York Public Library.

dance, betweene two of our company? *Duk.* No Epilogue, I
pray you; . . . But come, your Burgomaske; let your Epilogue
alone. The iron tongue of midnight hath told twelue./ Louers to
bed, 'tis almost Fairy time./ . . ."

Dover Wilson suggests that the Bergamask dance performs the
functions of an antimask, the grotesque and comic part of masque
entertainments, and that it is an introduction to the masque of
the fairies which follows it.[38] The suggestion is illuminating, but
the dance, probably a jig, is also to be considered as what Bottom
proclaims it to be—a part of the entertainment planned by the
rustics—an alternative afterpiece to their play. Jigs were usually
song-dances involving much pantomimic satire. No great degree
of imagination seems required to determine the subject for satire
in a wedding celebration, especially when we know that Morley,
in describing the Bergamask songs, which he called "Justinianas,"
referred to them as a "wanton and rude kind of musicke."[39] I
know of no contemporary song having words that would fit the
situation, but I offer an old song which has a tune admirably suited
to a humorous jig (see Plate X).

Quoth John to Joan, wilt thou have me? I prithee now wilt? And I'se
I've corn and hay in the barn hard by, and three fat hogs pent up

marry with thee, My cow, my calf, my horse, my rents, And
in the sty; I have a mare, and she is coal black, I

all my lands and tenements: O say, my Joan, say my Joan,
ride on her tail to save her back, Then

will not that do? I cannot come ev' - ry day to woo.

PLATE X.—*Wolsey's Wild.* This song appears in Chappell's *Popular Music of
the Olden Time,* I, 86, 87, and is assigned by him to the era of Henry VII
and Mary. The melody and two stanzas only are given above.

At the end of the Bergamask dance, a bell tolls the hour of midnight. It is the striking of the hour which separates the jig, aesthetically, from the music and dance which follow it. For, as the Duke proclaims, shifting from prose to blank verse, "The iron tongue of midnight hath told twelue. Louers to bed, 'tis almost Fairy time." It is fairy time. The mortals disappear, taking with them the world of reality and leaving in its stead a world peopled by creatures of the air, spirits of good and spirits of evil who, until cock-crow, flit unseen through the mansions of the living, locked often in silent struggles over the destinies of sleeping mortals. Lest the "damned spirits," mentioned earlier by Puck (III, ii, line 382), mar the auspicious occasion, Oberon and Titania, who "are spirits of another sort," come with their attendant fairies to exorcise the evil spirits from the happy household. Puck appears and explains the purpose of the fairy visitation.[40] The stage is suddenly filled with dancing fairies, flickering tapers, music and song. True to form, the fairies cast their beneficent spell to the sound of music:

> *Enter King and Queene of Fairies, with their traine.*
>   *Ob.* Through the house giue glimmering light,
> By the dead and drowsie fier,
> Eucrie Elfo and Fairie spright,
> Hop as light as bird from brier,
> And this Ditty[41] after me, sing and dance it trippinglie.
>   *Tita.* First rehearse this song by roate,
> To each word a warbling note.
> Hand in hand, with Fairie grace,
> Will we sing and blesse this place.

> ### The Song
>
> *Now untill the breake of day,*
> *Through this house each Fairy stray.*
> *To the best Bride-bed will we,*
> *Which by us shall blessed be:*
> *And the issue there create,*
> *Euer shall be fortunate:*
> *So shall all the couples three,*

Euer true in louing be:
And the blots of Natures hand,
Shall not in their issue stand.
Neuer mole, harelip, nor scarre,
Nor marke prodigious, such as are
Despised in Natiuitie,
Shall upon their children be.
With this field dew consecrate,
Euery Fairy take his gate,
And each seueral chamber blesse,
Through this Pallace with sweet peace,
Euer shall in Safety rest,
And the owner of it blest.
Trip away, make no stay;
Meet me all by breake of day.

Richmond Noble has described what, with two major reservations, we may safely accept as the way in which the little masque was performed.[42] Here is the text and assignment of lines as I believe them to have been written for the original performance of the play:

Oberon. Through the house give glimmering light,
　　　　By the dead and drowsy fire;
　　　　Every elf and fairy sprite,
　　　　Hop as light as bird from brier,
　　　　And this ditty after me,
　　　　Sing and dance it trippingly.
Titania. First rehearse this song by rote,
　　　　To each word a warbling note.
　　　　Hand in hand, with fairy grace,
　　　　Will we sing and bless this place.
　　　　Now until the break of day,
　　　　Through this house each fairy stray.[43]
Fairies. To the best bride-bed will we,
　　　　Which by us shall blessed be,
　　　　And the issue there create,
　　　　Ever shall be fortunate.
　　　　So shall all the couples three,

Ever true in loving be,
And the blots of Nature's hand,
Shall not in their issue stand.
Never mole, harelip, nor scar,
Nor mark prodigious such as are
Despised in nativity,
Shall upon their children be.

Oberon. With this field dew consecrate,
Every fairy take his gate,
And each several chamber bless,
Through this palace with sweet peace,
And the owner of it bless't
Ever shall in safety rest.[44]

Trip away; make no stay;
Meet me all by break of day.

If we begin the song with Oberon's lines, "Through the house
. . . " etc., the entire song will consist of five six-line stanzas
and a brisk closing couplet. These stanzas perform two functions;
the first two contain directions given by Oberon and Titania to
their attendants, that is, they explain what is to be done. The
fairies are to sing and dance through the house and are to bless
it. In the third and fourth stanzas, the fairies describe the nature
of their blessing. In the fifth stanza, Oberon repeats his commands
and concludes the song.

Although I suggest that the song began, structurally, with
Oberon's opening line, it is possible that Oberon and Titania do
not actually sing but rather intone their lines to the musical setting of the song.[45] The lines assigned the fairy king and queen
contain several commands for the attendant fairies to sing and
dance, which indicates that the actual singing and dancing has
not yet begun; also, it would not be in character for the fairy
monarchs to sing.[46] With the beginning of the third stanza, however, the fairy attendants apparently join hands and dance a
roundel while singing the third and fourth stanzas. The fifth
stanza and concluding couplet are again perhaps intoned by
Oberon, since in them are commands directed toward the lesser

fairies. The final couplet of the song is probably a "coda" such as we found in Titania's lullaby. It may be noted that, in both songs using this device, the couplets are set to different rhythms from those in the bodies of the songs. Apparently, the music also changed its rhythmic pattern. An example of this device, combining text and music, may be found in Johnson's setting of Ariel's song, "Where the bee sucks," in *The Tempest*.[47]

There is no stage direction in the Quarto and Folio texts indicating that the dance was accompanied by instrumental music, but it would be reasonable to assume that such was the case. The song, it appears, was written especially for the play: its structure is that of an ayre rather than that of a folk song. As was probably the case of Titania's lullaby, this song was set for an instrumental group similar to the one proposed for the other scenes employing music of this type.

The original musical setting for the song has been lost. The dance-song I use below for illustrative purposes was written for Middleton's play, *Blurt, Master Constable* (see Plate XI).

Before concluding our study of *A Midsummer Night's Dream*, a few words about the text used in the study are necessary. I purposely placed this explanation toward the end of the chapter because the evidence influencing my choice of texts is of a cumulative nature. As far as the passages quoted in this examination of the play are concerned, both the Q 1600 version and the Folio version appear to be, generally speaking, good texts, although both contain apparent errors. The discrepancies between the two texts I have indicated in footnotes. A comparison of the texts reveals that there are two general differences between them; the Quarto text is the more accurate in grammar, but it contains few stage directions; the Folio text contains several apparent errors in grammar and transcription, but its stage directions are more numerous and more revealing. The stage direction in V, i, of the Folio text, "Tawyer with a Trumpet before them," seems good evidence that the Folio text was based on a prompter's copy of the play.[48] Since our study is mainly one of the production of Shakespeare's comedies, I chose to follow the Folio text.

On the basis of the evidence presented in this study, the following conclusions regarding Shakespeare's use of music in *A Midsummer Night's Dream* seem to be inescapable:

1. Shakespeare used music in the play for the primary purpose of setting the fairies apart from the mortals.

2. A secondary use of music in the play was to stress the contrast between the dainty Titania and the boorish Bottom.

3. Another secondary use of music was to heighten the dramatic effect of the fairy spells and enchantments.

4. Still another secondary use of music was to symbolize the concord arising from the settlement of the fairy quarrel, and to foreshadow the resulting harmony between the mortals—thus emphasizing the turning point of the play.

PLATE XI.—*The Urchin's Dance.* This dance-song was written by Edmund Pearce, Master of the Choristers at St. Paul's, for the Paul's boys' production of Middleton's *Blurt, Master Constable* (see J. M. Gibbon, *Melody and the Lyric from Chaucer to the Cavaliers*, p. 132).

The evidence also supports two corollary conclusions: first, that in three instances—Bottom's song, the dance of Titania and Oberon, and the Bergamask dance—music should be performed although there is no stage direction calling for it in either the Quarto or the Folio texts; and second, that the stage direction in both texts for the performance of the final fairy song is apparently in error.

The over-all impression we gain from our examination of the music in the play is that Shakespeare employed music much more lavishly than he did in his preceding plays, and that the increase in the quantity of the music is equalled by the increased artistry with which the music was employed. We may readily believe that without the music in the play, performed as Shakespeare intended it to be performed, much of the lyrical charm and fantasy of *A Midsummer Night's Dream* would be lost.

Notes

1. Since most editors agree that the play was written for performance at a noble wedding, they attempt to establish its date in reference to some particular marriage. Henry Cuningham, editor of the Arden edition (pp. xxix, xxx), chooses the wedding of William Stanley, Earl of Derby, at Greenwich, January 26, 1595. Chambers (*William Shakespeare*, I, 358, 359) concurs, saying, "Either wedding [that of Elizabeth Carey, 1596, or that of the Earl of Derby and Elizabeth Vere] would fit such indications of date as the play yields. It belongs to the lyric group of 1594-6." Noble (*Shakespeare's Use of Song*, p. 52) notes the similarity of the concluding masque of the play and that in *The Merry Wives of Windsor* and, on that basis, selects the date 1598. Quiller-Couch and Wilson, editors of the New Cambridge edition (pp. 97, 98), also choose the date 1598, largely on the strength of Noble's suggestion. F. H. McCloskey ("The Date of 'A Midsummer Night's Dream,'" *MLN*, XLVI, 389) believes Bottom's song, "The Woosel cock so black of hew," is a parody of a song appearing in *The Arbour of Amorous Devices* (1597), and hence the play was written after the publication of that miscellany and before Meres' *Palladis Tamia* (1598), which mentions the play. The resemblance between the two songs is limited to one line—the first line of Bottom's song and the line, "The Throstle-cock so black of hew," in the *Arbour*. Burns Martin ("A Midsummer Night's Dream," *TLS*, January 24, 1935, p. 48) selects the double wedding of Lady Elizabeth and Lady Katherine Somerset to Henry Guildferd and William Petre on November 8, 1596. John W. Draper ("The Date of 'A Midsommer Night's Dreame,'" *MLN*, LIII, 266-268) computes the date of the wedding for which the play was written as May 1, 1595, using as a basis for his computations the astronomical allusions within the play. Neilson and Hill (editors of the Riverside Press edition, 1942, p. 88) concur in Chambers' selection of the wedding of the Earl of Derby, 1595, as the most plausible date.

2. Chambers, *Williams Shakespeare*, I, p. 359.

3. *Ibid.*

4. Quiller-Couch and Wilson, pp. 88, 92. Chambers, *William Shakespeare*, I, pp. 360, 361.

5. *Op. cit.*, I, p. 362. Chambers quotes a letter about the event from Dudley Carleton to John Chamberlain: "We had a play of Robin goode-fellow."

6. *Op. cit.*, I, p. 358.

7. Unless otherwise indicated, the quotations from the play used in this study are from the 1623 Folio. The line numbers follow those of the Globe edition. Throughout this chapter, the terms "Folio" and "Quarto" refer to the 1623 Folio and Fisher's 1600 Quarto, respectively.

8. *our* Q. *your* F.

9. *1. Fai.* Q. *2. Fairy.* F.

10. *2. Fai.* Q. *1. Fairy.* F.

11. Omitted Q. *Shee sleepes* F.

12. *NED.* Cf. Elson, *Shakespeare in Music*, p. 133.

13. See Arkwright, "Elizabethan Choirboy Plays and Their Music," *Proceedings of the Musical Association*, April 1914, p. 133.

14. See Chapter I, pp. 1, 2.

15. The stage direction states, *Fairies sing:* the following lines are not assigned to any individual by either text.

16. For example, Neilson and Hill, editors of the Riverside Press edition, 1942.

17. In dedicating his *First Book of Airs* (1597) to Sir George Carey, Dowland wrote: ". . . This small booke . . . I haue presumed to dedicate to your Lordship, who for your vertue and nobility are best able to protect it, & for your honorable fauors towards me . . . Neither in these your honours may I let passe the dutifull remembrance of your vertuous Lady my honorable mistris, whose singular graces towards me haue added spirit to my unfortunate labours, . . . your honourable hands have vouchsaft to uphold my poore fortunes, which I now wholy recommend to your gratious protection, with these my first endeuors, humbly beseeching you to accept and cherish them with your continued fauours." (Dowland, *First Book of Airs*, Part I, p. vii, as reprinted in Fellowes, *The English School of Lutenist Song Writers*.)

18. See Chapter II, p. 42.

19. See Chapter II.

20. *Enter Quince.* Q. *Enter Peter Quince.* F.

21. *Quin.* Q. *Pet.* F.

22. *with* Q. *and* F.

23. *Lets* Q. *Let us* F.

24. Omitted Q. *Musicke Tongs, Rurall Musicke.* F.

25. Quiller-Couch and Dover Wilson (New Cambridge edition, p. 157), quote Capell as saying the stage direction "is certainly an interpolation of the players."

26. See Chapter II, n. 139.

27. *Idem.*

28. *doe* Q. *doth* F.

29. Omitted Q. *Musick still.* F.

30. *Now, when* Q. *When* F.

31. This belief is treated at greater length, if superficially, by Naylor, *Shakespeare and Music*, pp. 34, 35, 104, 106.

32. *Op. cit.*, p. 53.

33. *NED,* "to bring into a state of slumber, rest, or peace by gentle motion to and fro."

34. *prosperitie* Q. *posterity* F.

35. From a photostat of a transcription furnished me by the New York Public Library.

36. *Shoute within: they all start up. Winde hornes.* Q. *Hornes and they wake. Shout within, they all start up.* F.

37. *Lyon.* Q. *Bot.* F.

38. *Op cit.,* pp. 140, 141.

39. *A Plaine and Easie Introduction . . . 1597,* p. 180.

40. Many editors note the similarity in purpose and subject apparent in the fairy masque and Spenser's "Epithalamion."

41. *NED,* "The words of a song as distinguished from the music or tune."

42. *Shakespeare's Use of Song,* pp. 52-54.

43. Will . . . place. *The Song. Now untill,* etc. Q. and F. Noble, p. 51, assigns the lines, "Now . . . stray." to Oberon. This not only breaks the unity of Titania's stanza, but also creates needless repetition in Oberon's lines.

44. *Euer shall in safety rest, and the owner of it blest.* Q. and F. The lines are reversed in most modern editions. Noble, p. 52, emends the stanza thus:

> Through this palace, with sweet peace,
>   Every fairy take his gait,
> And each several chamber bless,
>   With this field dew consecrate,
> And the owner of it blest,
> Ever shall in safety rest.
>   Trip away: make no stay:
>   Meet me all, by break of day.

Until more conclusive evidence can be brought to bear on the lines in question, I think they should be left in their places (excepting the reversed lines mentioned previously).

45. In the Quarto text, the stage direction, *The Song.,* falls in the midst of the stanza I assign to Titania. The stage direction is the only indication that the following lines are sung. Dr. Johnson made the suggestion, later employed by Kittredge, that the song, though indicated, was omitted from the text. The Folio, however, italicized the lines following the stage direction—a clear indication that its editors thought the lines were sung. The same lines were not italicized in the Quarto, but neither were the lines of Bottom's song, which were certainly sung. In view of the confusion apparent at this point, from the Quarto through subsequent editions, I feel free to suggest that the only apparent error in the Quarto and Folio texts of the song is the location of the stage direction. It should, I think, be placed two lines lower, as I have indicated. If I am right, the problem is clarified. An alternative conclusion, which I reject, is that intoning gave way to singing at exactly the spot indicated by the stage direction in the Quarto and Folio. My own suggestion involves a slight departure from the original texts but a far slighter degree of tampering than has been thought necessary by respected critics and editors from Johnson to Kittredge.

46. See Chapter I, p. 3.

47. The text and music are reprinted in Sir F. Bridge, *Shakespearean Music in the Plays and Early Operas,* p. 28.

48. For an explanation of this stage direction, see Lawrence, "Tawyer with a Trumpet Before Them," *TLS* (March 20, 1930), 241.

SIX

The Merchant of Venice

Y THIS TIME WE HAVE SOME IDEA OF WHAT TO look for in observing the way music is used in *The Merchant of Venice*. While the fairy element, so prominent in *A Midsummer Night's Dream*, is missing, we may yet look for music to emphasize critical points in the action and to augment lyrical passages. In considering this latter function of music in the play the Belmont garden scene immediately comes to mind. We will turn to it in time, and a rich store it is for our purpose, but there are several matters of equal interest which first deserve our attention.

For the purpose of our study, we again need to have in mind the date and sources of the play. Its date may be placed, by general agreement, during the period 1596-1597.[1] Modern texts of the play are derived from those of the Quarto of 1600 and the Folio of 1623. There is no comprehensive source; the play appears to be an interweaving of several folk-tale motifs of which two, the casket motif and the bond motif, are the principal ones. Analogues of the play have been found in Ser Giovanni's *Il Pecorone* (1558) and the *Gesta Romanorum*, a miscellaneous collection of forty-three anonymous stories translated into English in 1577 by Robinson. The play was revived for a court performance in the winter of 1604-1605.[2]

There are two strands in the plot of the play: one based on the casket motif, which involves Portia and Bassanio, and the other built on the bond motif, which involves Antonio and Shylock. The two strands are connected by the friendship between Antonio and Bassanio, and by Portia's solution of the legal problem raised by Shylock's demand for the pound of flesh. The Lorenzo-Jessica and Gratiano-Nerissa pairings may have been the result of Shakespeare's early delight in multiple love affairs. The two principal strands each have a climax in the play, and Shakespeare underscores one of them with music.

The climax in the Portia-Bassanio strand occurs when Bassanio makes his choice of the three caskets—a choice upon which, as it turns out, the happiness of all the lovers, and that of Antonio, depends. Portia and Nerissa have a direct and immediate interest in Bassanio's choice; hence we should notice the care with which Portia sets the scene for his decision, and the comments she makes while doing so.[3]

> *Portia.* Away then, I am lockt in one of them,
> If you doe loue me, you will finde me out.
> *Nerryssa* and the rest, stand all aloofe,
> Let musique sound while he doth make his choyse,
> Then if he loose he makes a Swan-like end,
> Fading in musique. That the comparison
> may stand more proper, my eye shall be the streame
> and watry death-bed for him: he may win,
> And what is musique than? Than musique is
> euen as the flourish, when true subiects bowe
> to a new crowned Monarch: Such it is,
> As are those dulcet sounds in breake of day,
> That creepe into the dreaming bride-groomes eare,
> and summon him to marriage. . . .

*   *   *   *   *   *   *   *   *   *   *

> *Here Musicke.*[4]
> *A Song the whilst Bassanio comments on the caskets*
> *to himselfe.*
> *Tell me where is fancie bred,*
> *Or in the hart, or in the head,*
> *How begot, how nourished? Replie, replie.*
> *It is engendred in the eye,*[5]
> *With gazing fed, and Fancie dies:*
> *In the cradle where it lies*
> *Let us all ring Fancies knell.*
> Ile begin it.
> *Ding, dong, bell.*
> *All. Ding, dong, bell.*

Bass. So may the outward showes be least themselues,
The world is still deceau'd with ornament. . . .

In this passage, as we have noted in other plays, the song underscores the climax of the scene; this is an obvious function of the song. But, in its use, we may also notice an influence of the folk-tale sources on Shakespeare's treatment of the scene.

In most folk tales in which the "task" motif appears, the hero is assigned a series of tasks which he must perform before he may win riches or a beautiful princess. Usually the tasks number three—the third time is the charm—and usually the hero is enabled to perform his tasks by the aid of some helper, supernatural or otherwise, such as an old woman, a talking bird, or other device.[6] In *The Merchant of Venice,* the task assigned involves a choice of the right casket from three possible ones. Bassanio is the third suitor shown in the play; the Princes of Morocco and Aragon make their wrong choices of the gold and silver caskets, respectively, and disappear. So far, the dramatic situation follows the folk-tale pattern; but now Bassanio must choose, and we look for the helping device. In his predicament the song seems to supply the necessary aid.

Several students of the play, Richmond Noble most fully, have suggested that Portia has the song performed in order to give a hint to Bassanio regarding his choice.[7] Noble suggests that the song urges the hearer "to beware of that which is pleasing to the sight, for it has no substance, . . ." and believes that Bassanio is clearly inspired by the song when he comments, "So may the outward showes be least themselues,/ The world is still deceau'd with ornament."[8] Dover Wilson has pointed out that Bassanio could easily have associated the dirge-like form of the song with the lead casket, a symbol of death.[9]

Shakespeare builds up a motive strong enough to cause Portia to skirt dangerously near a breach of her oath. We learn early in the play that Portia has seen and fallen in love with Bassanio even before he appears to make his choice of the caskets. We also know that Nerissa was favorably impressed by the young Venetian. Both Portia and Nerissa, by a process of elimination, would know

that the lead casket is the fruitful one. So would the audience.
With so many well-wishers, we would not expect Portia to be held
strictly to account if she dropped a subtle hint to Bassanio.

The supposition that the song gives Bassanio a clue is denied
by Poole, editor of the Arden edition, p. 103, because such action
would be a charge against Portia's good faith. In this connection,
we may note that Portia solves the legal suit of Shylock by an
extremely literal interpretation of the agreement between Shylock and Antonio; she cannot "teach" Bassanio "how to choose
right," but to a mind capable of Portia's lawyer-like superiority
over logic and meaning, a literal interpretation of her father's
instructions would allow more or less subtle hints.

The way in which the song was probably performed could
also have helped Bassanio to choose wisely. The song, whose
irregular structure suggests it was an ayre, is apparently sung by
a soloist from among Portia's train of attendants. He sings the
first three lines of the song as a question; the other attendants
apparently sing the two words, "Replie, replie," to separate the
question from the answer, which is sung by the soloist again.[10]
The first line of bell sounds is also sung by the soloist, who is
then joined by a chorus of slow "ding-dongs," apparently from
the assembled attendants. The slow tolling of the simulated bells,
perhaps from both sides of Bassanio, in Dover Wilson's interpretation would have the effect of saying, "Look at the lead casket!"
over and over again.

The Quarto and Folio texts do not indicate the nature of the
instrumental accompaniment for the song. The soloist, to judge
from the text, sings on the outer stage. The song is a short one.
Probably, the most convenient arrangement for the performance
of the song would have been for the singer to accompany himself and the chorus with a lute. The accompaniment would thus
be near the singer; in fact, the lute could be carried in by the
soloist. A lutenist would also be a natural part of the noble lady's
train.[11]

If, as the evidence seems to indicate, Shakespeare intended his
song to aid Bassanio in making the right choice, why did he decide

to use a song for this purpose? It is possible that the idea was suggested to him by a song written earlier by Sir Philip Sidney. The music and stanzas of Sidney's song, which he set to the tune "Wilhelmus van Nassau," are given in the accompanying illustration (Plate XII).[12]

The resemblance between Sidney's song and the dramatic situation in the play rests upon the paradox present in both works. In Sidney's lyrics, the lover is instructed to gain his mistress by

PLATE XII.—*Who Hath His Fancy Pleased.* Sidney set his song to the popular tune, "Wilhelmus van Nassau." The tune and one stanza are shown above as found in Gibbon, *Melody and the Lyric*, pp. 69, 70. The remaining stanzas follow:

She never dies, but lasteth
In life of lover's heart;
He ever dies that wasteth
In love his chiefest part.
Thus in her life still guarded
In never dying faith,
Thus in his death rewarded,
Since she lives in his death.

But eyes these beauties see not,
Nor sense that grace descries:
Yet eyes deprived be not,
From sight of her fair eyes.
Which as of inward glory
They are the outward seal;
So may they live still sorry,
Which die not in that weal.

Look then and die. The pleasure
Doth answer well the pain.
Small loss of mortal treasure,
Who may immortal gain.
Immortal be her graces,
Immortal is her mind;
They, fit for heavenly places,
This heaven in it doth bind.

But who hath fancies pleased
With fruits of happy sight,
Let here his eyes be raised
On nature's sweetest light.

(Drinkwater, ed., *The Poems of Sir Philip Sidney*, pp. 241, 242.)

dying; in Shakespeare's scene, Bassanio gains Portia and worldly wealth by choosing, at Portia's indirect suggestion, death as symbolized by the lead casket.[13]

Sidney's lyrics contain the following points:

1. The man who looks with Fancy's eyes is not acquainted with profound love until his eyes are "raised on nature's sweetest light," that is, inward grace.[14]

2. The lover, having perceived this "inward glory," ceases to look with Fancy's eyes, hence Fancy dies.

3. The lover also "dies" in that "he wasteth in love his chiefest part."

4. In "dying," the lover gains the immortality of his mistress' graces.

5. The lover has "small loss of mortal treasure," since he gains immortal treasures.

Shakespeare's song poses a riddle which is never clearly answered, perhaps intentionally so, but, taken along with its context, the following points emerge:

1. Fancy is fed with gazing, that is, superficial love is pleased by apparent beauty.

2. But with continued gazing Fancy, or superficial love, dies.

3. The lover (Bassanio), in loving profoundly, chooses the lead casket (death).

4. By choosing death, Bassanio gains Portia.

5. Bassanio sustains no loss of worldly wealth by refusing to pick the gold or the silver caskets, both symbols of mortal treasure.

The analogies between Sidney's song and Shakespeare's scene are the following:

1. Both were written with the idea of employing music.

2. In both, the lover is warned that superficial love, or Fancy, is destroyed by what it feeds on, that is, apparent beauty.

3. In both, the lover, in choosing love, also chooses death.

4. In both, the lover gains more than mortal treasure by choosing death.

5. In both, the lover rejects mortal treasure.

The paradox of the lover choosing death in choosing love is

a fairly common one in the literature of the period, as is the imagery and paradox surrounding the birth and death of Fancy. But the song by Sidney is the only one I know that combines these two paradoxes in such a way that they are analogous to Shakespeare's scene. The close analogy between the two works, and the earlier appearance of Sidney's song suggest the possibility that Shakespeare, in following his usual practice of stressing crucial scenes with music, realized the appropriateness of Sidney's song to the situation and decided to employ a similar song which would supply the music he wished, and which would also furnish Bassanio with the advice he needs in order to make the correct choice.

In Act V, i, we find music used for an entirely different purpose: as a setting for the apostrophe to music spoken by Lorenzo. The music there marks another step in the development of Shakespeare's conception of the dramatic role which might be played by music, for in the scene there is a passage written in the form of a dramatic recitative set to music, or dramma per musica, which in this instance apparently has as its primary dramatic function the dissipation of the tragic elements developed earlier in the play. The passage. is a nocturne, after whose incantation our hearts are relaxed and made receptive for the pleasantly humorous quality of the concluding scene. The hate, greed, and bitterness which mark the fourth act are replaced by a tender interlude containing music, poetry, moonlight, and young love.

The scene opens with a bit of badinage between Lorenzo and Jessica; the beauty and calmness of the night and its appropriateness for lovers' trysts is their subject. "On such a night" is the theme, and, as in a musical composition, the theme is given several variations. The lyricism of the dialogue is interrupted, momentarily, for the introduction of necessary information by Stephano and Launcelot. Then the music of the spoken lines reaches a higher pitch of lyricism as Lorenzo calls for Stephano's music to augment and support the dialogue: "*Loren.* Let's in, and there expect their comming./ And yet no matter: why should we goe in./ My friend *Stephen*, signifie [I] pray you/ within the house,

your mistres is at hand,/ and bring your musique foorth into
the ayre." While waiting for the musicians, Lorenzo anticipates
the subsequent joining of poetry and music by the delivery of a
twelve-line passage that all but sings itself:

> How sweet the moon-light sleepes vpon this banke,
> heere will we sit, and let the sounds of musique
> creepe in our eares soft stilnes, and the night
> become the tutches of sweet harmonie:
> sit, *Iessica*, looke how the floore of heauen
> is thick inlayed with pattens of bright gold,
> there's not the smallest orbe which thou beholdst
> but in his motion like an Angell sings,
> still quiring to the young eyde Cherubins;
> such harmonie is in immortall soules,
> but whilst this muddy vesture of decay
> dooth grosly close it in, we cannot heare it:

After the lines of Lorenzo, in which the music of the spoken word
is exploited to a high degree, the lyricism of the scene is lifted
to an even greater degree of intensity by the addition of instrumental music. After the musicians take their place on the stage,
Lorenzo gives them their cue to begin playing. "Come hoe, and
wake *Diana* with a himme,/ with sweetest tutches pearce your
mistres eare,/ and draw her home with musique. *play Musique.*"
Then, against the musical setting of the hymn to the moon, Lorenzo
begins his well-known discourse on the power of music, ending:

> Since naught so stockish hard and full of rage,
> but musique for the time doth change his nature,
> the man that hath no musique in himselfe,
> nor is not moued with concord of sweet sounds,
> is fit for treasons, stratagems, and spoiles,
> the motions of his spirit are dull as night,
> and his affections darke as *Terebus:*
> let no such man be trusted: marke the musique.

Portia and Nerissa enter, apparently talking as they advance
onto the stage. "*Por.* So dooth the greater glory dim the lesse,/ a

substitute shines brightly as a King/ untill a King be by, and then his state/ empties it selfe, as doth an inland brooke/ into the maine of waters: musique harke." Portia then comments on the greater beauty added to the music by the silence of the night, and concludes: "How many things by season, seasond are/ to their right prayse, and true perfection:/ Peace, how the moone sleepes with Endimion,/ and would not be awak'd. *Musicke ceases.*"[15]

With the suggested setting of the moon, the nocturne comes to an end. Almost immediately a trumpet signals the approach of Bassanio, and the action of the play resumes.

The brief explication of the passage in question has been made in order to indicate the extent to which the construction of the whole scene is motivated by the idea of music. Here we have a brief discourse on music—its origin, its power, its effects on the hearers—all presented in lyrical poetry, with a musical accompaniment provided by musicians seemingly brought onstage to personify the subject. We would not suppose that Shakespeare would have taken such pains in the construction and staging of this particular passage unless he intended the episode to perform a dramatic function. That function, I believe, is to restore the comic atmosphere to a play which, until the end of Act IV, has been growing more and more pregnant with tragic possibilities.

The Merchant of Venice is the first comedy by Shakespeare in which the life of a principal character is seriously endangered. The approach of death to Antonio is very near until the intervention of Portia. The comedy hence seems to be the first play of Shakespeare's which falls within the realm of tragicomedy. Giambattista Guarini, in his *Compendium of Tragicomic Poetry* (1599), describes the genre, saying in part: "He who composes tragicomedy takes from tragedy its great persons but not its great action, its verisimilar plot but not its true one, its movement of the feelings but not its disturbance of them, its pleasure but not its sadness, its danger but not its death; from comedy it takes laughter that is not excessive, modest amusement, feigned difficulty, happy reversal, and above all the comic order. . . ."[16] While there is no evidence that Shakespeare knew Guarini, both were working in a common genre which presented common problems. As Dr. Allen Gilbert remarks about the general applicability of Guarini's methods during Shakespeare's lifetime: "For the highest development of the new Renaissance drama one must go to the England of Marlowe, Shakespeare, Jonson, and Fletcher; none of them has left us such a defense of his methods as Guarini attempted. If we had such a discussion from their pens, we may suppose it would not have been essentially different from that of Guarini."[17]

Whether or not Shakespeare considered his play a tragicomedy, he was still confronted by the necessity for moving the emotions without disturbing them, of evoking the pleasure of tragedy without its sadness, of calling forth restrained laughter and "modest amusement." In other words, having developed the tragic elements of the play to a point just short of tragedy, he then was faced with the problem of dissipating the tragic emotions evoked in the audience and of replacing them with those proper to the type of comedy which he was writing. It was to solve this problem, I believe, that Shakespeare introduced the Belmont interlude and the music therein.

The way in which the music was performed is clearly indicated, at least in outline. At Lorenzo's request, Stephano brings his consort of musicians out on the stage. At the cue given by Lorenzo, "Come hoe, and wake *Diana* with a himne," the musicians begin to play: as the comments of the actors indicate, the musicians play until Portia gives them the cue to stop, "Peace, how the moone sleepes with Endimion,/ and would not be awak'd."

The consort was probably composed of from four to six string instruments. The music would necessarily have been subdued, else it would have covered up the dialogue which it accompanied.[18] A grouping of six viols—two treble viols, two tenor viols, and two viols da gamba—would have been appropriate.[19]

The nature of the music played by the consort cannot be determined with exactness, since the original score is not extant. The circumstantial evidence, however, points to a score which reflected the mood of the dramatic setting and the succession of sentiments expressed by the speakers. In general, we may assume that the music was calm and lyrical in nature. In particular, the dramatic and musical theories of the age suggest that the music and dialogue of this scene were more closely allied than would be necessary merely to express a common mood. In fact, the musical score may well have been composed for the scene in question or may have made use of several existing scores appropriate to the scene.

The composition of such a score would have fallen well within the province of the musical theory of the time, particularly as that theory was applied to the composition of musical settings for poetry. Thomas Morley, who provides us with the fullest exposition of the musical theory of his age, describes the proper procedure for writing such settings. He explains, in part:

> It followeth to shew you how to dispose your musicke
> according to the nature of the words which you are
> therein to expresse, as whatsoeuer matter it be which
> you haue in hand, such a kind of musicke must you frame
> to it. You must therefore if you haue a graue matter,
> applie a graue kinde of musicke to it if a merrie sub-
> iect you must make your musicke also merrie. For it
> will be a great absurditie to vse a sad harmonie to a
> merrie matter or a merrie harmonie to a sad lamentable or
> tragicall dittie. You must then when you would expresse
> any word signifying hardnesse, crueltie, bitternesse,
> and other such like, make the harmonie like vnto it,
> that is, somewhat harsh and hard but yet so it offend
> not. *Et seq.*[20]

That the theory expressed by Morley was practiced, in its essentials, by the musician-composers of the period has been established by the studies of Fellowes, Kastendieck, and Pattison.[21]

Morley was, of course, writing about the setting of poems as songs; but when we consider that the scene in *The Merchant of Venice*—at least that portion set to music—is pure lyrical poetry, and when we consider the planning that surely went on between Shakespeare and the musician who arranged or composed the music for the scene, it is easier to believe that the score would have followed Morley's precepts than to believe the contrary, even though the lines were to be spoken and not sung.

The setting of lyrical dramatic passages to a musical accompaniment was not a practice peculiar to Shakespeare; it appears elsewhere in the Elizabethan drama. We have earlier noted[22] a passage in Rowley's *When You See Me, You Know Me* (Q2, 1613), for which two consorts were employed, a "loud" consort and a "soft" consort. A similar combination of music and dialogue occurs in Marston's *Antonio and Mellida*, Part 2 ([1602] I, v, lines 475-513). The clearest example, which supports not only the point in view, but also indicates the versatility with which instrumental music was employed for dramatic purposes by Shakespeare's contemporaries, may be found in Campion's account of his *The Lords Mask* (1613):[23]

At the sound of a strange musicke twelue Franticks enter . . .
with others that made an absolute medly of madnesse; in
middest of whom Entheus *(or Poeticke furie) was hurried*
forth, and tost up and downe, till by vertue of a new change
in the musicke, the Lunaticks fell into a madde measure,
fitted to a loud phantasticke tune; but in the end thereof
the musick changed into a very solemne ayre, which they
softly played, while Orpheus *spake.*
    Orph. Through these soft and calme sounds, Mania, passe
With thy Phantasticks hence; heere is no place
Longer for them or thee; *Entheus* alone
Must do *Ioves* bidding now, all else be gone.
        [*Mania and Frantics depart.*]
    Enth. Diuinest *Orpheus,* O how all from thee
Proceed with wondrous sweetnesse! Am I free?
Is my affliction vanisht?
    Orph.   Too too long,
Alas, good *Entheus,* hast thou brook't this wrong.

The dialogue between Orpheus and Entheus continues for about twenty-six more lines, at the end of which the instrumental music is joined by a chorus of voices singing, "Come away; bring thy golden theft."

Of this passage Kastendieck remarks:

This must have been an attempt at recitative which flourished in Restoration opera. That the recitative should come in music after the reduction of voice parts from the madrigal to the solo of the ayre does not seem unusual. A single voice singing to an accompaniment might become still more simplified to a melodic line with an occasional chord of accompaniment. This of course is recitative.[24]

What Kastendieck refers to as an attempt at musical recitative was, in all probability, a full-blown example of dramatic recitative set to a musical accompaniment. Campion's stage direction prefacing the passage states definitely that Orpheus "spake" and that the music played was a "very solemne ayre."

It is unfortunate that the music originally used for V, i, of *The Merchant of Venice* cannot be ascertained. In the absence of the original music, I suggest an appropriate substitute would have been an ayre by Campion, "The Peaceful Western Wind," which meets the general, if not the particular, requirements of the dramatic setting of the scene. The melody of the ayre is given in the accompanying illustration (Plate XIII).

PLATE XIII.—*The Peaceful Western Wind.* This is the melody of an ayre printed in Campion's *Second Book of Airs* (c. 1613). The original song book is reprinted as a part of Fellowes' *The English School of Lutenist Song Writers,* from which the above illustration was taken.

We have now examined separately the two episodes in *The Merchant of Venice* which involve the use of music: When taken as a whole, the music in both instances evokes a similar emotional reaction from the audience. In the casket scene, the song contains the key which resolves the emotional tension created by Bassanio's predicament; in the garden scene the instrumental music and poetry resolve the emotional tension with which we are left at the end of the preceding act. In both episodes the effect is the same: music calms the emotions and changes the nature of them— from fear and uncertainty to happiness in the first instance, and from sadness and hate to joy and love in the second. For, if we may take Lorenzo's words as indicative of Shakespeare's intentions, there is "naught so stockish hard and full of rage, but musique for the time doth change his nature."

Notes

1. See Chambers, *William Shakespeare*, I, 373; G. L. Kittredge, ed., *The Merchant of Venice* (1945), p. vii; Pooler, ed., Arden edition, p. xiv.
2. Chambers, *idem.*
3. The text quoted from in this chapter is that of the Quarto of 1600 unless otherwise noted. The line numbering follows that of the Globe edition.
4. Omitted Q; *Here Musicke* F.
5. *eye* Q; *eyes* F.
6. See S. Thompson, *Motif-Index of Folk Literature*, III, H310-359, H505, H970-71; also Thompson, *The Folk Tale*, pp. 47-87 and 105-108.
7. *Shakespeare's Use of Song*, pp. 44-49.
8. *Op. cit.*, p. 45.
9. As quoted by Noble, "Shakespeare's Songs and Stage," *Shakespeare and the Theatre*, p. 125.
10. As suggested by Noble, *Shakespeare's Use of Song*, p. 49, and Reed, *Songs from the British Drama*, p. 277.
11. It will be remembered that David Rizzio, private secretary to Mary of Scotland, originally was retained by her as a lutenist. He was murdered in 1566. (S. Zweig, *Mary Queen of Scotland and the Isles*, pp. 112-114.)
12. As reprinted in J. M. Gibbon, *Melody and the Lyric*, pp. 69, 70.
13. *NED*, "Lead—*To lie, be wrapt in lead*: to be buried in a lead coffin. . . .
    1578 Chr. Prayers 83 We Earles and Barons were sometime:
    Now wrapt in lead, are turnd to slime."
14. The sense in which Sidney uses the term "fancy" may be suggested by the following lines from a poem in his *Arcadia*: "Beauty hath force to catch the human sight; Sight doth bewitch the fancy evil awaked:" (J. Drinkwater, ed., *The Poems of Sir Philip Sidney*, p. 271).
15. Omitted Q; *Musicke ceases* F.

16. As translated by A. H. Gilbert, *Literary Criticism: Plato to Dryden*, p. 511.
17. *Op cit.*, p. 505.
18. See Chapter II, pp. 18, 19, 35.
19. In this instance the presence of the consort on the stage would not interfere with the spoken lines. Here it personifies the subject under discussion; in a similar scene in *The Two Gentlemen*, the word play in the dialogue demands close attention.
20. *A Plaine and Easie Introduction*, p. 177.
21. *The English School of Lutenist Song Writers; England's Musical Poet, Thomas Campion; Music and Poetry.*
22. See Chapter II, pp. 40, 41.
23. Vivian, *Campion's Works*, pp. 90, 91.
24. *Op. cit.*, pp. 184, 185.

SEVEN

Much Ado About Nothing

HAKESPEARE USES MORE MUSIC IN *Much Ado* than he had in any previous comedy, save the masque-like *Midsummer Night's Dream.* But the significance of the music we will treat in this chapter rests upon more than its quantity. It rests upon the increasingly naturalistic way in which the music is introduced—the repetition of the emotion-soothing technique of the Belmont garden scene previously discussed—and upon the appearance of an adult actor-singer in Shakespeare's company for whom he seems to have created the role of Balthasar and to whom the two songs in the play are assigned.

Suppose we set forth through the familiar gates of Source and Date. We may note that the play is generally assigned to the period 1598-1599, and that its two primary sources are believed to have been Bandello's *Novelle* (1554), the twenty-second story, and Canto v of Ariosto's *Orlando Furioso* (1516).[1] No specific use of music appears in the sources, although Bandello's story begins and ends amid festivity, as does *Much Ado.*

Upon closer observation of the music used in *Much Ado,* it appears that the several performances of music therein are reflections of changing emotional appeals made during the course of the play. The instrumental music heard in the first two acts is used to suggest the stately merrymaking during the dinner and masque which takes place the first night of the play. The light-hearted song, "Sigh no more, ladies, sigh no more," is presented while the Prince, Leonato, and Claudio plot against Benedick's happy bachelorhood. The doleful hymn sung at Hero's supposed sepulcher is offered by the repentant Prince and Claudio, who believe they are responsible for her death. The final dance reflects the joyful mood of the play's conclusion and suggests that the lovers "live

happily ever after." The music hence appears in parallel to the
stately opening of the play, to the lightly humorous portion of
the plot in which Beatrice and Benedick are the protagonists, to
the ostentatious sadness of the sepulcher scene, and to the nuptial
festivity which concludes the play. But in fitting the music to the
tragicomic structure of the play, Shakespeare did not neglect its
possible uses for other dramatic purposes.

For example, the first appearance of music (I, ii) not only
helps to set the scene but also denotes a lapse of time between
the first and second scenes. The Prince and his fellow soldiers,
Claudio and Benedick, return to Messina after a victorious military campaign. In their honor, Leonato prepares a state banquet
and masque at his home. In the afternoon during which we may
suppose the Prince and his party arrive at Leonato's home, Claudio
meets and falls in love with Hero. Later, the Prince mentions the
forthcoming revelry as he talks to Claudio, I, i, lines 322-324:[2]
"*Pedro*. . . . I know we shall haue reuelling to night,/ I will
assume thy part in some disguise,/ And tell fair Hero I am Claudio,
. . ." At the conclusion of his speech, the setting changes. "*Enter
Leonato and an old man brother to Leonato. Leo.* How now
brother, where is my cosen your sonne, hath he prouided this
musique? *Old* He is very busie about it, but brother, I can tell you
strange newes that you yet dreampt not of. . . . the prince dis-
couered to Claudio that he loued my niece your daughter, and
meant to acknowledge it this night in a daunce. . . ." Shortly
after these lines are spoken, Antonio and Leonato leave the
stage; Don John and Conrade enter, followed a little later by
Borachio, who explains: "*Bor.* I came yonder from a great supper,
the prince your brother is royally entertain'd by Leonato. . . ."

In sequence of time, Don Pedro's promise to woo Hero for
Claudio is thus made some time before the banquet is to take place.
When Leonato and Antonio enter, however, the banquet is apparently in progress, and Leonato is busy playing the host. Immediately after Leonato and Antonio leave the stage, Don John, Conrade,
and Borachio enter; Borachio states that he has just come from
the supper.

It is hence evident that the music mentioned by Leonato opens the succession of scenes which revolve around the banquet and the following masque.[3] The music thus serves two purposes: it indicates that a period of time elapses between the Prince's promise to Claudio and the entrance of Leonato and Antonio which opens the next scene, and it aids in supplying the background of stately revelry against which the action of the next several scenes takes place.[4]

In order to serve the first dramatic function, the musicians probably began playing as soon as the Prince and Claudio left the stage at the end of I, i. After the music had continued for several minutes, Leonato and Antonio entered, and Leonato called attention to the performance. The music probably ceased shortly after the two old men began their conversation.

The broken consort, as we noticed earlier, was especially appropriate for the reception of noble persons;[5] hence we may assume that it would have been appropriate for Leonato's entertainment in honor of the Prince. It would also have been suitable to provide the dance music for the following masque. The composition of the broken consort could have been a treble viol, a viol da gamba, a treble lute, a mandore, a tenor recorder, and a drum or timbrel.

As the sound of music is supposed to come from the off-stage banquet, we may safely assume that the consort was also located off-stage. The music room of the playhouse could have been used for this purpose. The consort, of course, was hidden.

In order to set the scene of courtly entertainment, the musical score played by the consort should be one which combines a degree of pomp with festivity. The tune, "All You That Love Good Fellows" (see Plate XIV), with its march tempo and lilting melody would serve admirably for a state banquet in honor of a Prince who has just returned from the wars.

Music is next used in the play to indicate the dance which takes place immediately after the supper. Since the episode involves a problem in staging, we should examine its setting and action with care. The episode properly includes lines 87-163 of Act II.

According to both the Quarto and Folio texts, Leonato, Antonio,

Leonato's wife, Hero, Beatrice, and a kinsman are on the outer stage when the episode begins. They have come from the banquet, and Leonato has just told Hero that the Prince wishes to marry her, when the group is joined by the Prince, Claudio, Benedick, Balthasar, and, the Folio text adds, maskers with a drum, among whom are Don John and Borachio. All are apparently on their way to the masque, for Leonato, on seeing the noblemen, exclaims: "*Leonato.* The reuellers are entring brother, make good roome. *Enter prince, Pedro, Claudio, and Benedicke, and Balthaser, or dumb Iohn. Maskers with a drum.*"[6]

The members of the group then choose partners for the dance; the Prince chooses Hero and, after some conversation, they disappear from the scene. Likewise, Balthasar chooses Margaret, Antonio picks Ursula, and Benedick takes Beatrice. As the choices are made, each couple converses in turn. After the last lines spoken by Benedick and Beatrice, "*Beat.* . . . wee must follow the leaders. *Bene.* In euery good thing. *Beat.* Nay, if they leade to any ill, I will leaue them at the next turning," the Quarto stage direction states: *Dance   exeunt.*

PLATE XIV.—*All You That Love Good Fellows.* According to Chappell, *Popular Music of the Olden Time,* I, 149, this tune appears in several music books of the period. The above version is called "Sir Edward Noel's Delight"; it was taken from the *Friesche Lusthof* (1634).

The Quarto stage direction indicates that all of the couples perform a dance on the outer stage and then, with the exception of Don John, Borachio, and Claudio, all the persons on the stage leave in a group. This would present an awkward situation; the large group not taking part in the conversations would be hard put to act naturally, and the shifting of the conversation from one couple to the next would be difficult to manage. Also, such a large group leaving the stage at one time would present an unseemly appearance.

The alteration of the stage direction made in the Folio text clarifies the staging of the episode and suggests the manner in which it was originally acted. The Folio stage direction states: "*Beat.* Nay, if they leade to any ill, I will leaue them at the next turning.   *exeunt.   Musicke for the dance.*"

As is evident, the Folio stage direction would remove the possibility that the dance took place on the outer stage. It expressly states that the previous speakers and, we may assume, Leonato, his wife, and his kinsman, leave. Then the music begins. There is no stage direction calling for a dance; all that is called for is music for the dance.

The assignment of lines in the context of the stage direction gives us the probable movements of the actors on the stage. The Prince requests Hero to walk with him. He takes Hero's hand and they walk off the stage, speaking as they leave. Ostensibly, they go into the dancing room off stage. The Prince would normally precede the others into the adjoining hall. Balthasar and Margaret then follow the first couple off the stage, conversing as they walk. Then Antonio and Ursula follow, then Benedick and Beatrice, who remarks, ". . . wee must follow the leaders," and, finally, Leonato, his wife, and his kinsman, as would befit the host and hostess. Don John, Borachio, and Claudio are left on the stage.

The music for the opening dance is then heard. Against the background of the off-stage dance, in which the Prince and Hero are principal figures, Don John informs Claudio that the Prince intends to woo Hero for himself while pretending to woo her for Claudio. The music thus not only indicates the off-stage dance, but also creates a dramatic moment for Don John's false disclosure.

The opening dance of a courtly masque was usually a processional pavane; this form would hence be appropriate for the scene with which we are concerned. The melody of a pavane suitable for the occasion is shown in Plate XV. The consort that provided the music was doubtless the same as that which played the banquet music earlier in the play. As before, it was probably placed at some point within the tiring house—perhaps in the music room.

The performance of the song, "Sigh no more, ladies, sigh no more," is the next occurrence of music in the play. The song apparently serves no dramatic function other than to reflect the light and humorous spirit of the scene in which it is placed. Its significance, as far as Shakespeare's dramatic technique is concerned, lies in the fact that it marks the first time that Shakespeare clearly assigns a complete song to an adult actor, rather than to a professional musician or singing boy, and that the actor who sings the song portrays the role of a nobleman and not that of a commoner or page.[7]

The passage (II, iii, lines 38-90) begins when the Prince, Claudio, and Leonato enter a garden, supposedly to be entertained

PLATE XV.—*Pavane.* This pavane, an anonymous composition of the sixteenth century, is taken from Mabel Dolmetsch's *Dances of England and France from 1450 to 1600,* pp. 93, 94.

by music, but also in order to be overhead by Benedick, who had entered earlier and who had tried to conceal himself in the arbor: "*Enter prince, Leonato, Claudio, Musicke.*[8] *Prince.* Come shall we heare this musique? *Claud.* Yea my good lord: how stil the euening is,/ As husht on purpose to grace harmonie! *Prince.* See you where Benedicke hath hid himself? *Claud.* O very wel my lord: the musique ended,/ Weele fit the kid-foxe with a penny worth. *Enter Balthaser with musicke.*[9] *Prince.* Come Balthaser, weele heare that song againe. *Balth.* O good my lord, taxe not so bad a voice,/ To slaunder musicke any more than once."

After much urging by the Prince, Balthasar finally consents to sing, much to Benedick's disgust, who exclaims from his hiding place: "*Bene.* Now diuine aire, now is his soule rauisht, is it not strange that sheepes guts should hale soules out of mens bodies? well a horne for my mony when alls done."

The Song.

Sigh no more ladies, sigh no more,
Men were deceiuers euer,
One foote in sea, and one on shore,
To one thing constant neuer,
Then sigh not so, but let them go,
And be you blith and bonnie,
Conuerting all your soundes of woe,
Into hey nony nony.
Sing no more ditties, sing no moe,
Of dumps so dull and heauy,
The fraud of men was euer so,
Since summer first was leauy,
Then sigh not so, &c.

Prince. By my troth a good song.
Balth. And an ill singer my lord.

*   *   *   *   *   *   *   *   *   *   *

Bene. And he had bin a dog that should haue howld thus, they would haue hangd him, and I pray God his bad voice bode no mischeefe, I had as liue have heard the night-rauen, come what plague could haue come after it. *Prince* Yea mary, doost thou heare Balthasar? I

pray thee get vs some excellent musique: for to morrow
night we would haue it at the ladie Heroes chamber window.

As suggested previously, the song itself seems to have little
dramatic purpose. Most likely, as L. B. Wright believes, the song
was intended as a vehicle for some talented vocalist in the company.[10] Perhaps the singer had recently joined the company, for
apart from his music he takes little part in the action of the play
and is assigned only a few lines. In fact, Chambers refers to him
as a "mute" during his first appearance on the stage.[11]

The casting of the singer in the part of Balthasar may also
have been a departure from conventional practices. We noted
earlier that songs were seldom sung by actors playing the parts
of gentlefolk, and that the musical activities of noblemen of the
period were generally of an amateur and private nature.[12] Shakespeare seems to have taken steps to prepare his audience for such
a change from convention, for Leonato refers (I, ii) to Balthasar,
his nephew, as providing the music for the banquet; in the scene
now being examined Balthasar protests that he is not a skillful
singer, and (a point that is developed later) he does not enter the
stage with the household musicians, but enters a few lines after
them. Evidently, Balthasar was portrayed as a noble dilettante-
musician who had a pleasant voice and some musical training and
who had taken the household musicians under his supervision.

The performance of the music in the scene may be conjectured
on the basis of the stage directions, the comments on the music
given by the actors, and the setting of the passage. The scene is
laid in Leonato's garden; the occasion is supposedly a musical
performance before the Prince. We might hence expect the household musicians to play in the garden also, as their entertainment
is directed expressly at the Prince. This conjecture is supported
by the Quarto stage direction which brings the party on the stage:
Enter prince, Leonato, Claudio, Musicke.

The term "Musicke," in this instance, refers not to the sound
of music, but to the consort of musicians which follows the noblemen into the garden.[13] The term is used in the same sense, I
believe, by the Prince who in his opening line asks, "Come shall

we heare this musique?" Before the consort begins to play, however, Balthasar appears: *Enter Balthaser with musicke.*

Here we have what appears to be a duplication of stage directions. If the "musicke" is already on the stage, what is the
meaning of the "musicke" brought in by Balthasar? A plausible
supposition could be that the term used in connection with Balthasar refers to a sheet of notation—a song which he has recently written and which he is carrying around, possibly in hopes that he will
be requested to sing it.[14] This supposition would fit our previous
description of Balthasar as a musical dilettante. We may also note
that, as soon as the Prince perceives him, the Prince says, "Come
Balthasar, weele heare that song againe."

After some unnecessary coaxing, Balthasar agrees to sing. Evidently the consort plays a brief introduction to the song during
which Balthasar strikes an affected pose, for Benedick exclaims:
"*Bene.* Now diuine aire, now is his soule rauisht, is it not strange
that sheepes guts should hale soules out of mens bodies?" Balthasar then sings the song. At its conclusion, the Prince compliments
the singer and commissions him to arrange a serenade for Hero,
to take place the following night. Balthasar then leaves, followed,
possibly, by the musicians.

For some reason, which we may only guess, the Folio text
indicates an alteration in the musical performance outlined above.
The Folio stage direction which introduces the party into Leonato's
garden states: *Enter prince, Leonato, Claudio, and Iacke Wilson.*
The Quarto stage direction calling for the later entrance of Balthasar is omitted by the Folio text. It is generally agreed that Jack
Wilson was the name of the actor who took Balthasar's part in
a later production of the play.[15] The alteration hence implies that
Balthasar enters with the Prince and the others, and that he replaces the "Musicke" originally called for by the Quarto text.

Noble suggests the alteration was made in order to implicate
Balthasar in the plot against Benedick, and thus to establish a
more direct connection between the song and its context.[16] As an
alternate explanation, I suggest that in the production using the
Folio text the consort of musicians was not employed, and that the

Quarto stage directions were altered to cover the omission of the musicians originally used. According to our examination of the earlier scenes in which the consort played, the musicians played off-stage, hidden from the eyes of the audience. In these instances, the music of the missing consort could have been suggested by one or two instruments played by members of the company. In the garden scene, however, we have reason to believe the musicians originally appeared on the outer stage. In this case, the consort could not very well be suggested as in the previous scenes. The alteration of the Quarto stage directions would solve this problem without the necessity of changing the actors' lines. Balthasar could carry a lute or cittern as he enters with the others; the opening remarks of the Prince and Claudio would then refer to Balthasar instead of to the missing consort. The singer would, in this event, play his own accompaniment.

The song whose lyrics appear in the text may have been an ayre with its own musical setting, an ayre set to an existing tune, or a popular song. The simplicity and regularity of its structure, in any event, permits a comparatively wide choice of settings from among the tunes of the time. I suggest, as an appropriate tune, a setting of the song, "Hearts-ease," mentioned by Shakespeare in *Romeo and Juliet*. Shakespeare's words with the suggested musical setting, are shown in Plate XVI. An alternate setting made by Thomas Ford, a near contemporary of Shakespeare, is given in Plate XVII.

Before the next occasion arises for music in the play, the tragic elements therein become more prominent. As a result of Don John's false report of Hero's unchaste activities, the Prince and Claudio publicly shame and disavow her in the church where she is to be married. Hero faints, and the report is given out that she dies from the blow. The honor of Hero is vindicated when those valiant watchmen, Dogberry and Verges, uncover the treachery of Don John. The Prince and Claudio remorsefully attempt to console Leonato for the supposed loss of his daughter. Leonato exclaims: "I cannot bid you bid my daughter liue,/ That were impossible, but I pray you both,/ Possesse the people in Messina here,/ How innocent she died, and if your loue/ Can labour aught in sad inuention,/ Hang her an epitaph vpon her toomb,/ And sing it to her bones, sing it tonight: . . ." His words supply the motivation for the song which follows in V, iii.[17]

This song appears to serve two distinct dramatic purposes: it provides an effective instance of dramatic irony, and, as was also the case of the music in the garden scene in *The Merchant of Venice*, the song erases the effects on the audience of the tragic elements within the play.

In obedience to Leonato's request, the Prince and Claudio visit Hero's presumed sepulcher to "hang her epitaph vpon her toomb" and to "sing it to her bones." *Enter Claudio, Prince and three or foure with tapers.* After Claudio reads his epitaph, he commands:

> *Claudio* Now musick sound & sing your solemne hymne.
> *Song* Pardon goddesse of the night,
> Those that slew thy virgin knight,
> For the which with songs of woe,

Sigh no more ladies sigh no more, Men were deceivers ever, One foot in sea and one on shore, To one thing constant never. Then sigh not so but let them go, and be you blithe and bonny, Converting all your sounds of woe in-to hey non-ny nonny.

PLATE XVI.—*Sigh No More, Ladies, Sigh No More.* Shakespeare's lyric is here set to the tune "Heart's-ease," as given by Chappell, *Popular Music of the Olden Time,* I, 209, 210. According to Chappell, the original from which he made his setting may be found in a manuscript volume of lute music of the sixteenth century in the Public Library, Cambridge, England (D.d., ii.11).

Round about her tombe they goe:
Midnight assist our mone, help vs to sigh & grone.
Heauily heauily.
Graues yawne and yeeld your dead,
Till death be vttered.
Heauily heauily.[18]

[Claud.][19] Now vnto thy bones good night, yeerely will I do
this right.

    Prince. Good morrow maisters, put your torches out,
The wolues haue preied, and looke, the gentle day
Before the wheeles of Phoebus, round about
Dapples the drowsie East with spots of grey: . . .

The dramatic irony of this episode and its song arises from
its relationship to the serenade to Hero for which the Prince requested Balthasar to obtain musicians. The proposed serenade
has been considered an unresolved thread in the play's action,
since the serenade is never performed.[20] But, upon examination,
it appears to be an anticipation of the passage now under consideration.

The establishment of the relationship between the proposed
serenade and the song which apparently replaced it depends upon
the time sequence of the play. The interval of time between the
banquet and the Prince's request for the serenade is not definite,
but after the mention of the serenade, the action of the play follows a discernible schedule. The Prince speaks to Balthasar at
evening, appointing the serenade for "to morrow night." The
interrupted wedding, the shaming of Hero, the discovery of Don
John's plot to Leonato, and the imposition by Leonato of his
penance on Claudio and the Prince, all take place the following
day. In stating the terms of the penance, Leonato expressly states
that the visit to Hero's tomb should occur that same night. The
result is that the dirge is sung at the time originally chosen by
the Prince for his serenade to Hero.

The irony thus created is obvious. Instead of a merry serenade
under Hero's window in honor of a happily wedded Claudio and
Hero, we witness a mournful ritual performed, not under Hero's

marriage chamber, but before her tomb. The anticipatory remarks
made by the Prince (III, ii) and by Leonato (V, i) and the timing
of the doleful hymn, make it almost certain that Shakespeare had
this piece of dramatic irony in mind when he wrote the short
sepulcher scene. There is also evidence that he may have had a
more profound purpose in mind.

As was mentioned earlier, the scene with its song has the effect

PLATE XVII.—*Sigh No More, Ladies, Sigh No More*. This is Shakespeare's lyric, as set to music by Thomas Ford (d. 1648). The above illustration was taken from Gibbon, *Melody and the Lyric*, p. 117. The original is a manuscript in Christ Church, Oxford.

of calming the tragic passions aroused in the audience by Hero's dishonor and simulated death. The church scene is the climax of the tragedy in the play. The tragic mood is thence gradually dispelled; the dirge provides a ritualistic exorcism which drives away the last traces of the somber shadow that temporarily obscures the comic spirit of the play. This specific purpose seems intimated by the Prince's remarks at the conclusion of the hymn. As though impatient to be done with sadness, he exclaims, "Good morrow maisters, put your torches out,/ The wolues have preied . . ." In other words, evil has wasted its hours, and "the gentle day" will make an end to past sorrows. The remainder of the play is dominated by its comic elements.

The stage directions for the scene provide us with little information regarding the way the song was performed. We are told that the group on the stage at the time consists of Claudio, the Prince, an unnamed lord, and two or three others carrying tapers. Claudio calls for music; hence we may assume that he did not sing; nor would we suppose that the Prince sang. The casual enumeration of the other members of the group suggests that no organized body of musicians was used. It would therefore be reasonable to suppose that Balthasar was the unnamed lord, or the actor taking that part, who sang the song to the accompaniment of his lute or cittern. As we know, Balthasar was supposed to furnish the music for the missing serenade.

Mr. Moore suggests that the stage directions may indicate off-stage singing or, more likely, off-stage music for singing on the stage.[21] While such possibilities should not be discounted, the Elizabethan dramatists, when they used off-stage music, were usually considerate enough to indicate the source and function of the hidden music—information that is lacking in the present scene. There is also a question of verisimilitude involved. The music is not supernatural in origin, hence we should not expect it to materialize out of the air. The lament is apparently offered in the open air, to judge from the Prince's sweeping reference to the approaching dawn; thus it seems unlikely that the music would originate from "within." We therefore may believe that the musician, or musicians, could be seen by the audience.

The song itself is as extravagant as Claudio's courtship. In structure, it resembles one of the more complex ayres. Its subject matter, apparently a lament addressed to the goddess Artemis, is generally appropriate to the dramatic situation. Perhaps no particular song is necessary for the scene; the only general requirement seems to be that the song be an expression of grief. If this is so, the ayre, "Flow, My Tears (Lacrimae)," by Dowland, would be equally appropriate (see Plate XVIII).

The nuptial festivity attendant to the weddings of Claudio to Hero and Benedick to Beatrice concludes the play. The merriment and happiness which follows the double wedding is suggested by the dance called for by Benedick in his last lines. In effect, the dance performs the function of a "grand finale" participated in by all of the major characters.

PLATE XVIII.—*Flow, My Tears* (Lacrimae). From John Dowland's *Second Book of Airs* (1600), as reprinted in Fellowes' *The English School of Lutenist Song Writers.*

Appropriate to this scene would have been the "Cushion dance," a contemporary group dance in which the men and women kissed as they entered and left the center of the dancing area.[22] One of the tunes to which the dance was performed, called "Sweet Margaret Galliard," is given in Plate XIX. The musical accompaniment was, no doubt, played by the group of musicians heard earlier in the play. Benedick addresses his request for dance music to "pipers," a very general term which was applied to all sorts of instrumentalists.

Shakespeare's use of music in *Much Ado* is characterized by an increased awareness of the many ways in which music could be used in the drama. This awareness is indicated by the first appearance in the comedies of an over-all musical structure within the play, that is, the arrangement of the musical episodes so that they appear parallel to the successive emotional appeals made in the play. Other indications are presented by a detailed examination of the individual episodes within this general frame. For examples, the use of the music to create dramatic irony is exploited to a

PLATE XIX.—*Galliard, Sweet Margaret* (Cushion Dance). The cushion dance is mentioned in Lyly's *Euphues* (1580) and in Heywood's *A Woman Kilde with Kindnesse*. The tune is that given by Chappell, *Popular Music of the Olden Time*, I, 153-155, and was taken from *Nederlandtsche Gedenk-Clanck* (1626). The same tune appears, Chappell notes, in *Le Secret des Muses* (1615), where it is called "Galliarde Anglaise."

greater degree than was the case in the preceding comedies; music is also used, we find, to indicate a lapse of time and to smooth the transition from the first to the second scene of the play—a dramatic function which Shakespeare assigned to music for the first time in this comedy.

Regarding the part of Balthasar in the play, the evidence suggests that Shakespeare introduced the role to make use of the vocal talents of a particular member of the acting company. The creation of this role may have been an experiment. We also gain the impression that Balthasar was portrayed as an affected courtier, perhaps resembling the later Rosencrantz and Guildenstern.

The evidence concerning the text of *Much Ado* gives us reason to believe that the dance in II, i, was not performed on the stage, as indicated in several modern editions, but was only suggested by the playing of off-stage music. The hypothesis is also advanced that the alteration of the Quarto stage directions, made in the Folio text, II, iii, was designed to cover the omission of the musical group called for by the Quarto from the production of the play for which the Folio text was used.

We may also note that Shakespeare concludes *Much Ado* with a dance, which marks the first time he clearly uses a dance for this purpose.

Notes

1. Chambers, *William Shakespeare*, I, 387, 388; G. L. Kittredge, ed., *Much Ado About Nothing*, p. vii; G. R. Trenery, ed., Arden edition, p. ix; Neilson and Hill, eds., Riverside Press edition, p. 179.
2. Unless otherwise noted, the text used as the foundation for this study is that of the Quarto of 1600. The line numbers follow those of the Globe edition. By the term "Folio" is meant the Folio of 1623.
3. The appearance of music at this point may be evidence to support the hypothesis of Furness and Spedding that the division now marked I, ii, should actually be the beginning of Act II (H. H. Furness, ed., Variorum edition, p. 45 n.). Music was often performed between the acts of Elizabethan plays (See Chapter II, p. 36).
4. The use of off-stage music to suggest banquets or other festive occasions was a fairly common practice of the period (See Chapter II, p. 38).
5. See Chapter II, p. 28.
6. *Enter prince, Pedro, Claudio, and Benedick, and Balthaser, or dumb John.* Q; *Enter Prince, Pedro, Claudio, and Benedicke, and Balthasar, or dumbe Iohn, Maskers with a drum.* F.

7. Balthasar is apparently Leonato's nephew. See I, ii, lines 1-4. Cf. Noble, *Shakespeare's Use of Song*, p. 63, and p. 121 of this chapter.

8. *Enter prince, Leonato, Claudio, Musicke.* Q; *Enter Prince, Leonato, Claudio, and Iacke Wilson.* F.

9. *Enter Balthaser with musicke.* Q; Omitted F.

10. "Extraneous Song in Elizabethan Drama," *SP*, XXIV, 263.

11. *William Shakespeare*, I, p. 386.

12. See Chapter I, p. 3.

13. *NED*, "5. A company of musicians . . . *a* 1586 Sidney *Arcadia* III. (1629) 235 The musick entring alone into the Lodge, the Ladies were all desirous to see from whence so pleasaunt a guest had come."

14. *NED*, "7. 1655 (Title) Parthenia, or the Mayden-head of the First Musick that ever was Printed for the Virginals."

15. A definitive statement concerning the identity of Jack Wilson may be found in the Variorum edition, pp. 109-111, fn.

16. *Shakespeare's Use of Song*, p. 64.

17. A snatch of song is sung by Benedick (V, ii, ll. 26-29) before the lament is performed. Although the words of his song are confused with the text, they are probably a part of an extant song whose lyrics and tune were familiar to the audience. He sings: "*Bene.* The God of loue that sits aboue, and knowes mee, and knowes me, how pittiful I deserve." Benedick apparently bursts into song out of high spirits. Collier notes that there is a song in *The Handfull of pleasant delites* (1584), "The ioy of Virginitie: to The Gods of love." The tune would thus have been a familiar one. (Cited by Furness, Variorum edition, p. 269.)

18. *Heauily heauily* Q; *Heauenly heauenly* F.

19. *Lo.* Q; *Lo.* F. Generally believed to be incorrectly assigned to one of the lords in waiting. See Variorum edition, p. 276 n.

20. See Trenery, ed., Arden edition, p. 61, n. 1, and Furness, Variorum edition, p. 119, n. 90.

21. "The Songs of the Public Theaters in the Time of Shakespeare," *JEGP*, XXVIII, 186.

22. The dance is described more fully by Chappell, *Popular Music of the Olden Time*, I, 154.

EIGHT

As You Like It

ENERALLY BELIEVED TO HAVE BEEN WRITTEN IN
1599 or 1600, *As You Like It* has as its gen-
erally recognized source a prose novel by
Thomas Lodge, *Rosalynde, or Euphues' Gold-
en Legacy* (1590).[1]

Before considering the music of *As You
Like It* in detail, we may draw several inferences from a comparison of the music in *Rosalynde* and that in Shakespeare's play.
When Shakespeare turned to the novel, he found seven songs
spaced at intervals throughout it.[2] These songs, with the exception of the last one, are "artificial," amorous lyrics whose themes
are slight variations of the plight of the lover forsaken or ignored
by his beloved. The exception is a pseudo-bucolic song in imitation
of a folk type. There is little apparent connection between the
theme of the songs and the theme or moral of the novel, that is,
the weakness of a house divided.

Like *Rosalynde*, *As You Like It* contains songs spaced at intervals throughout the play—five of them, to be exact. But there
the similarity ends. The songs used by Shakespeare, whether imitations or genuine folk songs, have, with one exception, the flavor
of the folk and are performed in the play much as like songs
would have been performed by actual rustics. The exception is
the masque song, the hymn to Hymen, which falls in the conclusion of the play. The subject of the first two of Shakespeare's
songs is a restatement of the moral of the play, namely, the influence of nature on man is benign. The next two songs suggest
the joys and simplicity of rural life.

We may therefore draw one general conclusion: the songs in
As You Like It are popular generally, whereas the songs in *Rosalynde* are euphuistic, for the most part. Lodge deliberately used
an exaggerated literary style in order to appeal to a select circle

of readers. Shakespeare used a style more suitable to the medium in which he wrote and to the more representative audience to which he appealed.

Throughout the play, several simultaneous dramatic functions are assigned each piece of music. The cohesiveness thus created between the play structure and the music has the effect of moulding the various pieces of music into a unified structure closely paralleling that of the play. The dramatic theme of the play is not stated until its action moves to the forest of Arden. Coincident with the statement of the theme of the play, the first two songs relate the beneficent effect of nature on man. The merry life of the exiles is then portrayed on the stage and underscored by appropriate songs and instrumental music. When the exiled Duke and his party finally leave the forest to resume their positions in the affairs of men, the type of music changes from the rustic to the courtly, as exemplified by the music for the miniature masque performed toward the end of the play. It is a unique distinction of the songs in *As You Like It* that they are deliberately framed by being placed in individual short scenes. This may have been done in order to give prominence to the songs, which supply some variety in a rather ambling plot. On the other hand, the songs may have been set apart because the play was substantially complete in structure before the songs were introduced. Certainly, the plot would suffer little damage if the songs were removed. But whether or not the songs and music of the play evolved as Shakespeare wrote the play or were later interpolations, we find they fully exploit the dramatic situation at the moment they occur.

We observed in *Much Ado* that Shakespeare there used a unified musical structure. The same procedure is followed in *As You Like It*. Here, Shakespeare integrates the music in the play by associating it with lyrics which are variations upon a dominating theme, and by this means he contrives to give a connection, a continuity, to the several occurrences of music. The theme is the healing power of nature—the recurrent theme of the play as a whole.

As was also the case in *Much Ado*, each of the musical episodes in *As You Like It* is assigned other dramatic functions. For example, the first piece of music in the play, the song, "Under the Greenwood Tree," states the theme of the play; it aids in establishing the setting in the forest of Arden; it fills an interval of time while some necessary stage setting is performed; and it portrays the natures of two interesting characters, Amiens and Jaques.

The song with its context occupies a complete scene which must be examined as a unit in order to grasp the full significance of the music. The scene (II, v) begins with one stanza of the song:[3]

Scena Quinta

Enter, Amyens, Iaques, & others

Song.

Vnder the greene wood tree,
who loues to lye with mee,
And turne his merrie Note,
vnto the sweet Birds throte:
Come hither, come hither, come hither:
Heere shall he see no enemie,
But Winter and rough Weather.

Iaq. More, more, I pre'thee more.

Amy. It will make you melancholly Monsieur *Iaques*

Iaq. I thanke it: More, I pre'thee more,
I can sucke melancholly out of a song,
As a Weazel suckes egges: More, I pre'thee more.

Amy. My voice is ragged, I know I cannot please you.

Iaq. I do not desire you to please me,
I do desire you to sing:
Come, more, another stanzo: Cal you'em stanzo's?

Amy. What you will Monsieur *Iaques*.

Iaq. Nay, I care not for their names, they owe mee
nothing. Wil you sing?

Amy. More at your request, then to please my selfe.

Iaq. Well then, if euer I thanke any man, Ile thanke
you: . . .   Come sing; and you that wil not
hold your tongues.

Amy. Wel, Ile end the song. Sirs, couer the while,

the Duke wil drinke vnder this tree; he hath bin all this
day to looke you.

Iaq. And I haue bin all this day to auoid him: . . .
Come, warble, come.

Song.   *Altogether heere.*
Who doth ambition shunne,
and loues to liue i'th Sunne:
Seeking the food he eates,
and pleas'd with what he gets:
Come hither, come hither, come hither,
Heere shall he see. &c.

Iaq. Ile giue you a verse to this note,
That I made yesterday in despight of my Inuention.

Amy. And Ile sing it.

Amy. Thus it goes.

If it do come to passe, that any man turne Asse;
Leauing his wealth and ease,
A stubborne will to please,
Ducdame, ducdame, ducdame:
Heere shall he see, grosse fooles as he,
And if he will come to me.

Amy. What's that Ducdame?

Iaq. Tis a Greeke inuocation, to call fools into a circle. Ile go sleepe if I can: . . .

Amy. And Ile go seek the Duke,
His banket is prepar'd.   *Exeunt.*

Amien's song expresses the sentiments of the majority of the
noblemen-foresters. He invites the listener to participate in the
joys of a sylvan existence where the only enemies to be met are
winter and rough weather. The underlying theme of the play is
thus restated. Jaques disagrees with the popular belief and expresses his cynical opinion in the last stanza of the song.

The setting of the scene is also localized by the song. The
greenwood tree mentioned therein may or may not have had a
material representation on the stage, but a tree of some sort is a
part of the setting. Amiens tells us, ". . . the Duke wil drinke
vnder this tree. . . ." Possibly the song was designed to aid the

imagination of the spectator in creating a setting that had no substantial existence at all.

The setting of the scene is also suggested by the type of the song and the way in which it was probably performed. The song consists of two, or possibly three, stanzas and a refrain or chorus. Its subject and structure suggest a song suitable for singing by a convivial group. It is, perhaps, a drinking song appropriate for a group of mock foresters to sing or to enjoy as listeners.

The song seems to have been performed in a manner as simple as the life it extols. Amiens sings the first stanza as a solo. No instrumental music is mentioned by the text, nor does the type of song represented need an instrumental accompaniment. We may hence judge that Amiens sang without an accompaniment or, at most, with a single instrument played by himself. A cittern would have been suitable for the song and for the setting. The second stanza is sung by "all together," according to the Folio stage direction, although we are led to expect another solo by Amiens. The "others" present on the stage may have been lords and menials or, perhaps, only menials. We know that a banquet is being prepared while the song is sung; this would require some servants. In any event, the second stanza is sung by a group whose voices, we may believe, were not those of professional musicians—another indication that the setting of the song was a simple one.

There is some question as to whether or not the third stanza, a cynical parody by Jaques of the first two, was sung. It is not marked to be sung as are the earlier ones, but Amiens says, "Ile sing it," and the stanza is assigned to him, though as part of the spoken lines. The stanza may have been read by Jaques, as Noble suggests.[4] The mocking quality of the stanza could be best expressed by Jaques, I believe, and better expressed in spoken, rather than musical, delivery.

The tune to which the lyric was originally set is unknown. Gibbon has provided the words with a tune, printed in Playford's *The English Dancing Master* (1650), believed contemporaneous with the earliest production of the play. Of this setting, Gibbon remarks:

Chappell, whose knowledge of old tunes has never been equalled, suggests that this tune may date back to Elizabeth's day. Indeed his reasoning might be carried further so as to identify it with the ballad of "Robin Hood and the Monk" . . . which takes us back to the year 1450, as this has an "Under the greenwood tree" end-line and can readily be sung to this melody. Some lutenist may have written another tune for the actual production of *As You Like It*, but Shakespeare may very well have had the old tune in his head when he wrote the words of the song we know. His words exactly fit this traditional tune if the line "Come hither, come hither, come hither" is repeated, as lines and phrases are so often repeated when sung.[5]

Gibbon's setting is shown in Plate XX.

As was stated earlier, the song also serves to fill the gap in the action of the play caused by some necessary stage business. In this respect, the entire scene could be considered an entr'acte with music during which the stage is set for a following scene, the Duke's banquet in Scene vii. Before Amiens sings the second stanza of the song, he directs the serving men to begin setting the banquet table: "*Amy.* Wel, Ile end the song. Sirs, couer the while, the Duke wil drinke under this tree; . . ." At the conclusion of the scene, Amiens states: "And Ile go seek the Duke,/ His banket is prepar'd." Act II, v, hence appears to have as one of its pur-

PLATE XX.—*Under the Greenwood Tree.* This setting appears in Gibbon's *Melody and the Lyric*, p. 56.

poses the setting of the stage for Scene vii, which raises an interesting problem in production.

At the end of Scene v the stage is set for a banquet, yet in Scene vi we find Orlando and Adam lost in the forest and starving. How was Scene vi produced on the stage? If the play was first produced at the then new Globe playhouse, as Kittredge believes,[6] the normal acting space available would have included an outer stage, an inner stage, and an upper stage above the inner stage.[7] If the banquet was prepared on the outer stage, as the evidence in Scene vii would lead us to believe,[8] where did Orlando and Adam appear in Scene vi? The inner stage and the gallery above it would hardly have been suitable, at least not verisimilar. And Orlando and Adam would not have been shown starving with a banquet spread before them, as would be true if they appeared on the outer stage.

A possible explanation is that Scene v, containing the song, was inserted after the play was first written, and that the Folio text shows it inserted in the wrong place. The banquet scene should, logically, follow the song scene. Indeed, the line spoken by "*1. Lord*" in Scene vii suggests that he remained on the stage after the conclusion of Scene v and was joined by the Duke and other lords who enter at the beginning of Scene vii.[9] If so, the logical conclusion is that Scene vi is out of place and properly should precede the song in Scene v.

A brief description of the characters of Amiens and Jaques is also provided by the song and its context in II, v. The protestations and false modesty of Amiens in regard to his skill as a vocalist, coupled with the fact that in him we have another example of the nobleman-singer, reminds us strongly of Balthasar in *Much Ado*. We may hence suspect that the part of Amiens was originally taken by the same actor-singer who played the part of Balthasar, and that the portrayer of Amiens was perhaps kin to the posturing dilettante that is Balthasar.

The character of Jaques is more complex. We need not review here all of the qualities attributed to him by various editors and students of Shakespeare, but we may note that his remarks concerning the song sung by Amiens mark him rather precisely as a victim of one type of melancholia. His melancholy disposition, if we may be guided by Robert Burton,[10] is the result of too much unrelieved intellectual activity. Like Cassius, perhaps, he thinks too much. He likes music not because it relieves his melancholy but because it increases it. In other words he derives pleasure from being sad.

According to Burton, there were two effects music could have on the melancholy man, depending upon the nature of the music. If the music is sad or solemn it increases melancholy, as Burton and Lodge both assert.[11] If merry, music alleviates melancholy. Burton seems to describe the effect of music upon Jaques when he writes: "Many men are melancholy by hearing music, but it is a pleasing melancholly that it causeth; and therefore to such as are discontent, in woe, fear, or dejected, it is a most present remedy: it expels care, alters their grieved minds, and easeth in an instant."[12]

Jaques, we may believe, suffered from a mild melancholy, a sort of "Weltschmerz"; the world had grown stale to him. We may also note that Jaques has nothing to do with the merrymaking that takes place from time to time. In this connection, another passage by Burton is pertinent. In order to cure melancholia, he asserts: "Let them use hunting, sports, plays, jests, merry company", as Rhasis prescribes, "which will not let the mind be molested, a cup of good drink now and then, hear music, and have such companions with whom they are especially delighted, merry tales or toys, drinking, singing, dancing, and whatsoever else may procure mirth: and by no means, saith Guianarius, suffer them to be alone."[13]

Jaques thus seems to represent the completely cultured man who, with his world-weariness, is a dramatic foil to the idyllic simplicity represented by the forest of Arden. The implication made by Guianarius is a somber portent of the ultimate effect of Jaques' philosophy if we remember that Jaques refuses to go back to the great world and betakes himself to a monastery with the hope that in it "there is much matter to be heard and learn'd."

In Act II, v, therefore, we find an excellent example of dramatic economy. While the song which with its context constitutes the entire scene, adds little to the action of the play, it accomplishes much in the brief period of time allotted it. It restates the dominant idea of the play, it covers the setting of the stage for Scene vii, it delineates the characters of Amiens and Jaques, and it aids in establishing the sylvan setting in the forest.

In II, vii, Orlando carries in Adam to share the Duke's banquet. As the two hungry men eat, a song is sung: "*Du. Sen.* Welcome, fall too: I wil not trouble you,/ As yet to question you about your fortunes:/ Giue vs some Musicke, and good Cozen, sing.

Song.

Blow, blow, thou winter winde,
Thou art not so vnkinde, as mans ingratitude
Thy tooth is not so keene, because thou art not seene,
    although thy breath be rude.

Heigh ho, sing heigh ho, vnto the greene holly,
Most frendship, is fayning; most Louing, meere folly:
    The heigh ho, the holly,
    This Life is most iolly.

Freize, freize, thou bitter skie that dost not bight so nigh
    as benefitts forgot:
Though thou the waters warpe, thy sting is not so sharpe,
    as freind remembred not.
    Heigh ho, sing, &c.

Du. Sen. If that you were the good Sir *Rowlands* son,/ As you haue whisper'd faithfully you were, . . ."

In this song we again find a statement of the principal theme of the play. It is also no coincidence that the song, with its comments on man's ingratitude, should be sung immediately after Orlando carries Adam onto the stage, both having suffered extremely from man's ingratitude and feigned friendship. Clearly, the song is a commentary on the sad state of Orlando and Adam. The comment is an echo of the first speech of the exiled Duke, which is our first introduction to the forest of Arden (II, i, lines 5-11): "*Duk. Sen.* . . . Heere feele we not the penaltie of *Adam,*/

The seasons difference, as the Icie phange/ And churlish chiding of the winters winde,/ Which when it bites and blowes vpon my body/ Euen till I shrinke with cold, I smile, and say/ This is no flattery: these are counsellors/ That feelingly perswade me what I am:/ . . ."

In this song we also find another example of dramatic economy. As Noble has noted, the song replaces what otherwise would have been a repetitious account by Orlando of the circumstances leading to his appearance in the forest.[14] When the song is called for by the Duke, he has not questioned the two guests at his table. When the song is ended, however, he knows some of the story for he remarks to Orlando, "If that you were the good Sir *Rowlands* son,/ As you have whisper'd faithfully you were, . . ."

The song may also have served to cover the removal of the banquet from the stage. There is no stage direction in the Folio to this effect, but we know that the banquet is set forth during the course of a song, that the banquet is prepared by the time Orlando carries Adam onto the stage, that the Duke conducts Orlando and Adam to his cave after the singing of the song in question, and that the following scene is laid in Duke Frederick's palace. If there was no interruption between the two scenes, the banquet must have been cleared away while "Blow, blow, thou winter winde" was being performed.

The lyric of the song, in its appropriateness, suggests that it was written especially for the play. The mixture of cynicism and jollity set forth by the lyric does not find a general expression in English song until it appears in the cavalier lyrics. By their irregularity, the number of lines (9) and the rhyme scheme (aabccbddd), indicate that the song is an artistic imitation, rather than a true example, of a traditional song form.

The original music to which the lyric was set cannot be determined, nor have I been able to find a contemporary tune among the popular music of the period that would be entirely appropriate. The problem is complicated by the meter of the lyric which, in the stanza, calls for a 2/4 or, better, a 4/4 rhythm, and in the refrain, for a 6/8 rhythm. In order to provide a suitable illustration of the type of tune to which the lyric was set I have used part of a contemporary tune for the stanza of Shakespeare's song, and have written a melodic line to accompany the refrain. The contemporary tune is that set to the song, "Gathering Peascods," whose lyrics extol the delights of nature. This setting of "Blow, blow, thou winter winde" may be seen in Plate XXI.

The song was most likely sung by Amiens, although he is not mentioned by name. The Duke commands, "Give us some Musicke, and good Cozen, sing." The term "Cozen" supports the view that the song was at least sung by a nobleman, and Amiens is the singer of the group. The request of the Duke also indicates that an instrumental accompaniment was used for the song. The instrumental group need not have been large; a cittern or lute and a crowd would have sufficed and would have been appropriate to the rustic setting.[15]

The third song in the play has as its primary structural function the indication of a lapse of time. This song is also marked as a complete scene (IV, ii) in the Folio text, but the lines preceding and following the scene in question are necessary to establish its dramatic purpose.

PLATE XXI.—*Blow, Blow, Thou Winter Wind.* The first twelve measures of this setting were taken from an old dance tune found in Playford's *The English Dancing Master* (1650), as reprinted in Chappell, *Popular Music of the Olden Time,* I, 258. The last six measures (in brackets) were supplied by the writer to complete the musical setting.

At the end of IV, i, lines 180-185, Orlando and Rosalind are speaking:

>*Orl.* For these two houres *Rosalinde*, I wil leaue thee.
>*Ros.* Alas, deere loue, I cannot lacke thee two houres.
>*Orl.* I must attend the Duke at dinner, by two a clock I will be with thee againe.

.   .   .   .

Scena Secunda.

Enter Iaques and Lords, Forresters.

Iaq. Which is he that killed the Deare?
Lord. Sir, it was I.
Iaq. Let's present him to the Duke . . .; haue you no song Forrester for this purpose?
Lord. Yes Sir.
Iaq. Sing it: 'tis no matter how it bee in tune, so it make noyse enough.

Musicke, Song.

>*What shall he haue that kild the Deare?*
>*His Leather skin, and hornes to weare:*
>*Then sing him home, the rest shall beare this burthen;*
>*Take thou no scorne to weare the horne,*
>*It was a crest ere thou wast borne,*
>*Thy fathers father wore it,*
>*And thy father bore it,*
>*The horne, the horne, the lusty horne,*
>*Is not a thing to laugh to scorne.*   *Exeunt.*

Scoena Tertia

Enter Rosalind and Celia.

Ros. How say you now, is it not past two a clock? . . .

In trying to reconstruct the performance of this song, we must cope with a textual problem. The song appears to be a traditional one likely to have been sung by hunters or other convivial groups. The third line, however, does not seem to fit into the song, either in text or meter. The entire line appears to be a stage direction which has been confused with the original text of the song. The first part of the line may refer to some ritual of the hunt, the latter part to the way in which the song should be performed.[16] If the questionable line is omitted, the song becomes regular in structure and unified in text, as traditional songs usually are.

The hypothesis that the third line of the song is a stage direction is strengthened when we examine a musical setting of the lyric made by John Hilton (1599-1647), who arranged the song as a catch for four voices (see Plate XXII). It will be noted that Hilton's setting omits the questionable line. Since Hilton was probably familiar with the song as it was traditionally sung, his version, in addition to the other evidence we have observed, provides strong evidence that the third line of the song, as found in the Folio text, is actually a stage direction which should be removed from the song proper.

If we accept the third line as a valid stage direction, the way in which the song was originally performed is clarified. The "Lord" whom Jaques requests to sing was probably Amiens, who sang the first two lines solo. He was then joined by all the assembled noblemen-foresters in singing the refrain, or burden, beginning "Take thou no scorne. . . ."

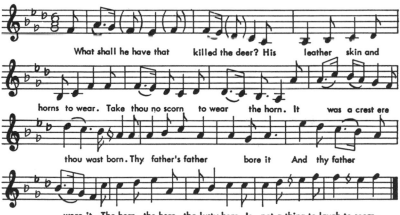

PLATE XXII.—*What Shall He Have That Killed the Deer?* This setting by John Hilton may be found in Playford's *The Musical Companion* (1672). It is reprinted in Gibbon's *Melody and the Lyric*, p. 111, from whence the above illustration was taken. The notes in parentheses are emendations by the writer of quarter notes appearing in Gibbon's illustration.

The Folio stage direction calls for "Musicke," which implies that the song had an instrumental accompaniment. Although this kind of song did not usually have instrumental support, the same musicians who accompanied the song, "Blow, blow, thou winter winde," may also have played for the song we now consider.

The well-known song, "It Was a Lover and his Lass," which next appears in the play, shows the most direct influence of Shakespeare's source, Lodge's *Rosalynde,* on the music of *As You Like It.* In the prose novel, a song is sung by Corydon, the old shepherd, as part of the wedding celebration at the close of the story. He accompanies himself with a crowd. His song is similar to the one used by Shakespeare. Lodge describes the scene: "About mid-dinner, to make them merry, Corydon came in with an old crowd, and played them a fit of mirth, to which he sung this pleasant song."

Corydon's Song.

A blithe and bonny country lass,
    heigh ho, the bonny lass!
Sate sighing on the tender grass
    and weeping said, will none come woo her.
A smicker boy, a lither swain,
    heigh ho, a smicker swaine!
That in his love was wanton fain
    with smiling looks straight came unto her.[17]

This song is unique among the other songs present in Lodge's novel, for it is a close imitation of a folk song, whereas the other songs, even though sung by rustics, are written in the same euphuistic style as their context.

When we compare Lodge's song with its Shakespearean counterpart, a curious reversal becomes apparent. The styles of the two songs are similar, but Shakespeare places his song before the wedding and introduces a hymeneal song in the courtly masque tradition after the weddings have been performed. We may also judge that "It Was a Lover and his Lass" had a comparatively elaborate musical setting, since two pages (probably skilled singing boys) are introduced for the main purpose of singing it. Thus, while Lodge ends his story by shifting from euphuistic songs to a traditional song style, Shakespeare, at the same point in the story, shifts from the rustic, as represented by the earlier songs in the play, to the more ornate and "artificial" songs which conclude the play. Our imaginations are removed from the fairy-tale existence led by the Duke and his party in the forest of Arden to a setting more akin to the life actually led by gentlefolk in Elizabeth's England.

The song, as we noted, is sung by two boys introduced as the Duke's pages. It is framed by a brief scene division, V, iii:

Scoena Tertia

. . . .

Clo. To morrow is the ioyfull day *Audrey*, to morow will we be married.

Aud. I do desire it with all my heart: and I hope it is no dishonest desire, to desire to be a woman of ye world? Heere come two of the banish'd Dukes Pages.

Enter two Pages.

1. *Pa.* Wel met honest Gentleman.

Clo. By my troth well met: come sit, sit, and a song.

2. *Pa.* We are for you, sit i'th middle.

1. *Pa.* Shal we clap into't roundly, without hauking, or spitting, or saying we are hoarse, which are the onely prologues to a bad voice.

2. *Pa.* I faith, y' faith, and both in a tune like two gipsies on a horse.

Song.

It was a Louer, and his lasse,
   With a hey, and a ho, and a hey nonino,
That o're the greene corne feild did passe,
   In the spring time, the onely pretty rang time,
When Birds do sing, hey ding a ding, ding.
Sweet Louers loue the spring,
And therefore take the present time,
With a hey, & a ho, and a hey nonino,
For loue is crowned with the prime,
   In spring time, &c.

Betweene the acres of the Rie,

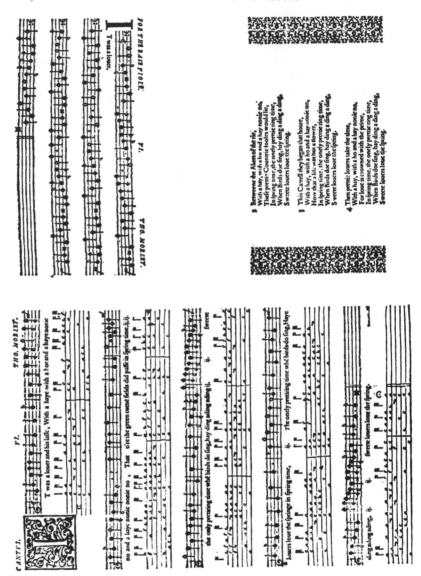

PLATE XXIII.—*It Was a Louer and His Lasse*. (See also ENDPAPERS.) Shown here is a reproduction of Morley's ayre, "It was a louer and his lasse," from his *First Book of Airs, or Little Short Songs* (1600). An original copy is in the Folger Shakespeare Library. The symbols between the lines comprise the lute tablature. The reversed part is an accompaniment for the viol da gamba.

With a hey, and a ho, & a hey nonino:
These prettie Country folks would lie.
  In spring time, &c.

This Carroll they began that houre,
With a hey and a ho, & a hey nonino:
How that a life was but a Flower,
In spring time, &c.

Clo. Truly yong Gentlemen, though there was no
great matter in the dittie, yet ye note was very vntunable
    1. *Pa.* you are deceiu'd Sir, we kept time, we lost not
our time.
    Clo. By my troth yes: I count it but time lost to heare
such a foolish song. God buy you, and God mend your
voices. Come *Audrie.*   *Exeunt.*

The two pages may have sung the song in unison, as Noble
suggests, but more likely they sang the verses alternately and
the refrain together. There would otherwise be little need for
two voices. The fact that two musicians are introduced into the
play for the primary purpose of singing the song argues that
it is probably an ayre whose music was unsuitable for amateur
voices. Although instrumental accompaniments were usually written for ayres, there is no evidence in the Folio text that instruments
were used with this one.

It has been believed for some time that the musical setting
for "It was a louer and his lasse," composed by Thomas Morley,
was perhaps written especially for the play and that there was
some direct collaboration between the two men. The facts are:

1. Morley's lyrics, despite a few slight variations in text, are
the same as those of Shakespeare (see Plate **XXIII**).

2. Morley's song was published in his *First Book of Airs, or
Little Short Songs* (1600), shortly after the play is believed to
have been written.

3. Shakespeare and Morley were neighbors during the period
of time in which the play and the book of airs appeared.[18]

4. There is a passage in *The Taming of the Shrew* closely resembling the gamut diagram in Morley's *A Plaine and Easie Introduction to Practicall Musicke* (1597).[19]

Regardless of the relationship of Shakespeare and Morley, the fact remains that we cannot say that Morley's music was composed especially for the play. Fellowes believes the song was not original with either Shakespeare or Morley, but was a traditional song whose lyrics were used by both dramatist and composer.[20] Morley's setting is a delightful one, though, and is chronologically the closest setting of any music written for a Shakespearean lyric.

On the day appointed for the marriage, Rosalind as Ganymede, true to her promise, divests herself of her disguise and appears as Rosalind, the daughter of the banished Duke and the beloved of Orlando. She appears accompanied by Hymen, the god of marriage, V, iv, line 113:

> *Enter Hymen, Rosalind, and Celia.*
> *Still Musicke.*
> Hymen. *Then is there mirth in heauen,*
> *When earthly things made eauen*
> *attone together.*
> *Good Duke receiue thy daughter,*
> *Hymen from Heauen brought her,*
> *Yea brought her hether.*
> *That thou mightst ioyne his hand with his,*
> *Whose heart within his bosome is.*

Orlando claims Rosalind for his bride, and the Duke accepts her as his daughter. Hymen then declaims:

> *Hy.* Peace, hoa: I barre confusion
> 'Tis I must make conclusion
> Of these most strange euents:
>
> .   .   .   .
>
> Whiles a Wedlocke Hymne we sing,
> Feede your selues with questioning:
> That reason, wonder may diminish
> How thus we met, and these things finish.
>
> *Song.*
> *Wedding is great Iunos crowne,*
> *O blessed bond of boord and bed:*
> *Tis Hymen peoples euerie towne,*

High wedlock then be honored:
Honor, high honor and renowne
To Hymen, God of euerie Towne.

The music in this miniature masque was probably performed as follows: Hymen, Rosalind, and Celia enter to the strains of soft and solemn music played, we may suppose, by a consort of three or four recorders hidden in the music room.[21] With this music for a background, Hymen speaks his opening lines. Here the music serves to identify Hymen as a deity and to solemnize the nuptial occasion in the absence of a Christian ceremony. In order to sustain the supernatural quality of Hymen's words, the "Still Musicke" probably accompanied his second speech which introduces the hymn to Hymen. Music that would have been suitable for the recorders and for the occasion is shown in Plate XXIV.

PLATE XXIV.—*Pavane in Six Parts.* This pavane by Henry LeJeune is reproduced from Naylor's *Shakespeare Music (Music of the Period)*, p. 33. Naylor states that the piece was written for hautboys, but it is also suitable for recorders if the two lowest bass parts be played an octave higher.

The song is sung by a chorus, to judge from Hymen's line, "Whiles a Wedlocke Hymne we sing." We have seen no evidence that would indicate that a group of skilled singers was used in the play at any time. On the contrary, we have seen that the preceding songs, excepting "It Was a Lover, . . ." were probably set to simple music which could be sung by the actors or by a talented actor-vocalist. We may hence suppose that the vocal setting for "Wedding is Great Juno's Crown" was simple and, perhaps, was sung in unison. The recorders could have furnished an appropriate accompaniment, but they would not have been necessary: the text contains no direction calling for the use of instruments with this song.

The original music for the hymn is not extant, but for illustrative purposes a hymeneal song by John Dowland is shown in Plate XXV. Dowland's ayre is written for a chorus of five voices and is probably more complex than was the musical setting for

PLATE XXV.—*Welcome, Black Night.* This nuptial hymn is by John Dowland. It appears in his *A Pilgrimes Solace (Fourth Book of Airs)* (1612), as reprinted in Fellowes' *The English School of Lutenist Song Writers.*

Shakespeare's song. It will serve, however, to impart some of the flavor of the music used by Shakespeare.

The dramatic functions performed by the "Still Musicke" and the wedlock hymn are several. To begin with, this portion of the scene is a wedding ceremony to which the music lends solemnity. Furthermore, the wedding is graced by the presence of a god whose deity is marked by the music accompanying his entrance upon the stage. The song, in addition to its ritualistic use, serves the more prosaic purpose of dramatic economy, for it replaces what would have been a difficult explanation for Hymen's presence in the play. Hymen states this function of the song when he says: "*Hy.* . . . Whiles a Wedlocke Hymne we sing,/ Feede your selues with questioning:/ That reason, wonder may diminish/ How thus we met, and these things finish."

The action of the play, following the multiple wedding, is given over to revelry (lines 182-204):

> *Du. Se.* . . . Meane time, forget this new-falne dignitie,
> And fall into our Rusticke Reuelrie:
> Play Musicke, and you Brides and Bride-groomes all,
> With measure heap'd in ioy, to'th Measures fall.
>   *Iaq.* Sir, by your patience: if I heard you rightly, . . .
>
> .   .   .   .
>
> *Du. Se.* Proceed, proceed: wee'l begin these rights,
> As we do trust, they'l end in true delights.   *Exit.*

The Duke calls for a dance, but Jaques forestalls the merriment, declaring that he will have nothing to do with the celebration. After this interruption, the Duke exclaims, "Proceed, proceed . . . " and the dance begins.

The clue to the nature of the music and dance employed in this episode is given by the Duke, who describes the scene as one of "Rusticke Reuelrie." The "Musicke" called for could have been supplied by the cittern and crowd suggested for an earlier scene of the play, perhaps augmented by a pipe and tabor. An appropriate dance would have been the "hey," a rustic measure for which a contemporary tune is shown in Plate XXVI.

As a dramatic device, the music of this final episode serves to conclude the play on a note of merriment and jollity befitting a comedy. It also provides a "grande finale" in which most of the actors are present on the stage to receive the applause of the audience.

Considered in retrospect, our study of the music in *As You Like It* provides a revealing glimpse of one aspect of Shakespeare's dramatic skill—the fashioning of a drama out of a prose narrative. Where Shakespeare picked up a euphuistic romance studded with courtly lyrics, he laid down a popularized play version sparkling with songs reflecting the spirit of English folk music.

The influence of *Rosalynde* may account for the quantity of songs in the play and perhaps for the emphasis placed on them by means of scene frames. Beyond this influence, however, Shakespeare and Lodge part company. Lodge's songs, with the exception

PLATE XXVI.—*The Haye.* The melody of this dance is taken from Arbeau's *Orchesography* (1588), p. 170. The harmonized version used above is from Naylor, *Shakespeare Music (Music of the Period)*, p. 58.

of Corydon's last song, are as "artificial" as his prose style; Shakespeare's songs have a flavor of the forest and the countryside. Lodge's songs serve, in the main, an ornamental purpose; Shakespeare's songs are primarily devices of dramatic economy by means of which much of the prose narration is telescoped or merely suggested. And, if repetition is an index to significance, the moral of the play is stated in several of its songs, whereas the songs in the prose novel have little relation to its didactic purpose.

Notes

1. See Chambers, *William Shakespeare*, I, 402-404; Kittredge, ed., *As You Like It*, p. vii; J. W. Holme, ed., *As You Like It*, Arden edition, p. viii. Quiller-Couch and Wilson, eds., *As You Like It*, New Cambridge edition, p. 103, suggest the year 1593 for the first composition of the play.
2. See T. Lodge, *Rosalynde* (1590), pp. 27-28, 49-50, 86-89, 116-117, 118-119, and 161-162.
3. The text of the play quoted in this study is that of the Folio of 1623 unless otherwise noted. The line numbers are those of the Globe edition.
4. *Shakespeare's Use of Song*, pp. 72, 73.
5. *Melody and the Lyric*, p. 55.
6. *As You Like It*, p. xvii.
7. As reconstructed by J. C. Adams in *The Globe Playhouse*.
8. In Scene vii, the Duke, Jaques, Amiens, and several lords are present at the banquet. They are apparently seated around the table when Orlando enters. Orlando commands, "Forbeare, and eate no more," under the impression that the banquet is in progress. Later the Duke says, "Sit downe and feed, & welcom to our table." The group does not begin to eat until Adam is brought in. It hence appears that seven or eight persons are seated around the table at one time. It is doubtful if the inner stage could have supplied the necessary space, whereas the outer stage would have provided ample room.
9. The Duke and attendant lords enter the stage at the beginning of Scene vii. He has been searching for Jaques. The "*1. Lord*" remarks, "My Lord, he is but euen now gone hence,/ Heere was he merry, hearing of a Song." This would imply that the speaker was one of those lords present in Scene v, and, therefore, that he did not enter with the Duke.
10. *The Anatomy of Melancholy* (1628).
11. Burton, pp. 367-374; T. Lodge, *A Defence of Poetry, Music, and Stage-plays*, pp. 19, 20.
12. P. 369.
13. P. 370.
14. *Shakespeare's Use of Song*, p. 73.
15. The crowd was considered a rustic instrument by the Elizabethans. It was a bowed, six-stringed instrument of rectangular shape. Two of the strings were drones. Like the rebec, and unlike the viols, it was held under the chin or resting against the shoulder of the player. (See Galpin, *Old English Instruments of Music*, pp. 73-79.)

16. See the Variorum edition, pp. 227-231.

17. *Rosalynde*, pp. 160, 161.

18. See Chambers, *William Shakespeare*, I, 402-405; Bridge, *Shakespearean Music in the Plays and Early Operas*, pp. 16, 19; E. Brennecke, Jr., "Shakespeare's Collaboration with Morley" and "A Reply and a Symposium to Ernest Brennecke's 'Shakespeare's Collaboration with Morley,'" *PMLA*, LIV (March, 1939), 139-152.

19. See Long, "Shakespeare and Thomas Morley," *MLN*, LX (January, 1950), 17-22, and rejoinders by Messrs. John R. Moore and Louis Marder in *MLN*, November, 1950.

20. Morley, *The First Booke of Airs*, Note VI, also p. 26 and note on p. 28, as reprinted by Fellowes, *The English School of Lutenist Song Writers*, 1st Series, No. 16.

21. Recorders were frequently used to provide music for solemn occasions. See Chapter II, pp. 21, 22.

NINE

Twelfth Night

welfth Night IS PERMEATED BY MUSIC. IT BEGINS
with music, it ends with music, and through-
out the play songs and snatches of songs as
well as instrumental music are scattered about
with what, at first glance, would appear to
be a casual hand. Though music is used ex-
tensively, it is marked by a restraint and a degree of naturalness
which, unless the spectator were interested specifically in the
music, would cause it to pass almost unnoticed. As is true of
costume, scenery, lighting, and other stage devices, dramatic music
is best employed when it does not attract attention to itself at
the expense of the play as a whole but rather is immediately
accepted by the audience as being so appropriate that it is taken
as a matter of course. Such is the music of *Twelfth Night*.

As we shall observe, the casualness with which music is employed in the play is not a result of indifference but of skill. This
study attempts to show that most of the music of the play may
be divided into two distinct groups, the sweet and plaintive music
associated with Duke Orsino and the lusty songs and ballads
assigned Sir Toby and his cronies. The Duke's music delineates
his character and hence aids in motivating his sudden change of
mistresses at the end of the play. The music of Sir Toby and his
friends, as well as the way it is performed, adds much to the comic
situations where it occurs. Actually, the two groups are musical
foils for one another.

The first notice of the play is John Manningham's record of
a performance in the Middle Temple on February 2, 1602. Parts
of a song by Robert Jones, printed in his *First Booke of Songs and
Ayres* (1600), appear in II, ii. The date 1600-1601 is generally
accepted for the composition of the play,[1] a fact which is important in our discussion of the sequence of the plays later on in
this chapter.

Shakespeare's source may have been Riche's *Farewell to the Military Profession* (1581), the "historie" of Appolonius and Silla, but Chambers believes his debt was not great.[2] I can find no connection between the music in *Twelfth Night* and Riche's work or any other sources usually suggested for the play.

As the play opens, Duke Orsino and his train enter to the sound of a consort piece played by the Duke's household musicians:

> *Enter Orsino Duke of Illyria, Curio, and other*
> *Lords.*
>
> Duke.
> If Musicke be the food of Loue, play on,
> Giue me excesse of it: that surfetting,
> The appetite may sicken, and so dye.
> That straine agen, it had a dying fall:
> O, it came ore my eare, like the sweet sound
> That breathes vpon a banke of Violets;
> Stealing, and giuing Odour. Enough, no more,
> 'Tis not so sweet now, as it was before.[3]

The stage directions and lines above provide enough information for us to determine the probable staging of the episode, the general nature of the instruments used in the consort and of the score it played, and one aspect of the Duke's character.

When the Duke enters, the musicians are most likely placed within the tiring house and not on the stage. There is no evidence in the stage direction that musicians are on the stage prior to the entrance of the Duke and the other Lords, or that the musicians enter with them. On the contrary, the Duke speaks of the music as he enters, an indication that he refers to music he had been listening to just before he appears in view of the audience. His remark, "That strain agen . . ." also suggests that a similar strain was heard before the actors come on the stage. It would hence appear that an instrumental prelude introduced the play, as was frequently the case in the productions of the Chapel Children,[4] and that the action of the play begins in the midst of a consort piece.

The Duke describes the sound of the music as having "a dying

fall" and as like "the sweet sound/ That breathes upon a banke
of Violets;/ Stealing and giving Odour." We may judge, then,
that the music was probably soft, sweet, and grave, with a touch
of sadness. Naylor suggests as an appropriate score for this scene
an instrumental work called "Lord Salisbury his Pavin" which
has a "dying fall" such as that mentioned by the Duke (see
Plate XXVII).

The consort best adapted to such a score would be one composed largely of recorders, since this family of instruments was
noted for its sweet and slightly mournful tones.[5] A five-piece
consort containing a set of recorders (treble, tenor and bass), a

PLATE XXVII.—*The Lord Salisbury his Pavin.* A reproduction of a pavane by Orlando Gibbons. This transcription appears in Naylor's *Shakespeare Music (Music of the Period),* pp. 10, 11. The original may be found in *Parthenia* (1611), a collection of virginal music. The "dying fall" occurs in the last eight measures of the composition.

treble lute, and a mandore or an archlute would meet the musical and dramatic requirements of the scene.

The dramatic function of the instrumental music is, for the most part, to provide an insight into the character of the Duke as a lover. His opening line, "If Musicke be the food of loue, play on," tells us that he is in love and that the music ministers to the emotions evoked by his love. His later remarks, as well as the plaintive type of music which delights him, indicate that he is, to quote Noble, "an exotic in search of a sensation."[6] He is in love with love and not with any particular mistress. The sudden switch of his interest from Olivia to Viola at the end of the play is thus partially motivated.

In marked contrast to the music which pleases the melancholy Duke, the next episode employing music (II, iii) presents a gay love song, a catch, and snatches of other convivial songs. This scene presents a carouse by Sir Toby, Sir Andrew, and Feste which, when interrupted by Malvolio, supplies the motivation for the practical joke later played on Malvolio by the two knights, the jester, and Maria. Such a rousing portrayal of "the good life" must needs have included songs.

The scene provides a crescendo of conviviality which brings first Maria who intends to quiet the roisterers (but who joins them), and then Malvolio who, roused out of his sleep, attempts to order Sir Toby out of the house. The increasing noisiness of the party is marked by the types of songs mangled by the tipplers.

The scene opens as Sir Toby and Sir Andrew are passing around the wassail bowl. They are soon joined by Feste, the jester (line 18): "*To.* Welcome asse, now let's haue a catch. *And.* By my troth the foole has an excellent breast. I had rather then forty shillings I had such a legge, and so sweet a breath to sing, as the foole has." After some wordplay, Sir Andrew continues: "*An.* Excellent: Why this is the best fooling, when all is done. Now a song. *To.* Come on, there is a sixe pence for you. Let's haue a song. . . . *Clo.* Would you haue a loue-song, or a song of good life? *To.* A loue song, a loue song."

Clowne sings.
O Mistris mine where are you roming?
O stay and heare, your true loues coming,
That can sing both high and low.
Trip no further prettie sweeting.
Iourneys end in louers meeting,
Euery wise mans sonne doth know.

    An. Excellent good, ifaith.
    To. Good, good.
    Clo. What is loue, tis not heereafter,
Present mirth, hath present laughter:
What's to come, is still unsure.
In delay there lies no plentie,
Then come kisse me sweet and twentie:
Youths a stuffe will not endure.

The words for this song are generally attributed to Shakespeare, and I see no reason to suppose otherwise. The rhyme scheme (aabccb) betrays more art than is generally found in folk lyrics, which generally employ simple couplets or alternate rhymes. The song, however, shows no indication that it was written especially for the play.

The musical setting is sometimes assigned to Thomas Morley, but the supporting evidence is inconclusive. There is an instrumental score, without words, in Morley's *First Booke of Consort Lessons* (1599) bearing the title, "O Mistresse mine."[7] Several attempts have been made to fit Shakespeare's lyrics to this melody, none of them completely successful. The treble viol part of Morley's score and attempted settings by Naylor and Bridge are shown in Plate XXVIII. Concerning the problem, Noble quotes from a letter by Edmund Fellowes:

In the first line of the treble viol, there is an awkwardness with the second syllable of "roaming"—up to that point it goes beautifully. This melody was set by Byrd, as you know, to a wonderful set of variations preserved in the Fitzwilliam Virginal Book. Byrd squared the whole rhythm, but there is a syllable short (for "roaming") exactly as in Morley's Consort Lessons. It can be no more than pure conjecture as to whether Morley was setting Shakespeare's words—there is no evidence whatsoever beyond whether the words will fit or no, and as far as one can see they do not fit exactly.[8]

The melodic theme for Byrd's variations and an illustration of its use as a setting for Shakespeare's song may be seen in Plate XXIX. If the melody by Byrd and that by Morley be compared, the melodic line of each will be found the same, although the time values of the notes differ.

The date Byrd composed his variations is not known; hence we do not know whether his score preceded or followed that of Morley.[9] No credit is given for the tune by either composer; it

PLATE XXVIII.—*O Mistris mine.* "O Mistress Mine"—the original melody in Morley's *First Book of Consort Lessons* (1599) and versions of Naylor and Bridge, as shown in Bridge, *Shakespearean Music in the Plays and Early Operas,* p. 77.

is possible that both found the tune among the folk or popular music of the time. This possibility leads Fellowes to suggest that Shakespeare also knew the anonymous folk song and virtually rewrote it.[10]

Actually, the only connection between Shakespeare's song and the tune by Morley is the similarity of the title of the instrumental score and the opening phrase of Shakespeare's song; the fit of the words to the tune is not snug enough to be conclusive. The title, "O Mistresse mine," could have been applied to innumerable songs of the period. In fact, there is a song in Morley's *Short Book of Airs* (1600) entitled "Mistress mine" which is distinct from the melody in his *Consort Lessons* and from Shakespeare's song.[11] The evidence is such that we must conclude that Shakespeare's song may have been set to a tune different from the one used by Morley and Byrd.

The actor who played the part of Feste in the original production of the play is generally supposed to have been Robert Armin, who replaced Will Kemp in the early part of 1600.[12] Armin apparently was not a trained singer in the sense that he had served a musical apprenticeship or had come to the Chamberlain's Men from one of the choirboy groups.[13] If he was as skillful a singer as Sir Toby and Sir Andrew proclaim, he may have picked up his musical training informally. At any rate,

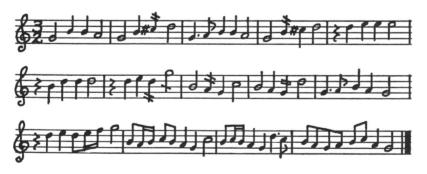

PLATE XXIX.—*O Mistris Myne.* This version is by William Byrd. It appears complete in the *Fitzwilliam Virginal Book*, No. 66. The illustration above was taken from C. Vincent's *Fifty Shakspere Songs*, pp. xxvii, xxviii.

his voice was suitable for the ayre and for the occasion in II, iii.

Feste evidently sang "O Mistris mine" without an accompaniment, since none is mentioned in the text. If the song had been set to music by a composer especially for the play, we should expect an instrumental accompaniment of some kind to have been specified.[14] The fact that none is indicated argues that Morley's setting was not written for *Twelfth Night*.

After the ending of Feste's love song, the party grows more boisterous; the three, well into their drink, decide to sing a merrier type of song:

> *To.* To heare by the nose, it is dulcet in contagion. But shall we make the Welkin dance indeed? Shall wee rowze the night-Owle in a Catch, that will drawe three soules out of one Weauer? Shall we do that?
>
>   *And.* And you loue me, let's doo't: I am dogge at a Catch.
>
> *Clo.* Byrlady sir, and some dogs will catch well.
>
> *An.* Most certaine: Let our Catch be, *Thou Knaue*
>
> *Clo.* *Hold thy peace, thou Knaue* knight. I shall be constrain'd in't, to call thee knaue, Knight.
>
> *An.* 'Tis not the first time I haue constrained one to call me knaue. Begin foole: it begins, *Hold thy peace.*
>
> *Clo.* I shall neuer begin if I hold my peace.
>
> *An.* Good ifaith: Come begin.   *Catch sung.*

The music for the catch sung at this time is shown in Plate XXX. Feste begins the catch and is joined, we may guess, by Sir Toby and then by Sir Andrew. The musical quality of their performance was not high, to judge from Maria's description of it as "catterwalling."

Sir Toby responds to Maria's attempt to quiet the noise by apparently bellowing out the lines from three popular ballads: "*To*, My Lady's a *Catayan*, we are politicians, *Maluolios* a Peg-a-ramsie, and *Three merry men be wee.* Am not I consanguinious? Am I not of her blood: tilly vally. Ladie, *There dwelt a man in Babylon, Lady, Lady.* . . . *To. O the twelfe day of December.* *Mar.* For the loue o'God peace."

The tune for the first two songs, and one stanza of the second, may be seen in Plate XXXI. Sir Toby's singing no doubt should make up for its lack of melody with its volume, for it brings a sleepy and angry Malvolio to the scene. After first insulting the musicianship of Sir Toby, Malvolio gives him a choice of giving up his roistering or of quitting the house. To this, Sir Toby, stung by the slur on his musical ability and by Malvolio's effrontery, shapes his retort in a mock-sad vein, using a popular ayre by Robert Jones for his reply. The clown, delighted by the device, picks up the words of the song. The two sing a slightly altered version of the song to its conclusion:

> *To.* Farewell deere heart, since I must needs be gone.
> *Mar.* Nay good Sir *Toby.*
> *Clo.* His eyes do shew his dayes are almost done.
> *Mal.* Is't euen so?
> *To.* But I will neuer dye.
> *Clo.* Sir *Toby* there you lye.
> *Mal.* This is much credit to you.
> *To. Shall I bid him go.*
> *Clo. What and if you do?*
> *To. Shall I bid him go, and spare not?*
> *Clo. O no, no, no, no, you dare not*
> *To.* Out o'tune sir, ye lye: Art any more then a Stew-

PLATE XXX.—*Hold Thy Peace.* Taken from Vincent's *Fifty Shakspere Songs*, p. xxix.

ard? Dost thou thinke because thou art vertuous, there
shall be no more Cakes and Ale?

A transcription of the ayre as written by Robert Jones is shown
in Plate XXXII.

The next scene (II, iv) is laid in Duke Orsino's palace. Again,
as in I, i, the Duke enters with a request for music:

Scena Quarta.

Enter Duke, Viola, Curio, and others.

Du. Giue me some Musick; Now good morow frends.

Now good *Cesario,* but that peece of song,

PLATE XXXI.—*Three Merry Men be We* and *There dwelt a man in Babylon.*
The words for "Three Merry Men be We" can be found in Peele's *Old Wives
Tale* (1595), the tune in Playford's *The English Dancing Master* (1650). This
setting is taken from Naylor, *Shakespeare and Music,* p. 182. The second song
fragment is from "The Ballad of Constant Susanna." Its tune is a corrupt form
of the popular tune, "Green Sleeves." One stanza of the ballad is as follows:

There dwelt a man in Babylon
Of reputation great by fame,
He took to wife a fair woman
Susanna she was callde by name.
A woman faire and vertuous,
Lady, lady!
Why should we not of her learn thus
To live godly?

(See Naylor, *Shakespeare and Music,* pp. 182, 183.)

That old and Anticke song we heard last night;
Me thought it did releeve my passion much,
More then light ayres, and recollected termes
Of these most briske and giddy-paced times.
Come, but one verse.

    Cur. He is not heere (so please your Lordshippe) that
should sing it?

    Du. Who was it?

    Cur. Feste the Iester my Lord, a foole that the Ladie
Oliuiaes Father tooke much delight in. He is about the
house.

    Du. Seeke him out, and play the tune the while.

Musicke playes.

Come hither Boy, . . .
How dost thou like this tune?

    Vio. It giues a verie eccho to the seate
Where loue is thron'd.

. . . .

    Du. O fellow come, the song we had last night:

FIRST LINE OF VERSE

Farewell, dear love, since thou will needs be gone. Mine eyes do show my

life is almost done. Nay, I will never die, So long as I ·can spy.

SECOND LINE OF CHORUS

Shall I bid her go? What and if I do? Shall I bid her go, and spare

not? O no, no, no, no, no I dare not.

PLATE XXXII.—*Farewell, Dear Love.* The melody for Shakespeare's version of
Jones's song is taken from Jones's *First Booke of Songs and Ayres* (1600),
where the complete original appears. The song book is reprinted in Fellowes'
The English School of Lutenist Song Writers.

Mark it Cesario, it is old and plaine;
The Spinsters and the Knitters in the Sun,
And the free maides that weaue their thred with bones,
Do vse to chaunt it: it is silly sooth,
And dallies with the innocence of loue,
Like the old age.

   Clo. Are you ready Sir?
   Duke. I prethee sing.   *Musicke.*

The Song.

Come away, come away death,
And in sad cypresse let me be laide.
Fye away, fie away breath,
I am slaine by a faire cruell maide:
   My shrowd of white, stuck all with Ew, O prepare it.
   My part of death no one so true did share it.

Not a flower, not a flower sweete
On my blacke coffin, let there be strewne:
Not a friend, not a friend greet
My poore corpes, where my bones shall be throwne:
   A thousand thousand sighes to saue, lay me ô where
   Sad true louer neuer find my graue, to weepe there.

When we attempt to reconstruct the performance of the music in this scene, we find ourselves concerned with a minor mystery. As the Duke enters, he calls for his musicians. (His request for "Musicke" must refer to the household consort; his command for the actual performance of music is not given until several lines later.) While the musicians come onto the stage, the Duke requests Viola (Cesario) to sing a song. We would expect Viola to sing at this time, for in I, ii, lines 55-59, Viola had told Antonio: "*Vio.* . . . Ile serue this Duke,/ Thou shalt present me as an Eunuch to him,/ It may be worth thy paines: for I can sing,/ And speak to him in many sorts of Musicke,/ That will allow me very worth his seruice." Viola does not sing, however. For some unknown reason Feste, with a hasty explanation, is substituted for the original singer. Quite clearly there has been a revision here.[15] Why was Viola's song re-assigned to Feste, who had been originally assigned many songs in the play?

An examination of the scene may provide a clue to the answer. The revision begins, probably, about line 8, at Curio's first speech. The introduction of Feste into the scene is a part of the revision, hence we may assume that the revised portions include at least those parts of the scene in which Feste appears. He leaves the stage at line 81. Now, if these portions of the scene are omitted, we find that the action of the play is not interrupted in the least. If we suppose that Viola sings the song at the Duke's request, and leave out the portions we believe comprise a revision, the scene would appear thus: "*Duke.* Come, but one verse." [Viola sings.] "Come hither, Boy. . . . *Vio.* And so they are: alas, that they are so:/ To die, euen when they to perfection grow./ *Duke.* Let all the rest giue place: Once more *Cesario,*/ Get thee to yond soueraigne crueltie."

Now, the omitted portions contain an explanation for the change in singers, lines 8-13, the instrumental music played as background for the Duke's musings (lines 15-42), the Duke's second description of the song (lines 43-51), and the brief conversation between the Duke and Feste (lines 68-81). We assume that the song sung by Viola occurred immediately after the Duke's first speech, instead of halfway through the scene. The significant omissions are thus the instrumental music and the second description of the song.

The reason for the addition of the music and song description to our conjectured original version of the scene can only be guessed at, but here is one explanation: for some reason the singing boy playing the part of Viola in the original version became unavailable. His song was assigned to Feste, but in order to explain the performance of the ayre by an adult voice when a rendition by a skillful singing boy was expected, the song was given a second description emphasizing its folk nature. The search for Feste was then utilized as an opportunity to insert the consort music which, perhaps, was a simplified version of the original score.

The purpose of the music in this scene is again to emphasize the moodiness and passivity of the Duke's character.

But to return to the performance of the music. The Duke calls for his musicians. While Curio goes to find Feste, the Duke requests the musicians to play the tune of the song. The music of this tune, to judge by the words later sung to it, was very likely slow and plaintive. The consort suggested for I, i, would be equally appropriate in this scene. The music probably continued until the entrance of Curio and Feste (line 42). Feste then sings the song accompanied by the consort.

The metrical construction of the song verses strongly suggests an ayre although its subject has a traditional flavor, and the Duke describes it as a folk song. The music to which the song was originally set has been lost. Moreover, the short lines, "O prepare it," "did share it," and "lay me ô where," "to weepe there," prevent the lyrics from being set to any of the traditional tunes of the period I have found, nor can any of the ayres I know supply a setting. On the theory that half a loaf is better than none, I have written a setting which I believe has some flavor of the original tune (see Plate XXXIII).

Feste again provides music for the next occasion (IV, ii), wherein he impersonates a parson and visits Malvolio, who has been locked in a dark room as a madman. Following his visit disguised as Sir Thopas, Feste is sent back to Malvolio without his disguise. He identifies himself by singing a snatch of an old ballad

PLATE XXXIII.—*Come Away, Come Away Death.* I have here set Shakespeare's words to a melody of my own devising. Afterward, I discovered that I had unconsciously based my melody on the Elizabethan tune, "Heart's-ease," mentioned in *Romeo and Juliet,* IV, v. The old tune may be found in Chappell's *Popular Music of the Olden Time,* I, 209, 210 (see Plate XVI).

as he approaches Malvolio's room (lines 78-85) : *"Clo.* Hey Robin, iolly Robin, tell me how thy Lady does. *Mal.* Foole. *Clo.* My Lady is vnkind, *perdie. Mal.* Foole. *Clo.* Alas why is she so? *Mal.* Foole, I say. *Clo.* She loues another. Who calles, ha?" The fragment of a tune to which Feste probably sang his lines is shown in Plate XXXIV.

When Feste leaves Malvolio, he does so speaking or singing the following lines (130-141) :

> *Clo.* I am gone sir, and anon sir,
> Ile be with you againe:
> In a trice, like to the old vice,
> your neede to sustaine.
> Who with dagger of lath, in his rage and his wrath,
> cries ah ha, to the diuell:
> Like a mad lad, paire thy nayles dad,
> Adieu good man diuell. *Exit.*

In view of Feste's past inclination to burst into song on the slightest occasion, it is possible that the jester sang the above lines; some modern editors mark the lines to be sung.[16] There is no evidence, however, beyond the metrical structure of the lines, which would indicate that they were supposed to be sung, nor has any traditional song or tune been found which could be identified

PLATE XXXIV.—*Hey Robin.* Feste's song is a part of a round for three or four voices, found in the British Museum, add. Ms. 31922, Folio 54. The above illustration is taken from Naylor, *Shakespeare and Music,* p. 184.

with the clown's lines. Despite what some editors have said, therefore, the lines lie outside the scope of this study.

The final occasion for music in the play is the epilogue sung by Feste:

Clowne sings.

When that I was and a little tine boy,
  with hey, ho, the winde and the raine:
A foolish thing was but a toy,
  for the raine it raineth euery day.

But when I came to mans estate,
  with hey ho, &c.
Gainst Knaues and Theeues men shut their gate,
  for the raine, &c.

But when I came alas to wiue,
  with hey ho, &c.
By swaggering could I neuer thriue,
  for the raine, &c.

But when I came vnto my beds,
  with hey ho, &c.
With tospottes still had drunken heades,
  for the raine, &c.

A great while ago the world begon,
  hey ho, &c.
But that's all one, our Play is done,
  and wee'l striue to please you euery day.

At the conclusion of the play all the actors leave the stage, except Feste, who remains to sing the epilogue. There is no indication in the Folio text that he has an instrumental accompaniment. A cittern or pandurina would have aided the singer, but it would not have been a necessity.

L. B. Wright and H. B. Lathrop describe this epilogue song as being entirely extraneous, and there does not seem to be any reason to doubt their conclusions. It is probably a popular song, not written by Shakespeare, to which was added the final stanza referring to the play. A slight variation of the song, in which the refrains are retained, was later used by Shakespeare in *King Lear* (III, ii).

The musical setting of the song was apparently a very popular tune; for it, or a quite similar tune, was used as a setting for Willy and Perigot's roundelay in the August Eclogue of Spenser's *Shepheardes Calender* (1579) beginning: "*Perigot.* It fell upon a holly eve,/ *Willye.* hey ho hollidaye,/ *Per.* When holly fathers wont to shrieve:/ *Wil.* now gynneth this roundelay."[17] The words of Corydon's song in Lodge's *Rosalynde* (1590) also could have been set to the same tune. It begins: "A blithe and bonny country lass/ Heigh ho, the bonny lass,/ Sat sighing on the tender grass/ And weeping said, will none come woo her."[18] Another lyric possibly written to be set to the same tune may be found in Deloney's *Garland of Good Will* (1593). It is entitled "A Pastoral Song" and begins: "Upon a down, where shepherds keep,/ Piping pleasant lays,/ Two country maids were keeping sheep/ and sweetly chanted roundelays."[19] And, finally, in *England's Helicon* appears "A Pastoral Song between Phillis and Amarillis, two Nimphes, each answering other line for line," by Henry Constable, which may be sung to the same tune. It begins: "Phillis: Fie on the sleights that men devise/ Heigh hoe sillie sleights/ When simple Maydes they would entice/ Maydes are young men's chiefe delights."[20]

The tune to which the epilogue song in *Twelfth Night* is now usually sung (when the epilogue is not omitted) may be seen in Plate XXXV. This tune is authorized only by stage tradition; there is no reason to believe it was used during Shakespeare's lifetime.

When we review the use of music and its performance in *Twelfth Night*, we are impressed by two facts: first that the music which receives extended description in the actors' lines is associated with the character of the Duke, whereas the music introduced with little or no description is associated with Sir Toby and his circle of friends; second, the complete songs in the Folio version are all sung by Feste, whose part was probably taken by Robert Armin in the first few productions of the play.

The fact that a large number of lines are expended in describing the music in three of the episodes we have examined argues that Shakespeare had a definite purpose in mind when he used that music and that he wanted his audience to be aware of his purpose. In the case of the instrumental music which opens the play, and the song, "Come away, come away Death," his purpose, clearly, was to underscore the melancholy and sentimental character of Duke Orsino by showing his reactions to the sound of sad and plaintive music.

The casual way in which the songs and snatches of ballads associated with Sir Toby are introduced suggests that they are primarily aids to setting and atmosphere, although they also serve to aid in the characterization of the comic figures of the play. The increasing noisiness of Feste, Sir Toby, and Sir Andrew in their carouse is marked by the songs they choose to sing: first a relatively sedate love song sung by Feste, then a lusty catch sung with more enthusiasm than art by all three, then maudlin scraps of ballads roared out by Sir Toby, and finally a comic dialogue song based on a popular ayre and aimed at Malvolio. The fragment of a song performed by Feste as he visits the cell of Malvolio is part of the mockery which pervades the scene. The concluding song of the play appears to be completely extraneous.

The fact that all the complete solo songs in the revised play,

When that I was a little tiny boy, With a heigh hol the wind and the rain, A foolish thing was but a toy, For the rain it raineth ev' - ry day, With a heigh hol the wind and the rain, And the rain it raineth ev'ry day.

PLATE XXXV.—*When that I was a little tiny boy.* The words are here set to the tune traditionally used on the stage. The origin of the tune is unknown. This setting was found in Chappell, *Popular Music of the Olden Time,* I, 225.

as well as bits of other songs, are assigned to one singer, and that one of the singers in the early productions of the play is generally believed to have been Robert Armin, is significant, for it leads to evidence that Robert Armin was connected with the Chamberlain's Men at an earlier date than has heretofore been believed:— that he was the actor who first played the parts of Balthasar in *Much Ado* and Amiens in *As You Like It*.

The known facts of Armin's career are few. He is believed to have been born about 1568.[21] On October 13, 1581, he signed an indenture of apprenticeship to a goldsmith, which lasted for a period of about eleven years.[22] His activities following the completion of his apprenticeship are obscure, but he evidently soon joined a company of players, for his play, *The Two Maids of Moreclacke,* was first acted in 1597-1598, and he is known to have acted with Lord Chandos' Men before 1600 and to have been a regular, and popular, player at the Curtain before that date.[23] In the spring of 1599, Will Kemp left the Lord Chamberlain's Men and was replaced by Armin as a regular member of the company about August, 1600.[24] T. W. Baldwin surmises that the Chamberlain's Men held Kemp's position open until he definitely decided to leave England about March of 1600, at which time the company offered his parts to Armin.[25] In 1603 Armin was listed as a shareholder in the Chamberlain's Men.[26] He died about November, 1615.[27]

The complete songs in *Twelfth Night* have an intrinsic musical value, and hence require a singer with at least a pleasant voice. Armin evidently had such a voice, perhaps trained informally during his earlier years as a player. Moreover, Feste's part was played by an adult actor; Armin was about thirty-two years old at the time the play is believed to have been first produced.

Now, let us consider the performers of the songs in *Much Ado, As You Like It,* and *Twelfth Night.* The dates of the plays are, respectively, 1598-1599, 1599, and 1600-1601. In 1598-1599, in *Much Ado,* we find Shakespeare unmistakably using for the first time an adult singer-actor to whom he assigns both of the complete songs in the play.[28] This seems to have been an experiment, for

the singer is introduced with apologies and with some good-
natured critical remarks on the·poor quality of his voice, which
had perhaps received no formal training. The actor may not have
been a prominent member of the company; he was employed primarily as a singer and not as an actor. The experiment was evidently a success, for in 1599, in *As You Like It*, we find that three
of the five songs therein are assigned to an adult singer (Amiens)
and while there is an apology made for the skill of the singer, it
is less prominent than the apology in *Much Ado*.[29] The songs
assigned to Amiens are comparatively simple and suitable to a
pleasant, though untrained, voice: in two of them, the choruses
are taken up by nonmusicians of the cast. The two songs not sung
by Amiens are the ayre, "It was a Lover and his Lass," sung by
two boys introduced especially for the purpose, and the choral
"Hymn to Hymen." Then in *Twelfth Night* (1600-1601), we find
the three complete songs sung by Robert Armin, who, so far as
we know, had received no formal musical training, who was an
adult with a pleasing voice, who is introduced with no apology
and, who, indeed, is given one of the prominent parts of the play.
It will not be idle speculation, then, if we make the tentative
statement that the same singer and actor took the parts of Balthasar, Amiens, and Feste in the initial productions of the three
plays with which we are concerned, and that the singer-actor was
Robert Armin. But let us see how this statement fits the known
facts of Armin's career.

At the time *Much Ado* is believed to have been first produced,
Robert Armin was a successful clown regularly performing at the
Curtain, possibly as a member of Lord Chandos' Men.[30] Shakespeare's company is also believed to have appeared at the Curtain
before moving to the Globe in 1599.[31] Armin perhaps remained
at the Curtain with some other playing company until he joined
the Chamberlain's Men in 1600. It could have been quite possible,
therefore, that Armin was employed as a singer by the Chamberlain's Men for their first production of *Much Ado* and that,
as a result of his success, he was again used for a larger part,
though still mainly as a singer, for the first production of *As You*

Like It in 1599. It is possible that, with Kemp's imminent departure in view, Armin as Amiens was being groomed to take over
Kemp's clown roles in the event Kemp permanently left the company.[32] In any event, when Kemp left, Armin joined the Chamberlain's Men in his place, receiving the major part of Feste in
which he appeared both as a singer and as a clown.

In view of the evidence set forth above, it appears quite likely
that Armin was associated with Shakespeare's company as a singer-actor as early as 1598, two years before he has been believed
heretofore to have worked with them, and that he took the parts
of Balthasar in *Much Ado* and Amiens in *As You Like It*, as well
as that of Feste in *Twelfth Night*.

Notes

1. See Chambers, *William Shakespeare*, I, 405, and Furness, ed., *Twelfth Night*, Variorum edition, pp. x, xi.
2. *William Shakespeare*, I, p. 407. Parrott (*Shakespearean Comedy*, p. 180) disagrees.
3. The quotations from the play appearing throughout this chapter are from the Folio of 1623, the only authoritative text. The line numbering follows that of the Globe edition.
4. See Wallace, "The Children of Blackfriars," *University Studies*, VIII, 71 ff.
5. See Chapter II, pp. 21, 22.
6. *Shakespeare's Use of Song*, p. 03.
7. Chambers, *William Shakespeare*, I, p. 405; Furness, ed., p. x; Noble, *Shakespeare's Use of Song*, p. 81.
8. *Shakespeare's Use of Song*, p. 82.
9. The period of the compilation of the *Fitzwilliam Virginal Book* has not been determined exactly.
10. *Idem.*
11. See Fellowes, *The English School of Lutenist Song Writers*, 1st Series, No. 15, pp. 36, 37.
12. Baldwin, *The Organization and Personnel of the Shakespearean Company*, p. 394; Chambers, *William Shakespeare*, I, p. 79; J. T. Murray, *English Dramatic Companies 1558-1642*, II, p. 31.
13. See pp. 183-185, below.
14. For example, the ayres "Who is Siluia?", "Tell me where is Fancy bred," "Sigh no more, ladies, sigh no more," and "Blow, blow thou Winter wind," are all set to consort accompaniments, as we know by stage directions.
15. Noted by Noble, *Shakespeare's Use of Song*, p. 80.
16. For example, Neilson and Hill, eds., Riverside Press edition, 1942.
17. See B. Pattison, "The Roundelay in the August Eclogue of 'The Shepheardes Calender,'" *RES*, IX, 54, 55.
18. See T. Lodge, *Rosalynde*, p. 161.

19. See J. H. Dixon, ed., *The Garland of Goodwill by Thomas Deloney*, p. 146.
20. See A. H. Bullen, ed., *England's Helicon*, p. 204.
21. Murray, II, p. 30.
22. Baldwin, *Organization and Personnel*, pp. 47n, 84, 152n.
23. Baldwin, "Shakespeare's Jester," *MLN*, XXXIX, 447-455.
24. Baldwin, *Organization and Personnel*, pp. 50, 84.
25. "Shakespeare's Jester," *MLN*, XXXIX, 447, 448.
26. Chambers, *William Shakespeare*, II, p. 78.
27. *Idem.*
28. See Chapter VII, pp. 126, 127.
29. See Chapter VIII, p. 145.
30. Baldwin, "Shakespeare's Jester," *MLN*, XXXIX, 447-455.
31. *Idem.*
32. As suggested by Baldwin. See *idem.*

TEN

Conclusion

HE FOREGOING EXAMINATION AND ATTEMPTED RE-construction of the music performed in seven of Shakespeare's comedies is an inquiry, as close as the subject permits, into the nature of the music employed by Shakespeare, the purposes for which he used music, and the value of that music as a dramatic element. In order to make such a study, it has been necessary to consider Shakespeare's use of music not as an isolated phenomenon but as a part of the musical and dramatic milieu of his age. As an inevitable concomitant of this study, a consideration of certain problems of text, production, and stage history has been necessary.

The Elizabethan dramatist was technically well equipped. Beyond the bare dramatic necessities—actors, stage, and story—he was equipped with a magnificent language, with brilliant costumes, and with music whose popularity is attested by the extent to which it was used. That the works produced by the major playwrights of the period constitute the greatest chapter of English dramatic history yet written should be proof that the tools of their craft were used fully and expertly, and that these tools were used partly to overcome the handicaps—if they were such—imposed by rudimentary stage scenery, clumsy machinery, and primitive lighting.

The use of music as a part of English drama can be traced from the origin of that drama in the medieval church to the present, though the two arts have diverged to a great degree since the Restoration. In the medieval church the music was supplied by the priests and the choirs; the later mystery cycles were accompanied by municipal and guild musicians; the interludes and moralities, by vagabond minstrels or the musicians of noble households. With the establishment of semipermanent companies of actors, and the construction of special playhouses in London late in the sixteenth century, the affinity between music and drama became closer as a result of the greater security thus given both actors and musicians.

The construction of the playhouses was a great boon to the playwright, since it gave him a fixed stage for the starting point of the action and setting of his plays, and provided more scope for his talents through the use of stage machinery and other devices. The permanent location of the playhouses in a thickly populated area also enabled him to draw upon a large force of musicians of all types and skills, and to construct his plays with specialized music in mind. It is no wonder, then, that the plays produced in London after the construction of the Theatre and the Curtain show an increasing use of stage devices and music.

A coincidental impetus to the use of music in Elizabethan drama was the formation of acting companies composed of choir-boys from the Chapel Royal and St. Paul's. It was only natural that the excellent musical training received by these boys should have been exploited by the dramatists who wrote plays for them. It was also natural that, as a result of their popularity, the adult companies should have emulated the children as far as they were financially able. The plays written for the singing boys by Edwards, Peele, and Lyly show clearly the impact on English drama made by the music of the "little eyases."

When we first hear of Shakespeare as a playwright, about 1592, the choirboy companies were entering a period of temporary obscurity, but their influence on Shakespeare's fellow dramatists was still strong. These men had discovered that music, which was casually used in plays prior to the emergence of the children's companies, could be woven into the texture of their plays, and that, in addition to its intrinsic value, it could be used to perform many purely dramatic functions. It could be used to reinforce the emotional impact of language, either in the form of song or as a support for spoken lines; it could contribute to the action of a play; it could augment settings, suggest off-stage action, create a supernatural atmosphere, cover the sound of stage machinery, and perform many other services. Moreover, a diversified body of music was at their disposal, including choral works, lutenists' ayres, street ballads, folk songs, and instrumental music of many kinds.

When Shakespeare began working on plays, therefore, he had in music a new, but proved, tool with which to work. He did not modify the tool appreciably, nor did he discover extraordinary uses for it. But his skill in its employment can seldom be questioned.

Now, what have we learned about the nature of the music performed in the seven plays comprising this study? In regard to the songs, we have found evidence that seventeen songs were performed (not counting fragments or possible songs omitted by the early texts) in the group of plays. If the total is broken down, the figures show a general increase, over the chronological period, in the use of songs. One appears in *The Two Gentlemen*, one in *Love's Labour's Lost*, three in *A Midsummer Night's Dream*, one in *The Merchant of Venice*, two in *Much Ado*, five in *As You Like It*, and four in *Twelfth Night*. The masque influence may account for the relatively large number of songs used in *A Midsummer Night's Dream*.

It is of course impossible to classify the songs with precision. On the basis of the tests we have used, however, the general statement can be made that the songs are a representative sampling of the vocal music of the period if we overlook the madrigals and ecclesiastical music, neither of which was employed to any extent in the Elizabethan drama. The types range from the elaborate song-dance-choral ayres of *A Midsummer Night's Dream* to the popular street song at the conclusion of *Twelfth Night*. The ayre is by far the predominant type.

Instrumental music is employed in the group of plays almost as extensively as vocal music. At least one performance by a consort occurs in each play, sixteen in the whole group. This figure does not include the use of solo instruments, which would probably increase the total figure. When the total figure is broken down according to play, the same general increase of music from play to play will be noted as was observed in the use of songs. The consort is used twice in *The Two Gentlemen*, once in *Love's Labour's Lost*, five times in *A Midsummer Night's Dream*, once in *The Merchant of Venice*, three times in *Much Ado*, three times in *As You Like It*, and three times in *Twelfth Night*. The masque influence may again explain the large figure associated with *A Midsummer Night's Dream*.

The types of music played by the consorts include accompaniments for ayres, dance music (both courtly and popular), background music for supernatural atmosphere and for banquets, and accompaniments for lyrical speeches.

Though it is difficult to determine the instrumentation of the consorts except in broad outlines, there is no evidence that instruments were employed that were not normally available to any of the dramatists of the period. A four- or five-piece ensemble composed of viols, lutes, and recorders would satisfy the dramatic requirements of all the occasions for which consort music was used, if we assume that the musicians could double on two or three rustic instruments such as the rebec, crowd, or pipe and tabor.

The technique of Shakespeare in his employment of music in the seven comedies we have studied has three major phases. In the first, comprehending *The Two Gentlemen of Verona*, *Love's Labour's Lost*, *A Midsummer Night's Dream*, and *The Merchant of Venice*, music signals the presence of critical or climactic situations in the plays. In *The Two Gentlemen*, the situation is Julia's discovery of Proteus' infidelity (IV, ii) during the course of a serenade. In *Love's Labour's Lost*, the climax of the comedy occurs in the Mask of the Muscovites (V, ii) during which the ladies of France heap scornful mockery on the King of Navarre and his friends to the accompaniment of dance music. The turning point of the plot of *A Midsummer Night's Dream* is the reconciliation of Oberon and Titania (IV, i), which is symbolized by a dance duet. And, of course, the highly dramatic moment when Bassanio must choose between the caskets in II, i, of *The Merchant of Venice*, is underscored by the enigmatic song, "Tell me where is Fancy bred."

The second phase of Shakespeare's dramatic use of music begins with *The Merchant of Venice* and ends with *Much Ado*. These two plays are the only early comedies by Shakespeare containing tragicomical elements. With the introduction of tragic elements into these plays, we also note a change in the over-all purpose for which music is used in them. Now the music serves as a sedative. In *The Merchant of Venice* (V, i), music of a sweet and lyrical nature follows closely after the tense trial scene in which Antonio almost loses his life. Likewise, in *Much Ado* (V, iii) the epitaph song serves as a musical catharsis to purge away the sadness of the preceding scenes in preparation for the happy conclusion of the play.

The third phase cannot be so well defined, for in it we find two extremes—the formalized arrangement of songs in *As You Like It*, and the naturalistic presentation of them in *Twelfth Night*. Perhaps this might be called an experimental phase wherein Shakespeare weighed the advantages of the stylistic use of music on one hand and its naturalistic use on the other. If so, we need only glance at the music in *The Winter's Tale, Cymbeline*, and *The Tempest* to see that his decision was made in favor of naturalism.

Within these three general phases, we find music employed for much the same purposes as in the works of other dramatists of the period. The serenade scene in *The Two Gentlemen of Verona* and the Mask of the Muscovites in *Love's Labour's Lost* are two examples of music entering directly into the action of the plays. Further use of music as an aid to forwarding action may be seen in the fairy songs (II, ii, and V, i) and the instrumental music in *A Midsummer Night's Dream* (IV, i). In *The Merchant of Venice* the song in the casket scene motivates Bassanio's choice of the right casket and thus forwards the action of the play. An instrumental consort playing within the tiring house indicates off-stage action in *Much Ado* (I, iii, and II, i). Malvolio's slur on Sir Toby's singing in *Twelfth Night* (II, iii) is a partial motivation for the practical joke later played upon him.

Music is used to an equal extent in character delineations. Perhaps the best known instance is the mournful music associated with Duke Orsino, and the lusty songs assigned Sir Toby and Feste, in *Twelfth Night* (I, i; II, iii; and II, iv). But equally effective are the dance songs used to portray the grace and airiness of the fairies (II, ii, and V, i) of *A Midsummer Night's Dream*, and the crude music supplied by Bottom and his fellows in the same play (III, i; IV, i; and V, i). In *As You Like It*, Jaques's comments on the song, "Under the greenwood tree," give us a revealing glimpse of his "humour."

We would not think that Shakespeare's prose and poetry needed reinforcement, especially in the lyrical passages, but we have found frequent occasions wherein lines are spoken against a background of consort music. The effect on Julia, of Proteus' unfaithfulness, in *The Two Gentlemen*, is made more poignant by the consort piece which underscores her comments. The badinage between Rosaline and the King of Navarre in *Love's Labour's Lost* is carried on to the sound of dance music. Probably the most effective use of music as an aid to language may be found in *The Merchant of Venice* (V, i). Here some of Shakespeare's most lyrical passages are made intensely melodic by the addition of an instrumental score. As we will remember also, many of the lines spoken by the Duke in I, i, and II, iv, of *Twelfth Night* are set to music.

The effectiveness with which settings could be suggested by music was recognized by Shakespeare. The banquet scene and the masque scene in *Much Ado* have appropriate music as a part of their settings. Likewise, the rustic settings of *As You Like It* are suggested by the songs, "Under the greenwood tree," "Blow, blow, thou winter wind," "Which is he that killed the deer," and the country dance music at the end of the play. The rowdy drinking scene (II, iii) of *Twelfth Night* is well defined by the types of songs used therein.

In addition to its use with the four dramatic components discussed above, we find music accomplishing many other purposes in the plays we have examined. Music creates a supernatural atmosphere for the appearances of the fairies in *A Midsummer Night's Dream*, and the entrance of Hymen in *Much Ado*; it aids in the creation of dramatic irony in *The Two Gentlemen of Verona* and *Much Ado*; it emphasizes the themes of *Love's Labour's Lost* and *As You Like It*; it denotes a lapse of time in *Much Ado* and *As You Like It*; and it covers the omission of repetitious or difficult explanations in *As You Like It*.

Out of all the music in the seven plays, only one song, the epilogue song in *Twelfth Night*, seems to be entirely extraneous.

Within the comprehensive scope of this study, we have found evidence bearing on the solution of several problems of text, production, and stage history. This evidence cannot, in most cases, be considered conclusive, but it supports the following statements.

In regard to text:

1. Two songs in *Love's Labour's Lost*, I, ii, line 127, and III, i, line 1, have been omitted, and the text of the song lyrics concluding the play is faulty because of absorbed stage directions.

2. The Folio stage direction, IV, i, line 31, of *A Midsummer Night's Dream*, though omitted by some modern editions, is legitimate and should be retained.

3. In the same play, IV, i, at line 86 and again at line 88, and in V, i, at line 369, music is performed though not indicated by stage directions in the Folio or Quarto texts.

4. Also in the same play, the stage direction for the last fairy song should be moved two lines lower.

5. Concerning the different stage directions appearing in the Quarto and Folio texts of *Much Ado*, II, iii, lines 38 and 44, the Quarto presents the preferable version.

6. In *As You Like It*, vi of II is out of place; it should precede, not follow, II, v.

7. The original version of II, iv, of *Twelfth Night* was revised in order to present Feste as the singer of the song therein.

In regard to production:

1. The performance of the serenade in *The Two Gentlemen of Verona* took place off-stage, not in view of the audience as modern editions present the scene (IV, ii).

2. The dance scene in *Love's Labour's Lost* should employ the dance figures of the galliard as a basis for its action (V, ii).

3. The music accompanying the fairy dance-songs and spells in *A Midsummer Night's Dream* should be supplied by musicians hidden from view of the audience (II, ii; IV, i; V, i).

4. The "Rural Musicke" requested by Bottom in the same play should be performed despite editorial emendations to the contrary (IV, i).

5. A distinct separation should be made between the Bergamask dance of the rustics and the fairy dance which follows it in *A Midsummer Night's Dream* (V, i).

6. In the masque scene of *Much Ado*, the dance music is played off-stage, and the progressive pairings of the characters on the outer stage are immediately followed, in each case, by the departure of the couples from the stage (II, i).

7. The lyrics for two songs are imbedded in the spoken lines of *Twelfth Night*; these lyrics should be sung (II, iv; IV, ii).

In regard to stage history:

1. Two songs were removed from *Love's Labour's Lost* between the time it was performed before Elizabeth and the time it was printed in the 1598 Quarto.

2. John Dowland may have collaborated with Shakespeare in arranging the music for *A Midsummer Night's Dream*.

3. The song "Tell me where is Fancy bred," in *The Merchant of Venice*, may have been suggested by an earlier song by Sidney.

4. The employment of an adult actor-singer in *Much Ado* and his reappearance in *As You Like It* and *Twelfth Night* mark the only significant departures by Shakespeare from the musical-dramatic conventions of his time.

5. The actor taking the parts of Balthasar in *Much Ado*, Amiens in *As You Like It*, and Feste in *Twelfth Night* was Robert Armin, whose connection with the Chamberlain's Men therefore began about two years earlier than has been believed heretofore.

The musical illustrations included in this study may alleviate some of the distress of the producer faced with the scarcity of authentic music for the comedies. The musical scores selected are appropriate to the scenes wherein they are placed. In the instance of the songs whose words have been retained in the early texts, the music set to them is usually very close to that used in the early productions of the plays concerned. In fact, the tunes set to the Spring and Winter song in *Love's Labour's Lost*, Bottom's song in *A Midsummer Night's Dream*, "Sigh no more, ladies" in *Much Ado*, and Feste's epilogue song in *Twelfth Night* may well have been the tunes to which these songs were originally sung.

In selecting illustrations of the instrumental music performed, we are aware that the guidance provided by the poetry in the selection of song tunes is missing; consequently, there is greater chance for error. An effort has been made to minimize this chance by basing the selection of instrumental music on information supplied by the actors' lines and the stage directions, and by following as closely as possible the dramatic conventions of the period governing each situation—a practice also followed in connection with the song settings and illustrations.

The transcriptions of music included in this study are hence not to be considered authentic in the strict sense of the word; they are Shakespearean and not Shakespeare's. They are, however, almost all contemporaneous and appropriate to the scenes in which they are placed.

This study is largely an assessment of probabilities. From it, however, one comprehensive and incontrovertible fact has emerged. The Elizabethan drama occupies a unique position in the history of both drama and music in that it is an art form which has firmly integrated the sister arts—poetry, drama, the dance, and music. We now have no exact counterpart for it. Opera has the music and, sometimes, a reasonably well-integrated dance, but it is not noted for drama or poetry. Musical comedy perhaps comes closest to resembling, musically, the Elizabethan plays, but so far as serious drama is concerned, there is little kinship between the two. The addition of sound to motion pictures has produced moments of well-balanced drama and music, but where is the poetry?

This comprehensive conclusion is supported, to a great degree, by an examination of one Elizabethan's use of music in his plays. But if and when similar studies are made of the use of music by other dramatists of the period, I have no doubt that the Elizabethan age will be known not only as the golden age of English drama and music, but also as the period which saw and heard that almost inextricable combination of the two typified by the comedies of William Shakespeare.

Annotated Bibliography

A larum for London (1602), edited by W. W. Greg, Malone Society Reprints. London: Oxford University Press, 1913. Contains musical stage directions.

ADAMS, J. C. *The Globe Playhouse: Its Design and Equipment.* Cambridge: Harvard University Press, 1942. Contains a description of the Globe music room and a study of musical activities on the Globe stage, based on interior evidence in plays produced in that playhouse.

——————. "The Staging of 'The Tempest,' III, iii." *RES,* XIV (October, 1938), 404-419. Description of the integration of action and music in a Globe Playhouse production, as determined by stage directions and dialogue when related to the construction of the playhouse.

ADAMS, J. Q. "A New Song by Robert Jones." *MLQ,* I (1940), 45-48. Music and lyric of an unpublished MS.

——————. *Chief Pre-Shakespearean Dramas; A Selection of Plays Illustrating the History of the English Drama from Its Origin Down to Shakespeare.* Boston: Houghton Mifflin Co., 1924.

ADSON, J. *Courtly Masquing Ayres comp. to 5 and 6 parts for Violins, Consorts, and Cornets. . . . London,* 1621. Photostats made from a transcription in the New York Public Library.

AGRIPPA, H. C. *Henrie Cornelius Agrippa, of the vanitie and vncertaintie of artes and sciences, Englished by Ja. San. . . . London, imprinted by Henry Wykes, 1569.* Huntington Library (Bridgewater 52038) STC 204. Not seen.

ALBRIGHT, V. E. *The Shakespearean Stage.* New York: Columbia University Press, 1926.

ALLISON, R. *An howres recreation in musicke, apt for instruments and voyces . . . By Richard Alison . . . London, printed by Iohn Windet . . . 1606.* Huntington Library (Bridgewater 60473) STC 356. Not seen.

ANDREWS, H. "Elizabethan Keyboard Music." *The Musical Quarterly,* XVI (January, 1930), 59-71. Contributions of lutenist techniques to the development of keyboard music.

ARBEAU, T. (Jehan Tabourot). *Orchesography* (1588). New York: Kamin Dance Publishers, 1948. One of the rare contemporary treatises on Renaissance dances and dance music. Contains woodcuts and music.

ARKWRIGHT, G. E. P. "Elizabethan Choirboy Plays and Their Music." *Proceedings of the Musical Association,* April, 1914, pp. 117-138.

BACON, F. *The Works of Francis Bacon, Lord Chancellor of England.* Philadelphia: Carey and Hart, 1842. 3 vols.

BALDWIN, T. W. "Shakespeare's Jester: The Dates of 'Much Ado' and 'As You Like It.' " *MLN,* XXXIX (December, 1924), 447-455.

——————. *The Organization and Personnel of the Shakespearean Company.* Princeton: Princeton University Press, 1927.

The Ballad of the Cloak, . . . To the tune of, From Hunger and Cold or Packington's Pound, 1681. Huntington Library (Bridgewater 134549). Not seen.

BANISTER, J., and T. Low. *New ayres and dialogues composed for voices and viols . . . London, printed by M. C. for H. Brome, 1678.* Huntington Library (Britwell 14243). Not seen.

BANTOCK, G. *One Hundred Songs of England*. Boston: Oliver Ditson Co., 1914. Includes several songs of the Elizabethan period, lyrics and music.

BANTOUX, G. *La Chanson en Angleterre au temps d'Elisabeth*. London: Oxford University Press, 1936. An extensive critical examination with reproductions of musical scores. Contains one chapter on songs in the drama.

BARING-GOULD, S. *English Minstrelsie: A National Monument of English Song*. Edinburgh: T. C. and E. C. Jack, Grange Publishing Works, 1895-1896. Vol. 1 of 8 vols. A description of English popular music from Chaucer to the Restoration, with music and pictures of instruments.

BARLEY, W. *A new booke of tabliture . . . London, printed for William Barley, 1596*. British Museum copy K. 1. c. 18, R218138, in the Huntington Library. Contains instructions for playing the lute and several popular ayres in tablature.

BARR, A. E. "Ballads and Ballad Music Illustrative of Shakespeare." *Harpers New Monthly Magazine*, LXIII (June, 1881), 52-61. An unscholarly description of ballad music drawn largely from Chappell's *Popular Music of the Olden Time*.

BARRIFFE, W. *Mars, his triumph . . . London, printed by I. L. for Ralph Mab, 1639*. Huntington Library, 17384 STC 1505. Not seen.

BARTLET, J. *A booke of ayres with a triplicitie of musicke . . . composde by Iohn Bartlet . . . London, printed by Iohn Windet for Iohn Brown, 1606*. Huntington Library (Britwell 13567) STC 1539. Not seen.

BASKERVILLE, C. R. "A Prompt Copy of 'A Looking Glass for London and England.'" *MP*, XXX (August, 1932), 29-51. Contains prompter's music cues.

——————. *The Elizabethan Jig and Related Song Drama*. Chicago: The University of Chicago Press, 1929. Includes a brief, but scholarly, description of the stage jig as it was performed on the Elizabethan stage.

BAYLISS, S. A. "Music for Shakespeare." *Music and Letters*, XV (January, 1934), 61. Not seen.

BEAUMONT, F. *The Works of Francis Beaumont and John Fletcher*. Variorum Edition. London: George Bell and Sons & A. H. Bullen, 1904. 3 vols.

BEVIN, E. *A briefe and short introduction to the art of musicke . . . London, printed by R. Young, 1631*. Huntington Library 69262 STC 1986. Not seen.

BOND, R. W. "Lyly's Songs." *RES*, VI (1930), 295-299. Discussion of omitted songs in Lyly's plays; a study in textual deduction.

BOYD, M. C. *Elizabethan Music and Musical Criticism*. Philadelphia: University of Pennsylvania Press, 1940. A study based on contemporary music instruction books, song books, their introductions, and other records. Has many quotations.

BRENNECKE, E., "Shakespeare's Collaboration with Morley." *PMLA*, LIV (March, 1939), 139-152. A review of facts pointing to an association between the two men.

BRETON, N. *The Arbor of Amorous Devices* (1597), edited by H. E. Rollins. Cambridge: Harvard University Press, 1936. A reprint of a collection of song lyrics. No music.

BRIDGE, SIR F. *Shakespearean Music in the Plays and Early Operas*. London and Toronto: J. M. Dent and Sons, Ltd., 1923. A discursive account of several songs mentioned by or used by Shakespeare, and amiable suggestions about Shakespeare's associations with contemporary composers.

——————. "The Musical Cries of London in Shakespeare's Time." *Proceedings of the Musical Association*, December, 1919, pp. 13-20. A description of street vendors' songs. No music.

BRIDGE, SIR F. *The Old Cryes of London; with musical examples.* Novello and Co., Ltd., 1921. Not seen.

BROOKE, C. F. T. *The Shakespeare Songs, Being a Complete Collection of the Songs Written by or Attributed to William Shakespeare.* New York: William Morrow and Co., 1929. A collection of lyrics only.

BROOKE, C. F. T., and N. B. PARADISE (eds.). *English Drama, 1580-1642.* Boston: D. C. Heath and Co., 1933.

BULLEN, A. H. (ed.). *England's Helicon. A Collection of Lyrical and Pastoral Poems; Published in 1600.* London: J. C. Nimmo, 1887. Song lyrics. No music.

——————. *Lyrics from the Dramatists of the Elizabethan Age.* London: J. C. Nimmo, 1889. Song lyrics. No music.

——————. *Lyrics from the Song Books of the Elizabethan Age.* New York: Charles Scribner's Sons, 1892. Song lyrics. No music.

——————. *More Lyrics from the Song Books of the Elizabethan Age.* London: J. C. Nimmo, 1888. Song lyrics. No music.

BURNEY, C. *A General History of Music, from the earliest ages to the present period. To which is prefixed a dissertation on the music of the ancients.* London: Printed for the Author, 1776-1789. Not seen.

BURTON, R. *The Anatomy of Melancholy; . . . by Democritus junior . . .* (1628). New York: Empire State Book Co., 1924. Contains a section treating the medicinal properties of music.

CASTELNUOVO-TEDESCO, M. "Shakspere and Music." *SAB*, XV (April, 1940), 166-174. A description of several musical compositions inspired by Shakespeare's plays and poems.

CHAMBERS, E. K. *The Elizabethan Stage.* Oxford: The Clarendon Press, 1923. 4 vols.

——————. *William Shakespeare: A Study of Facts and Problems.* Oxford: The Clarendon Press, 1930. 2 vols.

CHAPMAN, G. *The Works of George Chapman,* edited by R. H. Shepherd. London: Chatto and Windus, 1874-1875. 3 vols.

CHAPPELL, W. *Popular Music of the Olden Time.* London: Cramer, Beale and Chappell, n.d. 2 vols. A valuable history of early English popular music with copious musical illustrations drawn from contemporary music books. Well documented. Harmonization of the music is not authentic.

The Christmas Prince, edited by W. W. Greg, Malone Society Reprints. London: Oxford University Press, 1923. Text with stage directions pertaining to music; also a reporter's account of Cambridge festivities during which the play was given. Records of payments made to municipal musicians on this occasion.

COLLIER, J. P. "John Wilson, the Singer," *The Papers of the Shakespeare Society: Being Contributions Too Short in Themselves for Separate Publication.* London: Printed for the Shakespeare Society, 1853. An attempted identification of "Jack Wilson."

Course musicke plaid vpon the Odcombian hoboy . . . The punks delight, (Vaile bonnet iiging festivals) London, 1611. Huntington Library (Hoe 56406) STC 5807. Not seen.

COWLING, G. H. *Music on the Shakespearean Stage.* Cambridge: The University Press, 1913. A description of the use of music on the Elizabethan stages. Generally trustworthy, though lacking in documentation.

CUNNINGHAM, P. *Inigo Jones and Ben Jonson,* Shakespeare Society Publications No. 39. London: Printed for the Shakespeare Society, 1848. Contains

Jonson's description of the performance of several masques, including his explanations for the use of music in many instances.

DAY, C. L., and E. B. MURRAY. *English Song Books 1651-1702; A Bibliography with a First-line Index of Songs.* London: Printed for The Bibliographical Society at the Oxford University Press, 1940.

DEKKER, T. *The Dramatic Works of Thomas Dekker.* London: John Pearson, 1873. 4 vols.

DELONEY, T. *A Garland of Good Will* (1593), edited by J. H. Dixon. London: Printed for the Percy Society by T. Richards, 1851. A collection of song lyrics. No music.

————. *Strange Histories: consisting of ballads and other poems principally by Thomas Deloney. From the edition of 1607.* London: Reprinted by the Percy Society by C. Richards, 1841. Contains severals ballads with musical settings.

DENT, E. J. *Foundations of English Opera; A Study of Musical Drama in England During the Seventeenth Century.* Cambridge: The University Press, 1928. Includes a brief account of dramatic music prior to the Restoration.

DODGE, J. "Lute Music of the XVIth and XVIIth Centuries." *Proceedings of the Musical Association,* 1907-1908, pp. 123-153. A study of composition, with musical illustrations.

Dodsley's Old English Plays, edited by W. C. Hazlitt. London: Reeves and Turner, 1874. 15 vols.

Dodsley's Old Plays, Supplement of the Shakespeare Society, edited by T. Amyot *et al.* London: W. Skeffington, 1853. 4 vols.

DOLMETSCH, A. *The Interpretation of the Music of the XVII and XVIII Centuries Revealed by Contemporary Evidence.* London: Oxford University Press, 1946. A scholarly and full discussion.

DOLMETSCH, M. *Dances of England and France from 1450 to 1600: With Their Music and Authentic Manner of Performance.* London: Routledge and Kegan Paul, Ltd., 1949. An analytic description of dance forms, with contemporary music transcribed for piano by Arnold Dolmetsch.

DORIAN, F. *The History of Music in Performance; The Art of Musical Interpretation from the Renaissance to our Day.* New York: W. W. Norton and Co., Inc., 1942. Not seen.

DOUCE, F. *Illustrations of Shakespeare, and of Ancient Manners: With Dissertations on the Clowns and Fools of Shakespeare; On the Collection of Popular Tales Entitled Gesta Romanorum; and on the English Morris Dance.* London: Printed for Thomas Togg, 1839.

DRAPER, J. W. "The Date of 'A Midsommer Nights Dreame.'" *MLN*, LIII (April, 1938), 266-268.

DUNCAN, E. (ed.) *Lyrics from the Old Song Books.* London: G. Routledge and Sons, Ltd., 1927. Not seen.

————. *The Story of Minstrelsy.* London: The Walter Scott Publishing Co., Ltd., 1907.

D'URFEY, T. *Songs Compleat, Pleasant and Divertive; Set to Musick by Dr. John Blow, Mr. Henry Purcell, and other Excellent Masters of the Town.* London: Printed by W. Pearson, for J. Tonson, 1719. Contains several songs, with music, of an earlier date than indicated by the title page.

"Early Elizabethan Stage Music." *The Musical Antiquary,* I (October, 1909-July, 1910), 30-40. An account of music written for plays, with reproductions of musical scores.

EBISCH, W., and I. L. SCHUCKING. *A Shakespeare Bibliography.* Oxford: The Clarendon Press, 1931.
——————. *Supplement for the Years 1930-1935, to A Shakespeare Bibliography.* Oxford: The Clarendon Press, 1937.
ELSON, L. C. *Shakespeare in Music; A Collation of the Chief Musical Allusions in the Plays of Shakespeare, with an Attempt at Their Explanation and Derivation, Together with Much of the Original Music.* Boston: L. C. Page and Co., 1900. Written in popular style. Contains many pieces of contemporary music.
ELYOT, T. *The Governor* (1531). London: J. M. Dent and Sons, Ltd., 1937. Includes a discussion of music in education.
ENGELKE, B. *Musik und Musiker am Gottorfer Hofe.* Breslau: F. Hirt, 1930. A critical and historical account of musicians *ca.* 1580-1600. Many reprints of contemporary German, English, and Italian music.
EVANS, W. *Ben Jonson and Elizabethan Music.* Lancaster, Pa.: Lancaster Press, 1929.
——————. *Henry Lawes, Musician and Friend of Poets.* New York: The Modern Language Association of America, 1941. A critical biography of the musician with several MS songs written for masques and plays.
FELLOWES, E. H. *The English Madrigal Composers.* Oxford: The Clarendon Press, 1921. A biographical and critical study. No music.
——————. *English Madrigal Verse, 1588-1632.* Oxford: The Clarendon Press, 1920. A critical study. No music.
——————. "'It was a lover and his lass': Some Fresh Points of Criticism." *MLR,* XLI (April, 1946), 202-206. The popularity of Morley's setting as evidenced by later MS of the song found in the Edinburgh Library.
——————. *Orlando Gibbons.* London: Oxford University Press, 1925. Not seen.
——————. *Songs and Lyrics from the Plays of Beaumont and Fletcher, with Contemporary Musical Settings.* London: P. Etchells and H. MacDonald, 1928.
——————. *The English School of Lutenist Song Writers.* New York: G. Schirmer Co., 1920-1932. 1st Series, 16 vols. A scholarly collection of lutenists' song books, transcribed for piano and voice. Includes a general introduction and biographical and critical introductions to the individual song books.
——————. *The English School of Lutenist Song Writers.* London: Stainer & Bell, Ltd., 1925-1927. 2nd Series, 8 vols. A more authentic collection. Includes piano transcriptions and the original lute tablature, with biographical and critical introductions to the individual song books.
FITZGIBBON, H. M. "Instruments and Their Music in the Elizabethan Drama." *The Musical Quarterly,* XVII (July, 1931), 319-329. A description of several instruments and the dramatic effects appropriate to each.
FLATTER, R. *Shakespeare's Producing Hand: A Study of His Marks of Expression to be Found in the First Folio.* New York: W. W. Norton and Co., Inc., 1948.
FORSTER, M. "Shakespeare-Musik." *Germanische-romanische Monatsschrift,* XVI (July-August, 1928), 298-304. An interpretive and aesthetic evaluation of music written for Shakespeare's plays.
GALPIN, F. W. *Old English Instruments of Music: Their History and Character.* London: Humphrey Milford, 1926. One of the most detailed descriptions of early English instruments of music. The standard work.
GARVIN, K. "A Speculation about 'Twelfth Night.'" *N&Q,* CLXX (May, 1936),

326-328. That "Come away, come away death" is an English version of the French "chanson du travaille," a folk type of song.

Gaw, A. "The Impromptu Masque in Shakespeare." *SAB*, XI (July, 1936), 149-160. A conjecture re the use of supernumerary actors for masque scenes.

Geiringer, K. *Musical Instruments: Their History in Western Culture from the Stone Age to the Present.* New York: Oxford University Press, 1945. A cursory treatment.

Gibbon, J. M. *Melody and the Lyric from Chaucer to the Cavaliers.* London: J. M. Dent and Sons, Ltd., 1930. Popular history of music with many musical illustrations. Lacks complete documentation but is valuable for its treatment of dramatic music.

Gilbert, A. H. *Literary Criticism: Plato to Dryden.* New York: American Book Co., 1940.

Gow, A. "Is Shakespeare's 'Much Ado' a Revised Earlier Play?" *PMLA*, L (September, 1935), 715-738.

Graves, T. S. "The 'Act Time' in Elizabethan Theatres." *SP*, XII (July, 1915), 103-134. A study of between-the-act activities, including the performances of music.

Gray, A. K. "The Song in 'The Merchant of Venice.'" *MLN* (November, 1927), 458, 459. The sounds of the words provide a clue for Bassanio.

Greaves, T. *Songs of sundrie kindes . . . 1604.* Huntington Library 239390 STC 12210. Not seen.

Greene, R. *Alphonsus, King of Aragon,* edited by W. W. Greg, Malone Society Reprints. London: Oxford University Press, 1926. Contains revealing stage directions for the use of music.

——————. *The Plays and Poems of Robert Greene,* edited by J. G. Collins. London: The Clarendon Press, 1905. 2 vols.

Greg, W. W. *Dramatic Documents from the Elizabethan Playhouses.* Oxford: The Clarendon Press, 1931. Includes prompt copies containing musical stage directions.

——————. "Lyly's Songs." *TLS Corr.* (January 3, 1924). Not seen.

Grierson, H. J. C. "Shakespeare: Music and Songs." *TLS* (March 31, 1932), 229. Not seen.

Haas, R. M. *Aufführungspraxis der Musik.* Wildpark-Potsdam: Akademische Verlagsgesellschaft Athenaion m. b. H., 1934. A history of early music performance, illustrated with music and pictures of musical ensembles.

Harrison, G. B. *The Elizabethan Journals 1591-1603.* New York: The Macmillan Co., 1939. Contains accounts of court progresses and processionals employing music.

Harrison, T. P. "Concerning 'Two Gentlemen of Verona' and Monte-Mayor's 'Diana.'" *MLN*, XLI (April, 1926), 251, 252. Montemayor's work believed to be the source of Shakespeare's play.

Hayes, G. R. *King's Music; an Anthology.* London: Oxford University Press, 1937. Not seen.

——————. *Musical Instruments and Their Music, 1500-1750.* London: Oxford University Press, Humphrey Milford, 1928. 2 vols. A thorough description of viols. Well documented.

Henslowe, P. *Henslowe's Diary,* edited by W. W. Greg. London: A. H. Bullen, 1904-1908. Includes records concerning actor-musicians, purchases of musical instruments by actors, and a list of musical instruments owned by the Lord Admiral's Men.

——————. *The Henslowe Papers, Being Documents Supplementary to Hens-*

lowe's Diary, edited by W. W. Greg. London: A. H. Bullen, 1907. Additional records pertaining to actor-musicians.

HEYWOOD, T. *The Dramatic Works of Thomas Heywood.* London: John Pearson, 1874. 6 vols.

HILTON, J. *Catch that catch can . . . 1652.* Huntington Library (Bridgewater 145861). A collection of convivial songs arranged in simple harmonies.

HOLBORNE, A. *Pavans, galliards, almains, and other short aeirs both graue, and light, in fiue parts, for viols, violins, or other musicall wind instruments. Made by Anthony Holborne . . . London, imprinted by William Barley, the assignee of Thomas Morley, 1599.* Huntington Library (Rimbault-Britwell 14220) STC 13563. A collection of popular instrumental music. Cantus and bassus parts only.

HOLINSHED, R. *The Chronicles of England, Scotland, and Ireland.* London, 1587. 2 vols.

HOWES, F. *William Byrd.* London: Kegan Paul, 1927. Not seen.

In this boke ar conteynyd xx songes. [London] 1530. Huntington Library R217108 STC 22924. Not seen.

JACKSON, V. *English Melodies from the 13th to the 18th Centuries; One Hundred Songs.* London: J. M. Dent and Sons, Ltd., 1910. A collection of early lyrics and musical settings.

JAGGARD, W. "The Music to 'Macbeth.'" *N&Q,* CLXIII (December, 1932), 444, 445. Not seen.

JONSON, B. *Ben Jonson,* edited by C. H. Herford and P. Simpson. London: Oxford Press, 1932. 7 vols.

JUDD, P. "The Songs of John Danyel." *Music and Letters,* LVII (April, 1936), 118-123. Not seen.

KASTENDIECK, M. M. *England's Musical Poet, Thomas Campion.* New York: Oxford University Press, 1938. Contains well-documented descriptions of the contemporary performances of Campion's masques.

KIDSON, F. *Old English Country Dances, Gathered from Scarce Printed Collections, and from Manuscripts. With Illustrative Notes and a Bibliography of English Country Dance Music.* London: W. Reeves, 1890. Not seen.

KYD, T. *The Works of Thomas Kyd,* edited by F. S. Boas. London: Oxford Press, 1901.

LAMSON, R. "Some Elizabethan Tunes." *MLR,* XXXII (October, 1937), 584, 585.

LANDRY, L. "La sensibilité musicale au temps de Shakespeare." *Revue Musicale,* August, 1926. Not seen.

LANIER, S. *Shakespeare and his Forerunners; Studies in Elizabethan Poetry and its Development from Early English.* New York: Doubleday, Page and Co., 1902. Chapters 13 and 14, Vol. 2 of 2 vols. Treats Elizabethan music; follows Chappell.

LATHROP, H. B. "Shakespeare's Dramatic Use of Songs." *MLN,* XXIII (January, 1908), 1-5. A statement that Shakespeare's songs are often expressive of joyous and carefree moods.

LAWRENCE, W. J. "Music and Song in the Elizabethan Theatre," in *The Elizabethan Playhouse and Other Studies.* Stratford on Avon: 1912.

──────────. "Music in the Elizabethan Theatre." *The Musical Quarterly,* VI (1920), 192-205. A valuable account of production practices.

──────────. "Music in the Elizabethan Theatre." *Shakespeare Jahrbuch,* XLIV (1908), 36-50. A parallel study to the above.

──────────. *Old Theatre Days and Ways.* London: G. G. Harrap and Co., Ltd., 1935. Minor stage practices involving music.

LAWRENCE, W. J. *Pre-Restoration Stage Studies*. Cambridge: Harvard University Press, 1927. Essays on the stage jig and on the use of sound effects.

————. *Shakespeare's Workshop*. Boston: Houghton Mifflin Co., 1928. Includes a test for chronology of Elizabethan plays, based on the use of cornets in the plays.

————. *Speeding Up Shakespeare: Studies of the Bygone Theatre and Drama*. London: The Argonaut Press, 1937.

————. "Tawyer with a Trumpet Before Them." *TLS* (March 20, 1930), 241. An identification of the actor, "Tawyer."

————. "The English Theatre Orchestra: Its Rise and Early Characteristics," *The Musical Quarterly*, III (January, 1917), 9-27. An informative description of the organization and functions of the playhouse consorts.

————. *The Physical Conditions of the Elizabethan Public Playhouse*. Cambridge: Harvard University Press, 1927.

————. "Thomas Ravenscroft's Theatrical Association." *MLR*, XIX (October, 1924), 418-423. An account of Ravenscroft's collaboration with the Children of Paul's.

————. *Those Nutcracking Elizabethans: Studies of the Early Theatre and Drama*. London: The Argonaut Press, 1935. Stage practices, including the use of sound effects.

LINDSEY, E. S. "The Music in Ben Jonson's Plays." *MLN*, XLIV (February, 1929), 86-92. A description of the songs with their musical settings as found in contemporary song books.

————. "The Music of the Songs in Fletcher's Plays." *SP*, XXI, 2.

————. "The Original Music for Beaumont's Play 'The Knight of the Burning Pestle.'" *SP*, XXVI (October, 1929), 425-443. A description of the songs with the musical settings as found in contemporary song books.

LODGE, T. *A Defence of Poetry, Music, and Stage-plays*, Shakespeare Society Publications No. 48. London: Printed for the Shakespeare Society, 1853. One of the few critical works on the music of the time.

————. *Lodge's 'Rosalynde' Being the Original of Shakespeare's 'As You Like It.'* New York: Duffield and Co., 1907.

————. *The Wounds of Civil War* (1594), edited by W. W. Greg, Malone Society Reprints. London: Oxford University Press, 1910. Contains musical stage directions.

LONG, J. H. "Shakespeare and Thomas Morley." *MLN*, LX (January, 1950), 17-22. Morley's *Introduction to Practicall Musicke* suggested as the source of Hortensio's gamut in *The Taming of the Shrew*.

Look About You (1600), edited by W. W. Greg, Malone Society Reprints. London: Oxford University Press, 1913. Contains musical stage directions.

LYLY, J. *The Dramatic Works of John Lilly*, edited by F. W. Fairholt. London: Reeves and Turner, 1892. 2 vols.

Malone Society Collections, edited by W. W. Greg. London: Oxford University Press, 1908-1931. 2 vols. Includes records pertaining to the use of municipal musicians in play performances.

MARLOWE, C. *The Works of Christopher Marlowe*, edited by A. H. Bullen. London: John C. Nimmo, 1885. 3 vols.

MARSTON, J. *Antonio and Mellida* and *Antonio's Revenge* (1602), edited by W. W. Greg, Malone Society Reprints. London: Oxford University Press, 1922. Contain unusually revealing stage directions for the use of music.

————. *The Works of John Marston*, edited by A. H. Bullen. London: John C. Nimmo, 1887. 3 vols.

MARTIN, B. "A Midsummer Night's Dream." *TLS* (January 24, 1935), 48. On the date of the play.

MASON, G., and J. EARSDEN. *The ayres that were sung and played at Broughan Castle . . . 1618.* Huntington Library (Britwell 69281) STC 17601. Not seen.

McCABE, W. H. "Music and Dance on a 17th Century College Stage." *The Musical Quarterly*, XXIV (July, 1938), 313-322. Includes a clear, contemporary description of the composition and functions of the "whole" and the "broken" consorts.

McCLOSKEY, F. H. "The Date of 'A Midsummer Night's Dream.'" *MLN*, XLVI (June, 1931), 389-391.

MEYER, E. H. *English Chamber Music: The History of a Great Art from the Middle Ages to Purcell.* London: Lawrence Wishart, 1946. A scholarly history of early string ensemble music and performance.

MEYER, P. J. *The cries of London* [1795]. Huntington Library 239266. Not seen.

MIDDLETON, T. *The Works of Thomas Middleton*, edited by A. H. Bullen. London: John C. Nimmo, 1885. 8 vols.

MILLER, H. C. "A Shakespearean Music Lesson." *N&Q*, CLXV (October, 1933), 255-257. The musical background for the lute lesson in *The Taming of the Shrew*.

MONCUR-SIME, A. H. *Shakespeare: His Music and Song.* London: Kegan Paul, Trench, Trubner and Co., Ltd., 192-. A review of the music. Of doubtful value.

MONTEMAYOR, J. *Los Siete Libros de la Diana*, edited by F. L. Estrada. Madrid: Espasa-Calpe, S. A., 1946.

MOORE, J. R. "The Function of the Songs in Shakespeare's Plays." *Shakespeare Studies*, University of Wisconsin, 1916. A sensible analysis of the dramatic use of songs.

————. "The Songs in Lyly's Plays." *PMLA*, XLII (September, 1927), 623-640. A textual study of the songs and their contents.

————. "The Songs of the Public Theaters in the Time of Shakespeare." *JEGP*, XXVIII (April, 1929), 166-202. A careful and illuminating study of the nature and the use of the songs.

MORLEY, T. *A Plaine and Easie Introduction to Practicall Musicke . . . 1597.* Microfilm of the copy in the Folger Shakespeare Library. A contemporary music instruction book containing critical, theoretical, and sociological comments on Elizabethan music in general. Dialogue form.

MURRAY, J. T. *English Dramatic Companies 1558-1642.* Boston and New York: Houghton Mifflin Co., 1910. 2 vols.

NAGEL, W. *Annalen der englische Hofmusik von der Zeit Heinrichs VIII bis Tode Karls I (1509-1649).* Leipzig: 1894. Not seen.

NAYLOR, E. W. *An Elizabethan Virginal Book; Being a Critical Essay on the Contents of a Manuscript in the Fitzwilliam Museum at Cambridge.* London: J. M. Dent and Co., 1905. An analytical study of several musical works selected from those in the *Fitzwilliam Virginal Book*.

————. *Shakespeare and Music, With Illustrations from the Music of the 16th and 17th Centuries.* New York: E. P. Dutton and Co., Inc., 1931. An excellent background study. Includes an appendix with musical illustrations.

————. *Shakespeare Music (Music of the Period).* London: J. Curwen and Sons, Ltd., 1913. A collection of contemporary music used or alluded to by Shakespeare.

————. *The Poets and Music.* London and Toronto: J. M. Dent and Sons, Ltd., 1928. Not seen.

NICOLL, A. *The English Theatre: A Short History*. London: T. Nelson and Sons, Ltd., 1936.

NIERLING, J. "The Music for Shakespeare." *The Musical Quarterly*, XII (1926), 555-563. An attack on the way Elizabethan music is performed in modern productions of the plays.

NOBLE, R. "A Song in 'As You Like It.'" *TLS* (June 5, 1930), 478. Not seen.

——————. "Feste's Epilogue Song." *TLS* (July 10, 1930), 576. Not seen.

——————. "Shakespeare's Songs and Stage." *A Series of Papers on Shakespeare and the Theatre, Printed for the Shakespeare Association*. London: H. Milford, 1927. A discussion of stage employment of songs. Very brief.

——————. *Shakespeare's Use of Song, with the Text of the Principal Songs*. London: Humphrey Milford, 1923. A serious attempt to determine the methods of performance, text, and dramatic uses of the songs.

NORRIS, E. T. "Titus Andronicus." *TLS* (May 11, 1933), 331. Not seen.

PARROTT, T. M. *Shakespearean Comedy*. New York: Oxford University Press, 1949.

PATTISON, B. *Music and Poetry in the English Renaissance*. London: Methuen and Co., Ltd., 1948. A critical study of the relationship of the two arts.

——————. "The Roundelay in the August Eclogue of 'The Shepheardes Calender.'" *RES*, IX (January, 1933), 54, 55. The roundelay may have been set to a tune entitled "Heigh ho, holiday." Does not contain the music, nor will the lyrics fit the tune, "Heigh ho holyday" in Holborne's *Pavans, galliards, almains*. . . .

——————. "Sir Philip Sidney and Music." *Music and Letters*, XV (January, 1934), 75. Not seen.

PEACHAM, H. *Peacham's Compleat Gentleman* (1634). Oxford: The Clarendon Press, 1906. Includes a statement on the musical training necessary for the pre-Restoration gentleman.

PEELE, G. *The Works of George Peele*, edited by A. H. Bullen. London: John C. Nimmo, 1888. 2 vols.

PEERSON, M. *Mottects or graue chamber musique . . . 1630*. Huntington Library (Britwell 14225) STC 19552. Vocal music with instrumental accompaniment.

PHILLIPS, J. *Patient Grissell* (u.d.Quarto), edited by W. W. Greg, Malone Society Reprints. London: Charles Whittingham and Co., 1909. Contains stage directions for the use of music.

PLAYFORD, J. *A Brief Introduction to the Skill of Musick . . . London Printed by William Godbid for John Playford, and are to be sold at his shop in the Temple, 1667*. Microfilm of the copy in the Folger Shakespeare Library. Includes an excellent account of the construction and performance technique of the bass viol, as well as several pieces of music of the Elizabethan period.

——————. *Musick's delight on the citren, restored and refined . . . By John Playford Philo-musicae*. London, Printed by W. G. and are sold by J. Playford, 1666. Library of Congress. A collection of pieces in tablature.

——————. *The English Dancing Master*. London: Mellor, 1933. Not seen.

PROCTOR, T. *A Gorgeous Gallery of Gallant Inventions* (1578), edited by H. E. Rollins. Cambridge: Harvard University Press, 1926. A collection of song lyrics. No music.

PULVER, J. *A Dictionary of Old English Music and Musical Instruments*. London: Kegan Paul, Trench, Trubner and Co., Ltd., 1923. Not seen.

The Rare Triumphs of Love and Fortune, edited by W. W. Greg, Malone Society Reprints. London: Oxford University Press, 1931. Unusually descriptive stage directions for the use of music.

REED, E. B. (ed.). *Christmas Carols of the Sixteenth Century. Including Kele's Christmas carolles newly Inprynted, reproduced in facsimile from the copy in the Huntington Library.* Cambridge: Harvard University Press, 1932. Not seen.

——————. *Songs from the British Drama.* New Haven: Yale University Press, 1925. Includes lyrics and stage directions for the songs, notes about the songs, and an essay on Elizabethan music.

RENWICK, W. L. "Alphonso Ferrabosco." *RES,* XI (April, 1935), 184-185.

The Return from Parnassus, (1606), Cambridge play, edited by W. D. Macray. London: Oxford Press, 1936. Contains musical stage directions.

REYNOLDS, G. F. *The Staging of Elizabethan Plays at the Red Bull Theater 1605-1625.* New York: Modern Language Association of America; London: Oxford University Press, 1940. A description of staging, including the use of music.

RICH, B. *Rich's 'Apolonius & Silla,' an Original of Shakespeare's 'Twelfth Night,'* edited by M. Luce. London: Chatto and Windus, 1909.

RITSON, J. *Ancient Songs, from the Time of King Henry the Third to the Revolution.* London: Printed for J. Johnson, 1790. Includes many lyrics, some music, and an essay on ancient minstrelsy.

ROBINSON, C. *A Handful of Pleasant Delights* (1584), edited by H. E. Rollins. Cambridge: Harvard University Press, 1926. A collection of song lyrics. No music.

ROFFE, A. *The Handbook of Shakespeare Music, Being an Account of Three Hundred and Fifty Pieces of Music Set to Words Taken from the Plays and Poems of Shakespeare, the Compositions Ranging from the Elizabethan Age to the Present Time.* London: Chatto and Windus, 1878.

ROLLINS, H. E. (ed.). *The Paradise of Dainty Devices* (1576-1606). Cambridge: Harvard University Press, 1927. A collection of song lyrics. No music.

——————. (ed.) *The Phoenix Nest* (1593). Cambridge: Harvard University Press, 1931. A collection of song lyrics. No music.

SACHS, C. "Chromatic Trumpets in the Renaissance." *The Musical Quarterly,* XXXVI (January, 1950), 62-66. A description of an unusual type of trumpet.

——————. *The History of Musical Instruments.* New York: W. W. Norton and Co., Inc., 1940. One of the most scholarly works on the subject.

SALZMAN, L. F. "Dildos and Fadings." *TLS* (September 7, 1933), 592. Not seen.

SAUGNET, H. "La musique elizabèthaine" in "Le Théâtre Elizabèthain," *Cahier du Sud.* x. Numero Special, June 1933. Not seen.

SCHELLING, F. E. (ed.). *A Book of Elizabethan Lyrics.* Boston: Ginn and Co., 1903.

SCHOLES, P. A. *A list of Books about Music in the English Language Prepared as an Appendix to the Oxford Companion to Music.* London, New York: Oxford University Press, 1940.

——————. *The Puritans and Music in England and New England. A Contribution to the Cultural History of Two Nations.* Oxford: University Press, 1934. Not seen.

SCHOLL, E. "English Meter Once More." *PMLA,* LXIII (March, 1948), 293-326. The study of contemporary music as an aid to the metrical study of Elizabethan lyrics.

SCOTT, M. A. *Elizabethan Translations from the Italian.* The Vassar Semi-centennial Series. Boston and New York: Houghton Mifflin Co., 1916.

Selimus (1594), edited by W. W. Greg, Malone Society Reprints. London: Charles Whittingham and Co., 1908.

SHAKESPEARE SOCIETY. *Extracts from the Accounts of the Revels at Court, in the Reigns of Queen Elizabeth and King James I.* London: Printed for the Shakespeare Society, 1842.

SHAKESPEARE, W. *The National Shakespeare; a Facsimile of the Text of the First Folio of 1623.* London: W. Mackenzie, 1888-1889.

—————. *The Complete Plays and Poems of William Shakespeare*, edited by W. A. Neilson and C. J. Hill. Riverside Press Edition. Boston, New York: Houghton Mifflin Co., 1942.

—————. *The Complete Works of Shakespeare*, edited by H. Craig. New York: Oxford University Press, 1936.

—————. *The Plays and Poems of William Shakespeare, with the corrections and illustrations of various commentators: comprehending a life of the poet, and an enlarged history of the stage, by the late Edmond Malone.* London: F. C. and J. Rivington, 1821. Vols. 1-3 of 21 vols.

—————. *A Midsommer nights dreame. As it hath beene sundry times publickely acted, by the Right Honourable, the Lord Chamberlaine his seruants. Written by William Shakespeare. Imprinted at London, for Thomas Fisher, and are to be soulde at his shoppe, at the signe of the White Hart, in Fleetestreete, 1600.* Folger Shakespeare Library facsimile furnished to University of Florida Library.

—————. *A Midsummer Night's Dream*, edited by H. Cuningham, The Arden Shakespeare, XXV. London: Methuen and Co., Ltd., 1905. 39 vols.

—————. *A Midsummer Night's Dream*, edited by Sir A. Quiller-Couch and J. D. Wilson. Cambridge: The University Press, 1924.

—————. *As You Like It*, edited by J. W. Holme, The Arden Shakespeare, III. London: Methuen and Co., Ltd., 1906. 39 vols.

—————. *As You Like It*, edited by Sir A. Quiller-Couch and J. D. Wilson. Cambridge: The University Press, 1926.

—————. *As You Like It*, edited by G. L. Kittredge. Boston, New York: Ginn and Co., 1939.

—————. *The Comedy of Errors*, edited by H. Cuningham, The Arden Shakespeare, IV. London: Methuen and Co., Ltd., 1914. 39 vols.

—————. *The Comedy of Errors*, edited by Sir A. Quiller-Couch and J. D. Wilson. Cambridge: The University Press, 1922.

—————. *A Pleasant Conceited Comedie Called, Loues labors lost. As it was presented before her Highnes this last Christmas. Newly corrected and augmented, By W. Shakespeare. Imprinted at London by W. W. for Cutbert Burby, 1598.* Folger Shakespeare Library facsimile furnished to University of Florida Library.

—————. "Love's Labour's Lost," edited by E. Capell, *The Works of Shakespeare*, II. London: J. and R. Tonson, 1767. 10 vols.

—————. *Love's Labour's Lost*, edited by Sir A. Quiller-Couch and J. D. Wilson. Cambridge: The University Press, 1923.

—————. *Love's Labour's Lost*, edited by H. C. Hart, The Arden Shakespeare, XX. London: Methuen and Co., Ltd., 1930. 39 vols.

—————. *The most excellent Historie of the Merchant of Venice. With the extreame crueltie of Shylocke the Iew towards the sayd Merchant, in cutting a iust pound of his flesh; and the obtayning of Portia by the choyse of three chests. As it hath beene diuers times acted by the Lord Chamberlaine his Seruants. Written by William Shakespeare. At London, Printed by I. R. for Thomas Heyes, and are to be sold in Paules Church-yard, at the signe of the*

Greene Dragon, 1600. Folger Shakespeare Library facsimile furnished to University of Florida Library.

——————. *The Merchant of Venice*, edited by C. K. Pooler, The Arden Shakespeare, XXIII. London: Methuen and Co., Ltd., 1903. 39 vols.

——————. *The Merchant of Venice*, edited by G. L. Kittredge. Boston, New York: Ginn and Co., 1945.

——————. *Much adoe about Nothing. As it hath been sundrie times publikely acted by the right honourable, the Lord Chamberlaine his seruants. Written by William Shakespeare. Printed by I. S. for Andrew Wise, and William Aspley, 1600.* Folger Shakespeare Library facsimile furnished to University of Florida Library.

——————. *Much Ado About Nothing*, edited by G. R. Trenery, The Arden Shakespeare, XXVI. London: Methuen and Co., Ltd., 1924. 39 vols.

——————. *Much Ado About Nothing*, edited by H. H. Furness, Variorum Edition, XII. Philadelphia: J. B. Lippincott and Co., 1901. 24 vols.

——————. *Much Ado About Nothing*, edited by G. L. Kittredge. Boston, New York: Ginn and Co., 1941.

——————. *Twelfth Night*, edited by H. H. Furness, Variorum Edition, XIII. Philadelphia: J. B. Lippincott and Co., 1901. 24 vols.

——————. *Twelfth Night*, edited by G. L. Kittredge. Boston, New York: Ginn and Co., 1941.

——————. *Twelfth Night*, edited by M. Luce, The Arden Shakespeare, XXXV. London: Methuen and Co., Ltd., 1929. 39 vols.

——————. *The Two Gentlemen of Verona*, edited by R. W. Bond, The Arden Shakespeare, XXXVI. London: Methuen and Co., Ltd., 1906. 39 vols.

——————. *The Two Gentlemen of Verona*, edited by Sir A. Quiller-Couch and J. D. Wilson. Cambridge: The University Press, 1921.

SIDNEY, SIR P. *The Poems of Sir Philip Sidney*, edited by J. Drinkwater. London: G. Routledge and Sons, Ltd., 1910.

SIGISMUND, R. "Die Musik in Shakespeare's Dramen." *Shakespeare Jahrbuch*, XIX (1884), 86-112. A conjectural reconstruction of a philosophy of music based upon data in the plays of Shakespeare.

SIMPSON, C. M. "Tudor Popular Music: Its Social Significance." *Huntington Library Quarterly*, V (1941), 155-201. Not seen.

SISSON, C. J. *Lost Plays of Shakespeare's Age.* Cambridge: The University Press, 1936. Contains a rare text of an Elizabethan stage jig.

SORENSEN, F. " 'The Mask of the Muscovites' in 'Love's Labour's Lost.' " *MLN*, L (December, 1935), 499-501. Notes a resemblance of the mask to an earlier mask type popular at the court of Henry VIII.

SOUTHGATE, T. L. "The Evolution of the Flute." *Proceedings of the Musical Association*, 1907-1908, pp. 155-175. Contains a brief description of flutes and recorders.

STANFORD, C. V., and C. FORSYTH. *A History of Music.* New York: The Macmillan Co., 1925. Contains a colorful description of Elizabethan music and its performance. Stimulating, generally accurate, but largely undocumented.

STEELE, M. S. *Plays and Masques at Court During the Reigns of Elizabeth, James and Charles.* New Haven: Yale University Press, 1926.

STEELE, R. *The Earliest English Music Printing: a description and bibliography of English printed music to the close of the sixteenth century.* London: Printed for the Bibliographical Society at the Chiswick Press, 1903.

SULLIVAN, M. *Court Masques of James I; Their Influence on Shakespeare and the Public Theatres.* New York and London: G. P. Putnam's Sons, 1913.

Tancred and Gismund (1592), edited by W. W. Greg, Malone Society Reprints. London: Oxford University Press, 1914. A version of the play with stage directions for the use of music supplied by a contemporary reporter.

TERRY, C. S. "John Forbes's 'Songs and Fancies.'" *The Musical Quarterly,* XXII (October, 1936), 402-419. Not seen.

THOMPSON, S. *Motif-Index of Folk Literature; A Classification of Narrative Elements in Folk-tales, Ballads, Myths, Fables, Medieval Romances, Exempla, Fabliaux, Jest-books, and Local Legends.* Indiana University Studies, XIX (June, September, 1932). 6 vols.

————. *The Folk Tale.* New York: The Dryden Press, 1946.

THORNDIKE, A. H. *Shakespeare's Theater.* New York: The Macmillan Co., 1925.

TOURNEUR, C. *The Works of Cyril Tourneur,* edited by N. Allardyce. London: The Fanfrolico Press, 1929.

Two Elizabethan Stage Abridgements: The Battle of Alcazar and Orlando Furioso, edited by W. W. Greg, Malone Society Reprints. London: Oxford University Press, 1923. Contains musical stage directions.

VINCENT, C. *Fifty Shakspere Songs.* Boston: Oliver Ditson Co., 1906. Songs used or alluded to by Shakespeare. Lyrics and music.

VIVIAN, P. (ed.). *Campion's Works.* Oxford: The Clarendon Press, 1909.

WALKER, A. J. "Popular Songs and Broadside Ballads in the English Drama 1559-1642." Unpublished thesis, Harvard University, 1934. Not seen.

WALLACE, C. W. "The Children of Blackfriars, 1597-1603." *University Studies,* University of Nebraska, VIII (April, July, 1908). Monograph concerning the early stage history of the Blackfriars Children.

WARLOCK, P. *The English Ayre.* London: Humphrey Milford, 1926. An account of the emergence of the Elizabethan ayre as an "art song."

WEBSTER, J. *The Complete Works of John Webster,* edited by F. L. Lucas. Boston: Houghton Mifflin Co., 1928. 4 vols.

WELSFORD, E. *The Court Masque; A Study of the Relationship between Poetry and the Revels.* Cambridge: The University Press, 1927. Not seen.

WILLIAMS, L. "Published Shakespearian Music." *Quarterly Journal of Speech,* XIX (November, 1933), 503-513.

WILSON, R. *The Coblers Prophesie* (1594), edited by W. W. Greg, Malone Society Reprints. London: Oxford University Press, 1914. A play employing much music.

Wily Beguiled (1606), edited by W. W. Greg, Malone Society Reprints. London: Oxford University Press, 1923. A play in which music is used to a great extent.

Wit of a Woman, The (1604), edited by W. W. Greg, Malone Society Reprints. London: Oxford University Press, 1913. Contains musical stage directions.

WOOD, W. W. "A Comparison between Shakespeare and His Contemporaries in Their Use of Music and Sound Effects." *Summaries of Doctoral Dissertations,* Northwestern University, XII (1944), 33-38.

WOOLRIDGE, H. E. "The Polyphonic Period," *Oxford History of Music.* London: Humphrey Milford, 1929. Vols. 1 and 2 of 6 vols. Contains a cursory description of English secular music.

WRIGHT, L. B. "Extraneous Song in Elizabethan Drama after the Advent of Shakespeare." *SP,* XXIV (April, 1927), 261-274. Discusses the difference between public and private theaters in their use of extraneous songs.

ZWEIG, S. *Mary Queen of Scotland and the Isles.* New York: The Viking Press, 1935.

Index

15600